P9-AOJ-316

NOTORIOUS VOICES

Notorious Voices:

Feminist Biblical Interpretation,
1500–1920

Marla J. Selvidge

A Paragon House Book
CONTINUUM • NEW YORK

1996

The Continuum Publishing Company
370 Lexington Avenue
New York, NY 10017

Copyright © 1996 by Marla J. Selvidge

All rights reserved. No part of this book may be reproduced, in
any form, without written permission from the publishers, unless
by a reviewer who wishes to quote brief passages.

Printed in the United States of America

Library of Congress Cataloging-in-Publication Data

Selvidge, Marla J.
    Notorious voices: feminist biblical interpretation, 1550–1920 /
Marla J. Selvidge.—1st ed.
        p.   cm.
    Includes bibliographical references and index.
Paragon House ISBN 1-55778-630-5
Continuum ISBN 0-8264-0913-X
    1. Bible—Feminist criticism—History.   2. Women in
Christianity—History.   I. Title.
    BS521.4.S45   1995
    220.6'082—dc20   94-33899
                                                                          CIP

To: All the Mothers on Schram Street in Roseville, Michigan

who gathered regularly to drink coffee
and to discuss world problems
at my mother's kitchen table.

Especially,

Mrs. Cuma McGinnis
A proud substitute teacher who braved life in spite of Jim's illness.

Mrs. Nola Pannebecker
A tireless homemaker whose quick thinking saved my life.

Mrs. Henrietta Wolcanski
A homemaker and a friend who became family.

In Remembrance of:

Mrs. Esther LaRosa
A gas company clerk whose hands and heart
could make anyone happy.

and

Mrs. Lillian Seitz
A homemaker whose keen mind could discuss any issue in
psychology, philosophy, and history.

And to my Mother

Mary M. Gilreath Selvidge
A retired factory worker whose house is always filled with love.

Many thanks must go to the following:

Lori A. Fitterling, an interlibrary loan wizard, who searched tenaciously and retrieved clues, books, and information from around the globe.

Patricia L. Downing, who copied articles and resurrected many periodicals from the grave.

Linda L. Medaris, who punched in the numbers and produced a fifty page on-line search.

Avis R. Baker, whose keen eyes proofed this manuscript.

Pamela M. Vaught, who shared some of her summer budget with me.

Dr. Thomas C. Hemling, who actually listens to my stories.

Justin R. Karman and Shay Gaskin for placing the little pieces of paper in order for the Index.

And especially to my colleagues on the Research Council at Central Missouri State University, who awarded grants to me which funded all interlibrary loan, copying, and materials expenses. During the spring semester of 1994, they also honored me with a Summer Faculty Research Award newly created by Dr. Kathleen D. Easter, Dean of Graduate Studies and Research.

CONTENTS

INTRODUCTION   1

CHAPTER 1:   INTERPRETING THE BIBLE   11
    Notes   21

CHAPTER 2:   EGALITARIAN READINGS
    LITERAL APPROACHES TO THE BIBLE   23

    George Fox   25
    Margaret Askew Fell Fox   37
    Sarah Moore Grimké   44
    Lucretia Coffin Mott   54
    Phoebe Worrall Palmer   62
    Barbara Kellison   70
    Notes   76

CHAPTER 3:   GYNOCENTRISM
    WOMAN AT THE CENTER   86

    Mary Hays   88
    Elizabeth Cady Stanton   95
    Antoinette Louisa Brown Blackwell   105
    Notes   115

CHAPTER 4:   THE SUPERIOR FEMALE
    MATRIARCHAL READINGS   121
    Heinrich Cornelius Agrippa von Nettesheim   123
    Mary Astell   131
    Judith Sargent Murray   138
    Matilda Joslyn Gage   143

ix

Frances Elizabeth Caroline Willard   151
Charlotte Perkins Gilman   158
Notes   166

CHAPTER 5:   THE FEMALE AS DIVINE   174

Joanna Southcott   175
Anna Bonus Kingsford and Edward Maitland   186
Notes   195

CHAPTER 6:   AFRICAN-AMERICAN READING   200

Maria W. Miller Stewart   202
Notes   210

CHAPTER 7:   TRANSLATION AS INTERPRETATION   213

Julia Evelina Smith   214
Notes   225

CONCLUDING OBSERVATIONS   227

SELECTED BIBLIOGRAPHY   229

INDEX   237

INTRODUCTION

They hope for a time when barriers will be broken and the community will experience times of communal joy. This joy will spring forth out of respect and love for each person. Talents will be cultivated and life can be better if we listen and learn to foster change in each other. The community needs to relax its rigid perceptions of history, law, and the future.[1]

—FROM *Daughters of Jerusalem*

THE PROBLEM: TODAY

As a Missouri Humanities scholar I have crisscrossed the state giving lectures about women in the Bible and world religions. In spite of all the remarkable books written about women's history, problems, interpretations, and social status in the past twenty-five years, there are many, many women and men who have never read or heard a lecture about egalitarian models or stories of woman included in the Judeo-Christian scriptures. I am amazed at the number of people, born and bred within a church, who have never considered the historical-political importance of women within the history of Christianity.

Some of the women have sensed their own potential, but it has been submerged by a very strong cultural-religious bias against their leadership. That bias is based in the Bible. These women have lived their lives in "patriarchal" space without the benefit of an alternative critical view. Their narrow view of the Bible has been culturally conditioned; they can only see what they have been taught to see. This monolithic view has blocked and denigrated wonderful stories about women in the Bible from being considered important by the religious communities and the culture at large.

The idea for this book began over fifteen years ago when I was

1

taking my qualifying exams for a Ph.D. in Biblical Languages and Literatures. One of the tests included identifying and describing the contributions of fifty interpreters of the Bible during the past two millennia. All of the interpreters were male. I asked my professor to include a few women. He asserted that there were no worthy women and that perhaps I might be included in his list someday. My professor was unaware of the volumes of feminist works that had been developing since the early seventies.

And while the philosophical-historical-literary critical questions of feminism have advanced remarkably, producing thousands of books, my professor's attitude is still prevalent among many of the educators in the fields of Biblical Studies. Only recently, I was asked to review the new *Anchor Bible Dictionary* for the 1993 Central States meeting of the Society of Biblical Literature. My analysis of the dictionary discovered that modern commentaries continue the time-honored tradition of ignoring female scholarship, contributions, and methodologies.

Only one woman was listed as managing editor; the remaining ten editors were male. No females with Ph.D.'s in Biblical Studies were on the planning committee or board. There are approximately 835 scholars who contributed articles—only seventy-three were female, which is less than 9 percent. No major female writers, ancient or modern, were mentioned in over 2,000 reference entries at the front of the volume. Works by women were not considered to be classics or reference-worthy. Only one feminist journal was listed. Although there is an entry entitled "feminist hermeneutics," the articles on "hermeneutics" and "exegesis" do not take into consideration works by people doing feminist work. While the planners for this volume made an effort to include some women, they have omitted or ignored most of the great contributions of women throughout history. Their thoughts and critical ideas continue to remain on the periphery of this reference work.

THE PROBLEM: HISTORICALLY

During most of the past 2,000 years, Christian scholars and religious practitioners have chosen to ignore the majority of the woman stories

in the Bible. Those stories which were recognized generally portrayed women in a supporting role. Notorious, ancient, prophetic
voices challenge this androcentric view of the Bible. They question
the use and misuse of Scripture. They recognize the biased nature of
interpretation with its emphasis on original languages, choice of
Scriptures to emphasize, and the very biblical characters who were
held to be role models and leaders within Christianity.

In spite of their criticisms of the use of the Bible, these notorious
voices continued to claim the authority of Scripture in their lives.
They believed that there was a God who had ordered the universe.
But this God did not ordain anyone to be secondary or subordinate.
And the very Bible that had been used against them, to suppress, to
alienate, and subordinate them, contained the keys or verses to prove
their own egalitarian beliefs about the nature and relationship of
woman and man, society, and the Divine.

These notorious prophetic interpretations were often ignored and
suppressed by the prevailing religio-political power structures and
the general public. They were a minority that through the centuries
became squelched and silenced by those advocating the accepted
and approved way of interpreting Scriptures. It appears that every
time, throughout history, women and men gained some audience
and approval for egalitarian or matriarchal ideals rooted in Scripture, a forceful antiwoman or antifeminist campaign managed to
derail their efforts.

MODERN VOICES

In the past two decades Feminist Studies in all disciplines have blos-
somed. Thousands of books have been written on the topic. In the
field of Religious Studies, the new study, "Liberal Learning and the
Religion Major" completed in conjunction with the Association of
American Colleges, credits feminist scholars in the field of religion
with helping Religious Studies to become oriented toward multi-
cultural studies.[2] Feminist criticisms have not only raised questions
that deal with women but also minorities, the physically challenged,
and relationships among religious traditions.

FEMINISM AND FEMINIST BIBLICAL INTERPRETATION

Feminist scholarship and the recognition and acceptance of those efforts has matured in many ways during the past thirty years. The term feminist is a relatively new term, having its English-language birth at the turn of this century. Nineteenth-century suffragettes did not employ the term. They used the term "woman movement" as the banner for their efforts. To be historically accurate, the earlier interpretations of notorious, prophetic voices cannot be classified as feminist. Yet their goals, strategies, and conclusions could be placed squarely within feminism today.

To date, there is no universally accepted definition or description of the movement or the discipline. Dictionaries and encyclopedias recognize the pluralism of definitions and therefore choose to quote historic and contemporary opinions on the definition of feminism. Among the quotes in *A Feminist Dictionary* are:

> Feminism is a mode of analysis, a method of asking questions and searching for answers, rather than a set of political conclusions about the oppression of women.

> Feminism is a philosophy based on the recognition that we live in a male-dominated culture in which women remain unacknowledged, and where women are forced into sex roles which demand that they be dependent, passive, nurturant, etc. Men too must assume sex roles [but these] are not nearly as crippling as women's.

> Feminism is a theory that calls for women's attainment of social, economic, and political rights and opportunities equal to those possessed by men. Feminism is also a mode for a social state—an ideal, or a desired standard of perfection not yet attained in the world.[3]

The *Handbook of American Women's History* sums up the present day usage of the term "feminism": "Thus, since the 1960s in the wake of the modern women's movement, feminism has become the designated term for activities and issues connected with the entire spectrum of the struggle for the improvement of women's conditions in society."[4]

FEMINIST BIBLICAL INTERPRETATION

Feminism has produced many theories of interpretation and analysis. Feminist literary criticism "includes gender as a fundamental basis for literary analysis."[5] Elisabeth Schüssler Fiorenza attempts to describe the process of feminist biblical interpretation in her book *Bread Not Stone*: "In our struggle for self-identity, survival, and liberation in a patriarchal society and church, Christian women have found that the Bible has been used as a weapon against us but at the same time it has been a resource for courage, hope, and commitment in this struggle."[6]

Mary Ann Tolbert recognizes two approaches to feminist interpretation, those that argue for the equality of people and those that argue for female ascendancy. She struggles to define what she terms "feminist hermeneutics" and concludes that it is "a reading of a text (or the writing of an analysis, or the reconstructing of history) in light of the oppressive structures of patriarchal society. Such a reading can have either a predominately negative or a predominately positive orientation."[7]

Feminists who interpret the Bible today have taken a wide variety of approaches to rereading the text. Some have isolated stories and found positive life-giving examples in the text. Others have pointed to androcentric origins and androcentric models of leadership in the Bible that do not fit modern living. Some study words, others attempt to reconstruct history. Some compare the literature with ancient "feminist" literatures and draw conclusions about the origins of Scripture.

Feminist interpretations of the Bible are challenging the fundamental bases of American Judeo-Christian belief systems, theologies, and critical approaches to the Bible. Some view this massive scholarship as a threat to the existing religio-socio-theological structures of American life. Change always produces stress and that stress is evident in every segment of our society. Margaret Foster writes of her own experiences of that stress when she says: "[A]nd a feminist is no shrieking harridan obsessed with destruction but a man or a woman who strives to secure a society in which neither sex finds gender alone a handicap to their progress."[8]

Margaret Fuller, speaking from the nineteenth century, could have written these words today: "What woman needs is not as a woman to act or rule, but as a nature to grow, as an intellect to discern, as a soul to live freely and unimpeded, to unfold such powers as were given to her when we left our common home."[9]

CONTENTS OF THE BOOK

Notorious Voices, in chapter 1, gives the reader a brief introduction to the complicated approaches, views, and problems of interpreting the Bible. The remaining chapters catalogue the voices of women and men who looked to the Bible for authority to prove women's equality or superiority. They believed in a just God who ordered a universe for all people, not merely a select few. They offered alternative methodologies and views of those commonly held sacred literatures. All of them hoped for the improvement in lives of both women and men.

Most of the interpreters did not have the solid grounding in ancient languages, history, philosophy, and theologies that modern interpreters have amassed. Yet some of their strategies of interpretation are still used by feminists today. Other interpretations such as that of the Southcottians, who believed in a female Messiah, have not been pursued or adopted by contemporary critics.

Notorious Voices seeks to do what other books have ignored. It takes the reader back in time. People who lived in Europe and an awakening America between 1500 and 1920 voice their opinions about how Scripture should be interpreted on the topic of woman. While the term "feminism" may be a twentieth-century invention, its ideals and strategies were practiced long before the suffragettes won the vote, and long before Mary Daly, Elisabeth Schüssler Fiorenza, Phyllis Trible, Naomi Goldenberg, or Rosemary Radford Ruether penned their scathing critiques of the religious literatures and power structures of society.[10]

Notorious Voices examines historic traditionalists, radicals, and reformers within Christianity who used the Bible as the foundation for their views of woman. Their interpretative strategies included using accepted traditional methods of interpretation. George and Margaret Fox, Lucretia Mott, Sarah Grimké, Barbara Kellison, and Phoebe Palmer study the literal words of the Scriptures and produce surprisingly different arguments for their egalitarian viewpoints.

Notorious Voices contains chapters on gynocentric readings or revisionist readings by Mary Hays, Elizabeth Cady Stanton, and Antoinette Brown Blackwell. They demythologized and re-mythologized texts. Luckie Buchan, Joanna Southcott, Anna Bonus Kingsford, and Edward Maitland discovered that the Divine was indeed a Female. They conceived of the female as God, a Messiah, or the New Christ—she is the only hope for humanity. Heinrich Cornelius Agrippa von Nettesheim, Judith Sargent Murray, Matilda Joslyn Gage, Frances Willard, and Charlotte Perkins Gilman upheld motherhood and the Superior Moral Woman as the highest good and sought to help society educate all women through their matriarchal readings.

African American women, such as Maria Stewart, Sojourner Truth, and Amanda Berry Smith had a special cultural experience and so their view of Scripture includes the issues of slavery and racism. They understood the plight of all who were oppressed and used by a white male power structure. Women protested their unfair treatment by citing and refuting biblical stories and verses. These people were hopeful for the personal transformation of individuals and even of the world. Some viewed the Scriptures as foundational to equality in politics and government, others contended that freedom came through a personal transformation. Equality in society was not needed if you had equality before God.

One interpreter who did have considerable, though not necessarily formal, training in ancient languages and translations was Julia Smith. The last chapter of this book includes an analysis of her translation of the Bible. She may be the first woman in the United States to complete the tremendous process of translating the Old Testament from the Hebrew and the New Testament from the Greek into English and to publish them. Some of her translations are compared with the Revised Standard Version which emerged in the 1880s and the King James Version of the Bible.

Hundreds of other notorious interpreters were identified during the research for this study. Unfortunately, some of them did not meet the guidelines for this book or their manuscripts were unavailable. This study represents only a small percentage of the people who protested against the injustices of sexism and racism in their lifetimes by pointing to the Bible as their just defender.

METHODOLOGY

There is no text available today which surveys the ways in which women and men have interpreted the Bible between 1500 and 1920. There are many books which contain articles by scholars who attempt to define (or describe) feminist interpretation,[11] or recover women's history by creating anthologies that include sermons, letters, or other written works by famous or historic feminists.[12] Some works contain modern examples of a diversification of feminist interpretations.[13] Other books are histories of feminists from a particular country, time, and place.[14] There are a few histories of feminism written from a literary-critical or -political point of view.[15] Usually they mention religion or Christianity as a factor in the struggle for emancipation but do not analyze the biblical texts which were used by some of the leading feminists.

This book will survey the types of feminist or proto-feminist interpretations used by women (and some men) from the sixteenth century until the beginnings of the twentieth century. *Notorious Voices* discovers, describes, and gives examples of the major interpretative strategies used by people who sought a change in the status and relationship of women within religious communities and society. It will discuss the life and view of the Bible for each interpreter, identify the major problems in his or her literatures, give an excerpt of his or her writing, and then analyze the type of interpretation that is employed. Some of those literary or socio-political interpretations include allegory, typology, grammatical criticism, canonical criticism, retranslation, revisionism with women at the center of the narrative, matriarchal reading, proto-historical criticism, and mystical or symbolic prophetic readings.

Notes

1. Marla J. Selvidge, *Daughters of Jerusalem* (Scottdale, PA: Herald Press, 1987), 143.
2. *Liberal Learning and the Religion Major* (American Academy of Religion, 1990), 17–18.
3. "Feminism" in the *Handbook of American Women's History*, ed. Frances M. Kavenik (Boston: Pandora Press 1990), 206–207; and "Feminism" in *A Feminist Dictionary*, eds. Cheris Kramarae and Paula A. Treichler (Boston: Pandora Press, 1985), 159–160
4. *Handbook of American Women's History*, 206–207.

5. Ibid., 206–207.

6. Elisabeth Schüssler Fiorenza, *Bread Not Stone: The Challenge of Feminist Biblical Interpretation* (Boston: Beacon Press, 1984), x.

7. Mary Ann Tolbert, ed., *The Bible and Feminist Hermeneutics. Semeia 28* (Atlanta: Scholars Press, 1983): 119. See also several articles by feminist interpreters such as Bernadette J. Brooten, Carolyn Osiek, and Elisabeth Schüssler Fiorenza in Adela Yarbro Collins, ed., *Feminist Perspectives on Biblical Scholarship* (Chico, CA: Scholars Press, 1885).

8. Margaret Forster, *Significant Sisters: The Grassroots of Active Feminism 1839–1939* (New York: Knopf, 1985), 11.

9. Jane Rendal, *The Origins of Modern Feminism: Women in Britain, France, and the United States 1780–1860* (New York: Schocken, 1984), 282.

10. Mary Daly, *Beyond God the Father: The Church and the Second Sex* (Boston: Beacon Press, 1985); Rosemary Radford Ruether, *Religion and Sexism: Images of Woman in the Jewish and Christian Traditions* (New York: Simon and Schuster, 1974); Letty M. Russel, ed., *Feminist Interpretation of the Bible* (Philadelphia: Westminster, 1985); Carol P. Christ, ed., *Womanspirit Rising: A Feminist Reader in Religion* (New York: Harper and Row, 1992).

11. Josephine Donovan, ed., *Feminist Literary Criticism. Explorations in Theory* (Lexington: University of Kentucky Press, 1975); and *Feminist Theory: The Intellectual Traditions of American Feminism*, (New York: Ungar, 1985); Claudia V. Camp and Carole R. Fontaine, eds., *Semeia 61. Women, War, and Metaphor: Language and Society in the Study of the Hebrew Bible* (Atlanta: Scholars Press, 1993); Shari Benstock, ed., *Feminist Issues in Literary Scholarship* (Bloomington: Indiana University Press, 1987); Elisabeth Schüssler Fiorenza, *Bread Not Stone: The Challenge of Feminist Biblical Interpretation* (Boston: Beacon Press, 1984); Mary Ann Tolbert, ed., *Semeia 28. The Bible and Feminist Hermeneutics* (Chico, CA: Scholars Press, 1983); Susan Sellers, ed., *Feminist Criticism: Theory and Practice* (Toronto: University Press of Toronto, 1991); Marcia Broucek, ed., *Just a Sister Away: A Womanist Vision of Women's Relationships in the Bible.* (New York: LuraMedia, 1988).

12. Rosemary Radford Ruether, *Religion and Sexism: Images of Woman in the Jewish and Christian Traditions* (New York: Simon and Schuster, 1974); Ann Loades, ed., *Feminist Theology: A Reader* (London: SPCK, 1990); Rosemary Radford Ruether and Rosemary Skiller Keller, *Women and Religion in America.* 3 vols. (New York: Harper and Row, 1981–1990); Barbara J. MacHaffie, ed., *Readings in Her Story: Women in Christian Tradition* (Minneapolis: Fortress Press, 1992); Amy Oden, ed., *In Her Words: Women's Writings in the History of Christian Thought* (Nashville: Abingdon, 1994).

13. Elisabeth Schüssler Fiorenza, ed., *Searching the Scriptures: A Feminist Introduction* (New York: Crossroad, 1993); Patricia Demers, *Women as Interpreters of the Bible* (New York: Paulist, 1992).

14. Bass, Dorothy C. and Sanora Hughes Boyd, eds., *Women in American Religious History: An Annotated Bibliography and Guide to Sources* (Boston: G. K. Hall, 1986).; Ann M. Boylan, "Evangelical Womanhood in the Nineteenth Century: The Role of Women in Sunday Schools," *Feminist Studies* 4(1978): 62–80; J. R. Brink, ed., *Female Scholars: A Tradition of Learned Women before 1800* (Montreal: Eden Press Women's Studies, 1980); Barbara Caine, *Victorian Feminists* (New York: Oxford

University Press, 1992); Ginette Castro, *American Feminism: A Contemporary History* (New York: New York University Press, 1990); Richard L. Greaves, *Triumph over Silence: Women in Protestant History* (Westport, CT: Greenwood Press, 1985); Ann Green, *Women in American Religious History* (Boston: G. K. Hall, 1986); bell hooks, *Ain't I a Woman?: Black Women and Feminism* (Boston: South End Press, 1981); Gerder Lerner, *The Grimké Sisters from South Carolina: Pioneers for Women's Rights and Abolition* (NY: Schocken 1971); Philippa Levine, *Victorian Feminism, 1850–1900* (Gainesville: University Presses of Florida, 1989); Bert James Loewenberg and Ruth Bogin, eds., *Black Women in Nineteenth-Century American Life: Their Words, Their Thoughts, Their Feelings* (Philadelphia: Pennsylvania State University Press 1976); Florence M. Smith, *Mary Astell* (New York: Columbia University Press, 1912).

15. Karlyn Kohrs Campbell, ed., *Man Cannot Speak for Her: A Critical Study of Early Feminist Rhetoric,* 2 vols. (New York: Greenwood Press, 1989); Moira Ferguson, *First Feminists: British Women Writers 1578–1799* (Bloomington, Indiana University Press, 1985); Phyllis Mack, *Visionary Women: Ecstatic Prophecy in Seventeenth Century England* (Los Angeles: University fo California Press, 1992).

Chapter 1

INTERPRETING
THE BIBLE

WHAT IS INTERPRETATION?

What is interpretation? What is hermeneutics? Generally speaking, it is an attempt by a reader to have a conversation with a text. The goal is to find some type of meaning or understanding of the text. The *Interpreter's Dictionary of the Bible* (*IDB*) explains that an interpreter is "one who unfolds the meaning of what is said, seen or dreamed by another." Bernard C. Lategan in the new *Anchor Bible Dictionary* claims that, "Interpretation is essential to discerning the will of God."[1]

According to the *The Encyclopedia of Religion*, the study and practice of hermeneutics is much more complicated. It "refers to the intellectual discipline concerned with the nature and presuppositions of the interpretation of human expressions." This process of interpretation raises the issues of the "nature of the text, what it means to understand a text," and "how understanding and interpretation are determined by the presuppositions and beliefs (the horizon) of the audience to which the text is being interpreted."[2] Historically, interpreters of the Bible have attempted to differentiate between exegesis and hermeneutics. "Hermeneutics was the task of the theologian and exegesis was left to a biblical specialist.[3]

INTERPRETING THE BIBLE

Meaning and the study of interpretation or hermeneutics has been an important topic of discussion since the first works of the Bible were collected and edited. Even Jesus and Paul appear to have their own distinctive methodologies "derived from the Rules of Hillel."[4] The gospel writers portray a Jesus who believed in a literal interpretation of creation, quoted scriptures from the Old Testament to support his point of view, and applied those same Scriptures to his work and movement.[5] Paul also attempts to link the Jewish Scriptures with Christian ideologies. His methods are often "Christo-centered," including foreshadowing (typology), and allegory.[6]

For every passage of Scripture, readers can find an almost infinite number of interpretations during the past 2,000 years. Yet at the very basis of every interpretation is the relationship between the reader and the text. The text or the Bible can only supply answers to the questions posed to it by its readers. Sometimes the Bible does not appear to answer the questions; it is at this point that the readers decide to look elsewhere for answers or to create an interpretative system that will help to answer their questions.

Tracing the history of interpretation of all of those questions and relationships within the Bible would fill several volumes. Indeed, even after scholars discussed all the major interpretative strategies, there would probably be hundreds of other strategies which could be discovered in neglected texts about the Bible.

POPULAR VIEWS OF THE BIBLE: RULE BOOK, TRANSCRIPT OF GOD, AND OBJECT OF WORSHIP

For many the Bible holds the answers to all of their ethical dilemmas. It governs their actions in the now and the hereafter. These people often claim that the Bible is a transcript from God. It contains exact instructions from God to His people. The Bible, more than anything else within the Christian religion, becomes an object of worship. They want to know the exact meaning of interpretation of a story, a parable, or a letter. They want concrete answers that time will not erode.

Scholars themselves are not immune to this quest. Even, "The Emperor Constantine, spared nothing to procure for the Oriental churches correct copies of all the Bibles. Charlemagne and his successors have done the same for the Latin Bibles of the Western church."[7]

Becoming proficient in the exact interpretation and wording of a certain translation of the Bible becomes a life-long pursuit. Reciting certain passages of Scripture becomes a healthy way of repeating the words of God for the benefit of other people. Games have even been invented, such as "Bible Trivia" which help adherents to memorize the Bible.

Yet if students of the Bible are honest with themselves, they will have to admit that the interpretations they hold are based upon certain beliefs, or presuppositions about the Bible, or certain methodologies employed in studying the text. There is no such thing as a completely objective or perfect interpretation of the Bible.

Jews and Christians alike claim the Bible as a record of sacred history. Each would see themselves as chosen by God to perform a special mission on earth. They use the Bible to define their communities in terms of theology, rituals, sexual relations, morals, and even standards of clothing and appearance. In seeking personal guidance from its pages, they detect appropriate political and ecclesiastical structures.[8]

CRYSTAL BALL

The Bible is a very important part of our cultural heritage. People respect it so much that they often do not know what to do with it. For some, its passages are filled with enigmatic words that hold keys to the solutions of personal dilemmas or future events. Speculation about the end of the earth as portrayed in the book of Revelation surface every time there is a major political power struggle that results in war.

Others have a more direct approach to divining the future. In order to find an answer to a personal question they open the Bible at random and point to any verse on the page. As the theory goes, God should direct your hand to the perfect verse that will answer your question.

GOOD LUCK CHARM

Many people hold to superstitions about carrying a certain Bible verse in their wallets or purses as insurance. There are countless stories about how a lucky person was carrying a Bible in a front shirt pocket or a back pants pocket and it saved them from a random bullet or knife attack. These people, like the people who keep a leather-covered, gold-leaf Bible on their coffee tables, never study their Bibles. They keep them around for comfort and protection.

A POLITICAL TOOL OF THE FAITHFUL AND NOT-SO-FAITHFUL

Throughout the history of Judaism and Christianity, the Bible or the Book has been central to constructing the identities, rituals, ethics, and beliefs of its readers. For centuries peoples have searched its pages to find meaning for their lives, their families, and their countries. It has legitimated kings and queens, created cultural family norms, and offered a view of the future that made the here and now more bearable. Some feminists and liberation theologians would contend that it has subjugated women and entire nations and given a rationale for the destruction of earth's resources.

Thus, the Bible has been used as a political tool by the "religious" and the not-so-religious to bring about positive social change as well as to incite and prolong disastrous, debilitating wars. While many have used interpretations to give insightful advice on ethical dilemmas, there are others who would use interpretations to control, intimidate, and abuse. The sword of truth has often become "The Only Truth." Many, hoping to fulfill apocalyptic prophesies in the Bible, have come preaching peace in the name of a God and have left their listeners in a pine box.

Monarchs, popes, ecclesiastical authorities, as well as unlikely political alliances have governed people in the name of the God of the Bible. Their interpretations of the Bible became binding and thus were eventually accepted by the majority of Jews or Christians. Yet there were always dissenters who sought to promulgate or discover their own interpretations of the Bible.[9] Many of those dissenting voices were lost and now are beginning to find their way into the mainstream of biblical interpretation today.

OWNERSHIP OF THE BIBLE

[T]he proper place for the Bible is in the Church.[10]

The Church is not to determine what Scripture teaches, but Scripture determines what ought to be taught in the church.[11]

Does the Bible belong only to Jews and Christians? Do the churches and synagogues have a right to determine the meaning of the Bible for everyone? Much of the contents of the Bible may have been grounded, collected by, and edited by people within these religious traditions, but should they be the only legitimate interpreters? The Bible's influence has always gone beyond the sanctuary. It has influenced family law, literature, architecture, art, political structures, availability of food stuffs, clothing styles, and more. Thus, those people who have felt its touch upon their lives or heard its doctrines have a right to investigate it for themselves.

Many within the Judeo-Christian traditions would challenge the right of others to faithfully interpret their Word or Words of God. Interpreters must study ancient, dead, and esoteric languages in order to decipher the meaning of the texts. Entrance into a particular society of interpreters (denomination or order) is usually based upon gaining mastery of the tools as well as assenting to dogmatic beliefs about the teachings of the Bible and a particular church or synagogue. Without linguistic tools and historical awareness, the texts can be misinterpreted. For many who are unfamiliar with Greek, Hebrew, or Aramaic, an interpretation using these foreign-sounding words seems like magic. And magic can be very powerful!

In the name of objectivity and honesty, biblical interpreters continually seek to limit those who would determine "meaning" of the Bible. The old *International Standard Bible Encyclopedia* (*ISBE*) claims that the interpreters must be completely objective: "It is accordingly a purely reproductive process, involving no originality of thought on the part of the interpreter."[12] Yet within scholarly works which seek to give a survey of biblical interpretation in history, tendencies and biases toward particular people and methodologies is common. John H. Hayes agrees that religious communities influenced, even determined "the results of exegesis and interpretation."[13] S. J. Case in the *Dictionary of the Apostolic Church* (1:620) unashamedly boasts:

> Christians possessed a superior understanding, which allowed them to alter phraseology, to paraphrase freely, or even to cite loosely from memory. Thus their methods were more spontaneous than those of scribism, yet the general character of their interpretation was predominately Jewish. Its free handling of the text, its disregard for the original setting, its logical vagaries, its slight tendency to become artificial, were all Jewish traits.[14]

For instance, a recent article by an editor on the history of interpretation says, "Erasmus exemplified the finest in Renaissance scholarship that emphasized the original sources."[15] Yet as early as 1689 Richard Simon said, "Erasmus, who was well enough furnished with those sorts of manuscripts, is never the less guilty of gross errors."[16] For the same editor above, "Calvin was the greatest exegete of the Reformation."[17] Other works surveying the history of biblical interpretation barely mention Calvin[18] or severely criticize him for his subjectivism.[19] If you are a Lutheran then Luther's works are superb. If you are a Roman Catholic then "R. Simon, [quoted above] a French Oratorican priest . . . was the first to apply the critical method to the New Testament."[20] But the Baptist *Mercer Dictionary of the Bible* claims that modern historical criticism began with Samuel Reimarus's famous essay in 1778, "On the Purpose of Jesus and His Disciples."[21]

In determining the approved and proper method, scholars from competing religious traditions search different works and answer questions quite differently. The *ISBE* again gives its own opinion: "In the legitimate sense of the term, every interpreter of the Bible is 'prejudiced,' i.e., is guided by certain principles which he holds antecedently to his work of interpretation."[22]

Scholars often voice their fears about others who interpret the Bible differently. In the 1682 edition of Richard Simon's *A Critical History of the Old Testament*, his blunt assessment of Protestantism reads this way: "Those Protestants without a doubt are either ignorant or prejudiced who affirm that the Scripture is plain of itself. As they have laid aside the Tradition of the Church, and will acknowledge no other principle of Religion but the Scripture itself, they were obliged to suppose it plain and sufficient for the establishing of the truth of faith without any Tradition."[23]

He even asserts that the early Fathers of the church were not scholars. Their mission was primarily religious or Religion, not a literal understanding of the text: "[I]t is certain that most of the Fathers have not had all the necessary helps nor time enough to search into the great difficulties in the Scripture."[24]

In the end Richard Simon concludes that all are biased: "But after all I found that no one had hither to thoroughly searched into the criticism of the Scripture; every one has commonly spoke according to his prejudice."[25] At the end of his book he acknowledges that some Protestant authors are worth reading even though they "are very conceited and deluded."[26]

In the old *Schaff-Herzog Encyclopedia*, Henry S. Nash speaks of something termed "eisegesis and dislocations"[27] which he claims is born out of a subjective rather than a completely objective view of Scripture. Raymond Brown in his article on "hermeneutics" in the *Jerome Biblical Commentary* also expresses concern over an abuse of the Bible. He recognizes a tendency among some interpreters to study texts that only have theological value for the reader. "In its consequences for theology such a selectivity on the basis of relevance is truly frightening."[28]

More recently, Elisabeth Schüssler Fiorenza criticizes her feminist sisters for not following her own prescribed methodology: "Women's Bible commentaries focus on the women characters in the Bible as well as on what biblical authors have written about women. Such a methodological focus on woma[e]n is in danger of identifying women's reality with women's representation and of succumbing to the totalizing power of the grammatically masculine so-called generic text."[29]

Josef Blank in the book *Conflicting Ways of Interpreting the Bible* also points out that interpreters are biased: "Behind it all we have to deal with the problem that the historico-critical method is never a neutral, value-free instrument of research which can be used in a purely technical way."[30]

Carl Braaten eloquently summarizes the interpreter's dilemma: "If reason precedes faith, the simple believer is made dependent upon the oscillating opinion of historical scholars; on the other hand, if faith is primary, the suspicion arises that faith projects its own basis and content out of itself."[31]

DEFINING THE METHODOLOGIES

Attempting to find uniform definitions of the major interpretative strategies used in and outside religious circles over the past 2,000 years is next to impossible. Scholars generally describe (not define) the methodology and its results. Neither can this chapter survey all of the major methodologies. Although somewhat reductionist, major methodologies before the explosion of the historical-critical method will be considered under these categories: Literal, Ethical-Theological, and Symbolic. Some of the other names of approaches to interpreting the Bible include Socinian, pneumatic, scholiastic, artistic, exposition, allegoresis, numerology, etymology, tropology, aetiology, anagoge, illumination, materialist, psychohistorical, African American, ideological, and liberation theology perspective. More recent methodological approaches not fully developed during the period under consideration by this book, include criticisms of form, rhetorical, redaction, canonical, source, structuralism, reader-response, materialistic, tendency, psychological, sociological, semiotics, and others.

TRANSLATION

At best, every English version of the Bible was translated by people with focal points of differing lengths. Those spectacles do not always produce clear and precise translations. Although the scholars study the Greek, Hebrew, and Aramaic, they must decide which groups or editions of manuscripts will be used in a translation to be included in the Bible (textual criticism). While we recognize that our interpretations of the Bible are conditioned by numerous cultural experiences, we must also realize that the translator is no different or less influenced than we are.[32]

LITERAL INTERPRETATION

Many readers of today and yesterday claim to discover the literal interpretation of the Bible. What does the term "literal" mean? Does it mean "physical, plain, textual, grammatical, or philological?" Raymond Brown suggests that "it is the sense which the human author directly intended and which his words convey."[33] But how do you know what the author intended? And more importantly, how do you develop a methodology that will uncover this meaning?

ETHICAL-THEOLOGICAL

The Bible has often become a source of ethical theory and practice for its readers. Many would ask the Book, how should I live my life as a Christian or a Jew? Indeed, the first five books of the Old Testament (Hebrew Bible or First Testament) are commonly termed the "law." Throughout history, theologians looked to the Bible for a basis in dogmatic theology, in practical psychology and devotion. Ancient interpreters labeled this approach "tropological."

Many people looked to the future to inform and interpret the present. Rubem Alves terms this a hope for the "presence of the absent."[34] People hope for a perfect world and perfect life which has been won by the death and resurrection of Jesus. They interpret many passages of Scripture as applying to this distant future home and life. This approach has many names: teleological, anagogical, mystical, eschatological, heavenly, and metaphysical theological speculation.[35]

SYMBOL

This category is discussed more than any other by authors who have researched the history of interpretation. Perhaps it is because so many passages within the Bible remain opaque and interpreters want to penetrate the dark window to understanding. If they do not know what the text originally meant to the author then it must have some meaning or it would not be included as sacred Scripture? This type of approach to the Bible has many categories: typology, allegory, spiritual exegesis, figurative, analogy, Christological, and intellectual.

In order to rescue the Old Testament or Hebrew Bible, many Christians believed that everything in the Old Testament corresponded to elements or activities found in the new. They found Jesus and the cross in every book. A death, a flower, a stream, everything had meaning because it pointed to the Jesus event. This approach totally divorced the passage from its literal and historical context. But it is very effective because, in essence, the reader or interpreter can make the text say anything he or she wants it to say.

An old quotation used by many attempts to explain typology or allegory this way: "Thus Jerusalem signifies the city, the Church, a settled and moral order, and the everlasting life."[36] Raymond Brown attempts to improve this quotation by explaining the different types of interpretative approaches which have been employed. "When Jerusalem is mentioned in the Bible, in its literal sense it is a Jewish city: allegorically, however, it refers to the Church of Christ, tropologically Jerusalem stands for the soul of man; anagogically it stands for the heavenly city."[37]

WOMEN AND THE HISTORY OF INTERPRETATION

Interestingly and sadly, only one major resource used in the preparation of this chapter on the history of interpretation includes mention of methodologies employed by women before the historical critical period. R. Simon compares his work on the New Testament to the ". . . Ladies in St. Jerome's time: Who not content to read, the Scripture in the Vulgar tongue, dispersed among the People, they diligently enquired after the corrected Copies, learning those very Tongues in which they were writ. I assert nothing, which cannot be maintained by the Letters of those Pious Ladies. . . ."[38]

While feminist criticism is touted as a new methodology employed by scholars of the late nineteenth and twentieth centuries, we will learn that its strategies were employed centuries earlier.

Notes

1. Interpretation, *Interpreters Dictionary of the Bible* (NY: Abingdon Press, 1962): vol. 2, 724.
2. Van A. Harvey, "Hermeneutics," in *The Encyclopedia of Religion*, Mircea Eliade, ed. (New York: Macmillan Publishing Co, 1987)6:279–280.
3. Robert M. Grant, *A Short History of the Interpretation of the Bible* (New York: Macmillan, 1966), 11.
4. E. Glenn Hinson, "Interpretation, History of," *Mercer Dictionary of the Bible*, Watson Mills, ed. (Georgia: Mercer University Press, 1990), 408.
5. Grant, *History of Interpretation*, 18–27.
6. Ibid., 28–42.
7. Richard Simon, *A Critical History of the Text of the New Testament* (R. Taylor, N.P. 1689), p. 5 of the unnumbered preface.
8. See John B. Gabel and Charles B. Wheeler, *The Bible as Literature. An Introduction.* Second Edition (New York: Oxford University Press, 1990), 249–265.
9. Paul D. Hanson, *The Dawn of Apocalyptic* (Philadelphia: Fortress Press, 1975), 1–32.
10. Grant, *History of Interpretation*, 13.
11. "Exegesis or Hermeneutics," in *The New Schaff-Herzog Encyclopedia of Religious Knowledge*, Samuel M. Jackson, ed. (New York: Funk and Wagnalls, 1909)4:241.
12. "Interpretation," *International Standard Bible Encyclopedia*, James Orr, ed. (Chicago: Howard-Severance Company, 1915), 3:1489.
13. Carl R. Halladay, *Biblical Exegesis: A Beginner's Handbook* (Atlanta: John Knox Press, 1973), 19.
14. S. J. Case, "Interpretation," *Dictionary of the Apostolic Church* (New York: Charles Scribners Sons, 1915), 1:620.
15. David Alan Black and David S. Dockery, *New Testament Criticism and Interpretation* (Grand Rapids, MI: Zondervan Publishing House, 1991), 47.
16. Simon, *History of the Text*, p. 2 of the unnumbered preface.
17. Black and Dockery, *New Testament Criticism*, 47.
18. *Schaff-Herzog Encyclopedia*, 4:244.
19. Grant, *History of Interpretation*, 13.
20. Frederick Gast, "Modern New Testament Criticism," *Jerome Biblical Commentary*, (New York: Prentice Hall, 1968) 2:8(5a).
21. E. Glenn Hinson, "Interpretation," *Mercer Dictionary of the Bible*, 410.
22. "Interpretation," *International Standard Bible Encyclopedia*, 3:1489.
23. Richard Simon, *A Critical History of the Old Testament*. English Translation from the French (London: 1682), Preface labeled "b" or approximately, p. 8.
24. Ibid, 10.
25. Ibid, 12.
26. Ibid, 140.
27. Henry S. Nash, "Exegesis and Hermeneutics," *Schaff Herzog Encyclopedia*, 4:240.
28. Raymond Brown, "Hermeneutics," *Jerome Biblical Commentary* (New York: Prentice Hall, 1968), 2:609.
29. Elisabeth Schüssler Fiorenza, ed. *Searching the Scripture: A Feminist Introduction* (New York: Crossroad, 1993), 20.

30. Joseph Blank, "The Authority of the Church in the Interpretation of Scripture," in *Conflicting Ways of Interpreting the Bible,* ed. by Hans Küng and Jurgen Moltmann (New York: Seabury Press, 1968), 68.
31. Carl Braaten, *New Directions in Theology Today, vol. 2, History and Hermeneutics* (Philadelphia: Westminster Press, 1974), 49.
32. Ralph W. Klein, *Textual Criticism of the Old Testament. From the Septuagint to Qumran* (Philadelphia: Fortress Press, 1974).
33. R. Brown, *Jerome Biblical Commentary,* 2:607.
34. Rubem Alves, *What Is Religion?* (New York: Maryknoll, 1984), 6 and following.
35. Werner G. Jeanround, "Interpretation, History of," *Anchor Bible Dictionary,* David Noel Freedman, ed. (New York: Doubleday, 1992), 3:429.
36. *Schaff-Herzog Encyclopedia,* 4:241.
37. R. Brown, *Jerome Biblical Commentary,* 2:612.
38. R. Simon, *History of the Text,* pp. 3–4 of the unnumbered preface.

Chapter 2

EGALITARIAN
READINGS

Literal Approaches to the Bible

INTRODUCTION

The collection of writings in this chapter span about a two-hundred-year period in England and America. All of the writers, except Phoebe Palmer, trace their religious roots to Quakerism; even Barbara Kellison claims to know of Quaker literatures. All of their strategies attempt to take the Bible literally, producing interpretations that follow the biblical text ever so closely. They believed that their faith in the Christian God had produced a Bible that treated all people equally and their works attempted to prove it to anyone inside and outside of Christianity.

George Fox, the founder of Quakerism, wrote many letters and treatises to members of the Society of Friends all over the world on behalf of women in the seventeenth century in England. He upheld the right of women to preach, teach, administer money, as well as to nurture and lead Quaker communities. He found Scriptures that supported every one of his positions while belittling those who would suppress the active worship of females.

Margaret Askew Fell Fox, also in the seventeenth century, argues for the right of women to preach in public. Women have always preached, as in the examples of Mary and Martha, Anna, the women at the tomb, and others. Stepping out of a literal mode, Margaret Fox asserted that the Church is the image of woman. She was created by

God and no one would be against women speaking in their own Church if they were listening to God.

Another Quaker, Sarah Moore Grimké, living in the early nineteenth century, penned a brilliant defense of the equality of women based upon the Bible. Her interpretative strategies are sophisticated and complicated. Men and women are equal based upon her readings of Genesis 1, Ephesians 5:22, I Corinthians 11 and 14, and I Timothy 2.

Lucretia Mott, writing about a half a century later, wrote many discourses and gave numerous speeches on the equality of women. Taking the Bible from Genesis to Revelation, she demonstrated how the laws and stories were given and apply equally to men and women.

A Pentecostal preacher within Methodism, Phoebe Palmer, followed many of the same strategies as the Quakers, yet she claimed that she was not really arguing for the right of a woman to preach before a mixed audience of males and females. Her historic book, *The Promise of the Father*, cites extraordinary women in both Testaments who were called by God for a special mission. She points out that Paul's writings are contradictory, stretching the interpretation of the "keep silent" passages to any time a woman opens her mouth to sing, teach her children, or to even write books. Listing a few historic women who rose to leadership within their cultures, her real purpose in writing the book was to catalogue the extraordinary women living during her own lifetime. If God calls a woman, how can anyone stop her?

And finally, Barbara Kellison (a pseudonym), of Madison County, Iowa, authored a tract in 1867, published in Dayton, Ohio, defending the rights of women in the church. Her approaches are as varied and complicated as Sarah Grimké's. She focuses on her opponents objections and refutes them one by one by pointing to specific words and contexts within biblical passages. She includes the creation story, stories about prophetesses, other women whose voices were heard within congregations, the mythology of the weaker vessel, and a warning about the day of judgment to those who would stand in the way of women.

GEORGE FOX (1624–1691)
AND
MARGARET ASKEW FELL FOX (1614–1702)

Our most considerable enemy nowe in our view are the quakers.
I thinke their principles and practices
are not very consistent with civil government,
much less with the discipline of an army.[1]

—OLIVER CROMWELL, 1656

HISTORICAL SITUATION: THE SEVENTEENTH CENTURY IN ENGLAND

Quakerism was spreading like wildfire throughout the English colonies. By 1660, there were reports of between 60,000 to 150,000 Quakers making there way through the burroughs. While George Fox is credited as the founder of the Quakers, the movement itself was much larger than the man. Itinerate Quaker preachers made their way through the towns preaching a gospel of liberation from everything. They often enrolled stray Levellers, Baptists, Diggers, Familialists (Family of Love), and others who had worked for the disestablishment of the state church.[2]

Their strategies often included stealing pulpits, pulling down ministers from their pulpits, refusing to pay tithes, and even running naked across the green. They refused to recognize the upper class or gentry and did not use appropriate language or bows to acknowledge their presence. Their sermons questioned the primacy of the Scriptures. They taught about an inner light, the Holy Spirit, who was above the Scriptures.[3] And as one writer protested: "They even permitted their women to preach; 'a monstrous practice,' condemned as against nature."[4]

GEORGE FOX

> *I would to God all the Lord's People were Prophets;*
> *And Surely the Lord's People are made up of*
> *both men and women.*
>
> —GEORGE FOX

"In 1640, when Fox was eleven, public distaste explodes and Archbishop Laud is impreached and imprisoned; in 1640 a censorship that has been in force for years is lifted; in early 1642 the bishops are excluded from the House of the Lords, and by that summer, civil war, with all the consequent extra mobility and disruption of traditional standards and hierarchies, has broken out; in 1643, espiscopacy is abolished and mostly Presbyterian Assembly of Divines is set up to reform the Church of England. By 1644 numerous radical religious movements are beginning to emerge. In 1646 when Fox is seventeen, the Levellers, the first democratic political movement in modern history, develops, led by John Lilburne and in 1649 the first communist community is set up by the Diggers, led by Gerrard Winstanley. (Both of these men are later to become Quakers.) By the end of the year the King is beheaded, Oliver Cromwell has been Lord Protector and the whole country has been set on its head."[5]

George Fox led his own personal revolution against the injustices resulting from the corruption of the reigning institutionalized religions in the seventeenth century. Men and women, including himself and his wife Margaret, were imprisoned for their faith. Both Margaret and George lost all of their property to the state because of holding unauthorized or illegal religious meetings. This did not stop him from continuing his mission and indicting religious and state authorities for what was in his view "diabolical" activities:

Now hear you magistrates, priests and people, which do put into prison sons and daughters for prophesying, and the Lord's people, You shew a contrary spirit, you shew a spirit that hath erred from Moses' Spirit. . . .[6]

And come, ye clerks, and parson, and vicars for the whore hath many garments, and decks herself with many colours, as the beast had many names, and likenesses, and colours; so you have many changings.[7]

BIOGRAPHY

"George Fox, the weaver's son, apprentice to a shoemaker and dealer in wool, had little book-learning beyond the Bible, but he had as a young man acquired first-hand knowledge of varieties of religious experience by walking through the Midlands to seek out and converse with "professors" of Puritanism in all its forms."[8]

Born into a family in Leicestershire, England with five brothers and sisters, George did not follow in the footsteps of his father who was a weaver and a Puritan church warden. While his family thought that he should become an ordained minister, he chose instead to become a shoemaker and a sheepherder.[9] He could not bear to be ordained by a church where people led such hypocritical lives. When he was about nineteen years old he left his job, family, and home in search of a true religion and religious experience. He remembered that day vividly: "At the command of God, on the ninth day of the seventh month 1643, I left my relation, and brake off all familiarity or fellowship with young and old."[10]

Eventually George found answers to his questions through mystical experiences which he termed "openings." These were personal meetings with the Divine which produced an "inner light."

George taught that everyone who knew Jesus possessed an inner light which should be cultivated and allowed to shine. He rejected institutional hierarchies, ordained clergy, sacramental systems, and refused to fight in wars or make vows.[11] He, with likeminded separatists, formed an association by the name of the "Children of Light," which was later termed Friends, Quakers.[12]

Fox spent most of his life carrying his message throughout Britain, North America, northern Europe, and other parts of the world including islands in the Caribbean. In addition, he wrote over 270 tracts and 400 letters.[13]

During his itinerate ministry he traveled with virtually no money or clothing.

> His privations were great: a night in a haystack in rain and snow, a day's journey through deep snow, a vigil sitting among furze bushes till it was day; another night under a haystack, footsore and weary, a night with three companions under a hedge,—such were some of the experiences of these months. He was dressed in leathern breeches and

doublet, and a white hat, the leathern dress being chosen for its simplicity and durability.[14]

He was often met with verbal hostility, physical violence, and imprisonment. Here is a typical account of one of the altercations: "At Mansfield-Woodhouse, near Mansfield, when he spoke in the church, the congregation fell on him in a great rage, beat him with their hands, Bibles, and sticks and nearly smothered him. They then put him in the stocks, and afterwards stoned him out of the town. He soon found himself in more serious trouble."[15]

Here is a sample of one of his sermons that might have incited a congregation to riot against him.

> And come, priests, vicars, and curates, and parsons, are you not they that will no go without a bad, and those which have taken the people's money for that which was not bread, and the messengers of Satan, and his ministers of unrighteousness, which Satan hath transformed himself into, that takes and will have money of them, and means, whom you do not work for, and where you have neither plowed nor threshed, and where you never planted, and have made the gospel chargeable? Come up, guilty, or not guilty? answer for yourselves, and come up, priests, and curates, and vicars, and parsons, are you not such as go in long robes, fashions and lusts of the world, with your ribands and points, and double cuffs, and wearing of gold rings, in the lusts of the flesh, and pride of life, and the lust of the eyes, which is not of the father but of the world, more like your mountebanks, and fiddlers, and stage-players, than like unto sober men that preach the gospel? guilty, or not guilty?[16]

His first imprisonment was in 1650 for breaking the Blasphemy Act. The sentence was for six months but it lasted almost a year.[17] Between 1650 and 1674 (George was between 36 and 50 years of age), he was sentenced to prison at least eight times for breaking laws for preaching, plotting against Charles II, holding illegal religious meetings, and other infractions.[18]

Eleven years after the death of Margaret Fell's husband, George married her. He was ten years her junior: "I had seen from the Lord a considerable time before, that I should take Margaret Fell to be my wife . . . yet I had not received a command from the Lord for the accomplishment of it then."[19]

After one week of a honeymoon, they left each other for their own itinerate ministries. George landed in prison and Margaret was sent to jail. Most of their married life was spent evangelizing in different parts of the world. They communicated mainly through letters.[20]

Always on the move, except when imprisoned, George kept in touch with many of the Quakers through letters. According to Susan Mosher Stuard, early in his career George advocated equality for women and men. She suggests that his letter "Concerning Sons and Daughters, and Prophetess speaking and prophesying in the law and the Gospel" was one of his earliest letters on the subject.[21]

VIEW OF THE BIBLE

George Fox studied his Bible fervently. He cared little for formal education or interpretations written by others. He agreed that it was difficult to understand the Bible but the educated clergy in England did not know as much as he did because they were "unlearned" in the things of Christ. To Fox, the "teachers of the world are ignorant of the Prophets." Take for example the apostle Peter; he was "unlearned in letters" but he was "learned" in Christ.[22] He gained his knowledge by waiting on the Lord. He would often seek guidance from God on a specific verse of Scripture by withdrawing by himself into the countryside. This personal illumination was a revelation in itself and was from what he determined to be a higher plane than his so-called educated opponents.

Fox set his readers straight on every issue by employing a variety of methodologies that forced his readers back to their Bibles. He believed that they were living in a new time or dispensation (time of Gospel, Day of Christ, the time of his Grace),[23] yet vacillated on his view of the Old Testament or Hebrew Bible. He wanted to keep only certain parts of the Hebrew Bible as authoritative. It is Word of God but some of the Word no longer applied to the lives of Christians. He used some Hebrew stories[24] as authoritative for the lives of his constituents. The people of Israel were but "figures and Shadows of the Substance, Christ Jesus, the Holy one."[25] Yet, in other publications, he claims that people are not bound by the law.[26]

For example, when attempting to prove that women should meet together separately and be included in the worship services he cites Exodus 38:29. Women in the Old Testament are actively participating in worship: "And in the time of the Law, the Women were to offer up Sacrifices and Offerings, as well as Men, upon God's altar, as you may see Hannah."[27]

Yet, in other tracts, he warns the people not to live by or under the law. In the sermon, "The Woman Learning in Silence," he says, "but if you are led by the spirit, then you are not under the law."[28]

Women and men in the time of the Law were partners or "meet helps" to one another, "in the Work and Service of the Holy Things about the Tabernacle and Sanctuary, and the Women had their Assemblies."[29] For Fox, the God of the Old Testament is certainly the same God of the New Testament.

THE PROBLEM

A collection of letters written between 1672 and 1676 to Friends Meetings in Barbados, New England, Virginia, and other parts of the world, reveals that George Fox attempted to solve many community issues. Some of those issues included the issues of separate women's meetings, preaching, teaching, authority of women, governing, and administering monies collected for welfare purposes.[30]

INTERPRETATIVE STRATEGY

George may have had an inner light but he knew how to appeal to the authority of the Bible. He challenged his hearers to read the Bible closely. Obviously from the reports that he had been getting, Quakers did not know what the Bible said about women; if they did, there would not be any issues to solve. In order to break their stereotypical views of the role of women within Christian communities, he acted like a father, scolding them for their attitudes and actions.

Some of his strategies included interpreting volatile Scriptures by referring to the immediate context. Several Scriptures are compared with each other to show their inconsistencies. Often his philosophy of the inner light experience allowed him to add his own, new interpretations to verses long-used against women. His egalitarian view of the Christian community helped him to create an androgynous vocabulary. Finally, he began to discover feminine imagery for God in both the Old and New Testaments.

Fox clearly saw that the woman controversies originated with the men and not the women. He challenged the spiritual status of the males within the community by pointing to characters or stories within the Bible in which men supported women. These stories became models or examples of appropriate Quaker living. If the men were actually believers, they would encourage, not discourage, the women in their work. Their attitudes degrade woman. He calls them "niggards," and claims that they may have a "dark spirit."[31]

EQUALITY IN TRANSLATION AND EXAMPLE (ROLE MODELS)

Fox firmly believed that equality between the sexes should be a foundational belief in all of the meetings. He recognized the power of language to evoke symbols. While in the process of interpreting the Bible, he created an androgynous vocabulary. George constantly used words such as "fellow laborers," "meets help," and "laborers and helpers in the Gospel."[32] He also took liberties with texts such as John 1:12 which he freely translated "and all that receive him, he gives them Power to become the Sons and Daughters of God."[33]

Role models of effective female leaders can be traced back to the Old Testament. Fox was trying to help his readers understand that women have always had leadership positions. For instance, women who lived hundreds of years ago were respected as powerful forces in the community of Israel.

Women stories found in the Old Testament are testimonies to the fact that men obeyed and listened to the opinions of women. He cited examples of stories where women gave directions or were in charge of some important activity. His very long list included: Sarah, Deborah, the Elder Women, and then others in the New Testament: Dorcas, Mary Magdalene, the other Mary, and the four daughters of Philip. There were also many partners such as Abraham and Sarah, Isaac and Rebecca, David and Abigal, Elijah and the widow, and others. He recalled a litany of honorable women who counseled

men. There were Rachel and Leah, the midwives in Exodus, Miriam
the prophetess, Deborah the judge, Hannah, Ruth and Naomi, and
Huldah:[34] "Neither King nor Priests despise this Prophetess's Teaching [Huldah] and Instruction, but obeyed it, as you may see what a
large Sermon she preached to them."[35]

And she was not the only woman to preach. There was Jephthah's
daughter who preached to him and Sampson's mother counseled
Manoah: "And here you may see the steadfastness of this Woman's
faith, beyond her Husband's, as in Judges 13."[36] Other women who
taught lessons were the woman of Canaan, and the woman who
anointed Jesus, the woman with the issue, and the women who testi-
fied to the resurrection of Jesus.[37]

MOTHERS AS ELDER WOMEN

Fox recognizes a diversity of female roles within society. He uses the
image of a mother who nurses her children and suggests that
women can do the same thing for the meetings. She can nourish by
teaching and preaching: "And the Elder Women in the Truth were
not only called Elders, but Mothers. Now a Mother in the Church of
Christ, and a Mother in Israel, is one that gives Suck, and Nourishes,
and Feeds, and Washes, and Rules, and is a Teacher in the Church,
and in the Israel of God, and an Admonisher, an Instructor, an
Exhorter."[38]

THE WOMEN'S MEETINGS

George, himself, set up the first separate Women's meetings. They
became a trademark for the early Quakers because women discovered independence and self-esteem in meetings that were totally
managed by themselves.[39] On the issue of separate meetings for
women, he wrote in 1674,

> But there is some dark Spirits that say, That for women to meet
> together to worship God, apart from Men, is monstrous and ridicu-

lous: But this dark Spirit has not defined what Worship is; for if a Company of Women should meet together, and some of these Women should kneel down, and lift up their Hands and Eyes to God . . . this is Worship: And if the dark Spirit calls this Monstrous and Ridiculous, because Men is not with them, then it will follow, it will be monstrous and ridiculous to pray to God, or to worship God, except Men be with them.[40]

PREACHING

Many suggested that women did not have the right to preach but Fox found plenty of evidence to refute this opinion.

And all that be of his Mind in the Lord, will encourage either Women or Widows, or Virgins, that have received the Gospel, to labour in it; and all that have not the Mind of the Apostle of the Lord, will discourage Womens labouring in the Gospel, and not entreat others to help them; but such will give them Liberty to labour in the Power of Darkness and to Slothfulness, and Carelessness; which the Wo is unto, and not the Blessing.[41]

Now Old Ely was not against the Assemblies of the Women . . . though some Men now-a-days may be against Womens Meetings or Assemblies in the Gospel-times, and against Womens speaking or Prophecying, but they are ignorant of the universal Spirit, and of their Service and labour to God . . . and are of a narrow Spirit, and are not the true Servers of God themselves; for if they were, they would have all People to serve God in his Power.[42]

Listening to the gossip about the women must have been more than he could bear. In this short paragraph Fox set up Moses and Aaron as godly examples that would have never delineated a specific role for women: "Now Moses and Aaron, and the Seventy Elders, did not say to those Assemblies of the Women, We can do our Work our selves, and you are more fitter to be at home to wash the Dishes; or such-like Expressions; but they did encourage them in the Work and Service of God, in those things which God had commanded them in the time of the Law."[43]

ADMINISTERING MONEY

Apparently the men and some husbands did not like the idea of women managing funds to support the Women's meetings or other types of philanthropic activities. Fox sets them straight by suggesting that a husband who is indeed a Christian would never prevent his wife from helping someone in need. He also points to Luke 8:1–3 which tells the story about how women financed the career of Jesus:

> And there is no Believing Husband will hinder his Believing Wife, being Heirs of Life, to administer some of their temporal thing to them that are in Necessity.[44]

> Now, would not some Niggards be ready to say, These Women [Mary, Joanna, and others who provided for Jesus out of their own pockets] pickt their Husbands Pockets; and others with Judas, who carry the Bag, may say, We must have one Purse, and is not our Gift and Benevolence sufficient?[45]

SUBORDINATION OF WOMEN, USURPING AUTHORITY, AND WOMEN TEACHING MEN

The Eve story has been used as grounds for a God-ordained subordinate position of women to men. Paul reiterates that belief in his letters by suggesting that there is a hierarchical order in marriage. Fox denies both of these interpretations. Eve may have been at fault in the Creation story, but it is of no consequence to Christians. In Christ all people are restored and thus men and women are partners or equals within Christianity: "For Man and Women were helps meet in the Image of God, and in Righteousness and Holiness, in the Dominion before they fell; but after the Fall, in the Transgression, the Man was to rule over His Wife; but in the Restauration by Christ, into the Image of God, and his Righteousness and Holiness again, in that they are helps meet, Man and Woman, as they were in before the Fall."[46]

Fox actually uses Pauline letters to refute Paul and the Creation story, although he does not quote the Scriptures word for word. In

Ephesians 5:24 (which Fox believes was written by Paul) women are to be submissive. Yet in I Corinthians 11:12 it states that males and females have a complementary relationship:

> And some Men may say, Man must have the Power and Superiority over the Woman, because God says, The man must rule over his Wife; and that Man is not of the Woman, but the Woman is of the Man: In deed after Man fell, the Command was; but before Man fell, there was no such Command; for they were both meet helps, and they were both to have Dominion over all that God made. And as the Apostle saith, for as the Woman is of the Man, his next Words are, so is the Man also by the Woman; but all thing are of God.[47]

The following passage is found in I Timothy 2:12 and is interpreted as prohibiting women from preaching in the assemblies: "But I suffer not a Woman to teach nor to usurp Authority over the Man; but learn in Silence, &c. For the Woman being deceived, was first in Transgression, &c."[48]

Fox argues again that the story of Eve does not apply. If a woman has learned the ways of Christ and is in subjection to the Spirit then she may teach and preach.[49]

ISSUE: KEEPING SILENT IN THE CHURCH (I CORINTHIANS 14:34)

Traditionally, I Corinthians 14 has been interpreted as prohibiting women from discussing issues or preaching in church.[50] If all people have the inner light of God, how can this be true? By closely reading the context of I Corinthians 14, Fox draws the conclusion that it is not only women who are asked to remain silent; there are times when all people are told to be silent in the church. He quotes I Corinthians 14:27, "So, here the Men must keep Silence in the Church in this case, as well as the Women."[51] He argues that everyone who becomes a Christian possesses the inner light, therefore everyone can speak for Christ, including women: ". . . if male and female have received the testimony of Jesus, they have received the spirit of prophesy."[52]

Using a contextual and logical approach to the documents, Fox listed evidence from I Corinthians 11:5 concluding that women can prophesy when their heads are covered. It does not make sense for a woman to be told to remain silent and then to ask her husband at home in I Corinthians 14:34 when Paul has already mentioned that women are prophesying or preaching in a community environment. He suggested that this verse was not meant as a prohibition of uplifting or helpful speech: "But when they have learnt of Christ their Husband at home, they are not forbidden of Christ from Prophesying or Praying; but to lie, babbling, and prating in the Church, such Speaking in the Church is a Shame."[53] The "silence" phrase is issued to those that would use destructive speech which would undermine or destroy the meeting.

Fox also claimed that I Corinthians 11 and 14 are illogical because widows and virgins don't have husbands. Why would they be prohibited from prophesying? And what about the husband who is not a Christian? How can a nonbeliever interpret or "sanctify" a Christian woman?

GOD IN THE IMAGE OF A FEMALE

The gentle and intuitive Fox recognized that within himself there were traits traditionally assigned to woman. He believed that the experience of the "inner light" freed men and women from typical cultural roles and expectations. In the midst of his own struggle to find freedom, he discovered the feminine side of God within the biblical teachings.[54] Here he quotes Proverbs 9:3 to prove that females are sent by the Divine and are of the Divine. To accept them is to accept the will of the Divine: "Wisdom she hath sent forth her Maidens. . . ."[55] "Here you may see the Wisdom of God sends forth Maidens though the Wisdom of the World will not receive them (that makes Ministers by their Wisdoms) and such as will not receive Wisdom, will not receive her Maidens, Prov. 9. 1.2.3."[56]

Fox believed the equality of males and females within Christ, this image was also reflected in the Divine. If there was a place for men to rule, there was also a place for women to rule: "[F]or that male in whom Christ doth reign, rule, and speak, he will own Christ in the female, there to reign, to rule and speak, and come to see the apostle's doctrine."[57]

SUMMARY

This humble and yet great man believed that his God taught equality, and for his entire life he not only preached equality, he lived it. His message lives on in his works as people continue to learn from this "uneducated" man. From the burroughs in England to the missionary fields of Barbados, Fox argued for the respect and honor of women. He believed that by denying women equality, men were flying in the face of the Almighty. In fact, the reflection of the Almighty may be seen in the face and activities of a woman, especially a mothering woman.

This radical stance brought violence and anguish into his own life. But his efforts opened the minds of both women and men toward the possibilities of a different kind of life as a Quaker. His enthusiastic support cracked the doors for women and built a foundation upon which later Quakers, such as Sarah Grimké and Lucretia Mott, could light a revolution that would change the lives of women forever in faraway America.[58]

MARGARET ASKEW FELL FOX

Fox's first disciple was probably a woman, and if Fox was the father of Quakerism, Fell was its mother.[1]

BIOGRAPHY

Margaret Askew married Thomas Fell in 1632 when she was seventeen or eighteen years old.[2] He was a member of the Long Parliament, Judge of Assize of the Chester and North Wales Circuit, Vicechancellor of the Duchy and Attorney for the County Palatine of Lancaster and was sixteen years older than Margaret.[3] She was a member of an old and wealthy family living on Marsh Grange, calling herself a Seeker for many years before meeting George Fox.

Together they produced nine children, and offered their home as a place of solace for Friends.[4] Judge Fell attempted to protect her and the new movement but never identified himself with it.[5] He died in 1658 and with his passing, she lost her political security.

Margaret's first encounter with George Fox was in 1652 when she was "convinced" and became a Friend. Within a few years, all of her household were convinced. Several of her children began to publish tracts and correspond with leaders within the movement. Margaret and George married in 1669. She was fifty-five and George was forty-five. Historians credit George with the founding of Quakerism, but it was Margaret who administered the finances, indeed donated her own fortune, kept track of correspondence at her home at Swarthmore, visited meetings, and spoke out publicly in defense of Quakers. Even after the death of George in 1691 she continued with her vigilant activities.

Margaret was often arrested, questioned, and jailed for her activities among the Quakers. In spite of this harassment, beginning in 1660 she continued her seditious activities by traveling thousands of miles preaching to Friends Meetings.[6] In 1664 she was arrested, tried, and found guilty of refusing to take an oath of allegiance as well as of holding unauthorized meetings of Friends in her home. Her property was confiscated and she was imprisoned for four years. After the death of Charles II, her land and house were restored to her.

Margaret wrote sixteen books and and at least twenty-seven pamphlets and epistles enlightening and defending the Quaker faith.[7] Only one of her pamphlets will be analyzed here, *Women's Speaking Justified*. It is reported to have been written during prison in about 1666, many years before her marriage to George and prior to his writings defending the status of women.

> Let this word of the Lord,
> which was from the beginning,
> stop the mouths of all that oppose
> Womens Speaking
> in the Power of the Lord.[8]

THE PROBLEM

> And how are the men of this generation blinded. . . . and pervert the Apostle's words.[9]

Margaret was outraged by the violent treatment Quaker women received by powerful religious leaders and the government. She contended that they had no right to prevent women from speaking in the churches—God had ordained them. Her words betray a personal encounter with both physical and mental abuse. Men despise women[10] and harass women. She vilifies her oppressors as "ministers of darkness"[11] "spirit of darkness,"[12] "dark priests,"[13] "seed of the serpent," and the "Pope's Wife."[14] They are incompetent because they have forgotten, misinterpreted, and distorted the message of the apostles, of Jesus, and of the teachings in the law or Old Testament with regard to women:

> Whereas it hath been an objection in the minds of man, and several times hath been objected by the Clergy, or Ministers, and others, against Womens speaking in the Church; and so consequently may be taken, that they are condemned for medling in the things of God; the ground of which objection, is taken from the Apostles words . . . But how far they wrong the Apostles intentions in these Scriptures, we shall shew clearly when we come to them in their course and order.[15]

VIEW OF THE BIBLE

The Bible and its words are from the beginning.[16] Margaret accepted the divine authorship of the Bible and believed that God the Father created male and female.[17] For instance, in the creation story she assumed that God is speaking. If God did not recognize a distinction between male and female then why should anyone else? In reading Paul, she also assumed the letters are his literal words while numbering him among the apostles.[18]

INTERPRETATIVE STRATEGY

Margaret's pamphlet seems to use certain volatile words that could potentially conjure up emotions within the audience. Perhaps this pamphlet was written in order to be used for preaching or reading to the public. While scriptural words and phrases are quoted, and sometimes the passage is cited, she often blended many Scriptures together as if they came from the same passage.

Ms. Fox's interpretative strategy is complicated and varied, using ancient methods of interpretation as well as anticipating modern historical-critical practices. She interpreted many passages in light of a particular historical situation while resisting the tendency to universalize or symbolize passages that might have damaged the status of woman within the church. At the same time, she employed typological interpretation to prove the divine legitimacy of woman preaching in the church. She called for a logical approach to the Scriptures while pointing to female role models and drew the obvious conclusion that the Apostles must have listened to Mary and the others; if they had not listened then how do we know about the gospel today?

I CORINTHIANS 11 AND 14

Margaret and George made similar points regarding key passages from I Corinthians 11, 14 and I Timothy. After studying the context of the passages in Corinthians, she rejected the commonly held interpretation that women should keep silent in the churches. She concluded that the verses in I Corinthians 14 apply only to a particular Jewish historical situation that occurred among groups that have not experienced the inner light or the Spirit. There are also inconsistencies in I Corinthians 11 and I Corinthians 14. Women are praying and prophesying in 11 but are supposedly told to keep silent in I Corinthians 14. She points to the context within I Corinthians which suggests that men are also entreated to "keep silent" in order to preserve the dignity of the service.[19]

In a later addition to her pamphlet she adds additional thoughts about I Corinthians 11 and 14. Both are inconsistent because Paul "contradicts himself." The verse about keeping silent and consulting your husband at home could not apply to widows or to virgins or to people such as Philip's four daughters who were prophetesses. Women cannot be prohibited from speaking because the law does not apply to them; they are led by the Spirit of God.[20]

I TIMOTHY 2

In the problem Pauline or Pseudo-Pauline passages which place women in a lower social position then men, Margaret turns to I Timothy 2:13: "I permit no woman to teach or to have authority over men; she is to keep silent. For Adam was formed first, then Eve; and Adam was not deceived, but the woman was deceived and became a transgressor." (*RSV*)

She reinterpreted the meaning of the terms Adam and Eve—they are no longer names which are symbolic of the whole human race. Adam and Eve are symbolic only of the relationship of a husband and wife. On the issue of "ursurping authority over a man" in I Timothy, she particularizes rather than universalizes the issue. The problematic passage refers only to married women and their relationships with their husbands at home. It has nothing to do with relationships and activities in the church.

I Timothy suggests ways in which women should dress, jewelry they should wear, and how they should style their hair: "I desire . . . that women should adorn themselves modestly. . . ." I Timothy 2:8–9

According to Margaret these passages refer only to women who have been "undecent and unreverent," certainly not to all women everywhere.[21] These verses should not be used to keep women from exercizing their potential within the communities.

GENESIS 2: THE SERPENT AND THE SEED

Her most unusual approach to arguing for women's equality was the use of allegory or symbolism in the Creation story. She bases her conclusions upon the words "serpent" and "seed." Who are the seed of the woman? Obviously the answer is "all people." Therefore to silence women is to silence one half of the "seed" and thus, to allow the serpent or to allow the devil to speak. Genesis 2:15 reads, "I will put enmity between you and the woman, and between your seed and her seed; he shall bruise your head, and you shall bruise his heel." (*RSV*) She freely retranslates this verse, ".... He hath put enmity between the Woman and the serpent, and if the Seed of the Woman speak not, The Seed of the Serpent speaks."[22]

THE CHURCH AS A FEMALE

Margaret also pointed out that the Bible uses feminine imagery when referring to the church. She cited Old Testament passages as a foundation for her typology. For her, the church began during Old Testament times among the Hebrews: "Moreover, the Lord is pleased, when he mentions his Church, to call her by the name of Woman, by his Prophets, saying, I have called thee as a Woman forsaken, and grieved in Spirit, and as a wife of Youth, Isa. 54. Again, How long wilt thou go about, thou back-sliding Daughter? For the Lord hath created a new thing in the earth, a woman shall compass a Man, Jer. 31.22."[23] Woman is the church for Margaret. And women are indeed stronger then men or "encompass" or overtake men.

THE TRUE CHURCH

Now the true Church or the true wife of Christ is found in churches that allow women to preach: "But Christ, who is the Head of the Church, the True Woman which is his Wife, in it do Daughters Prophesie, who are above the Pope and his Wife and a top of them; And here Christ is the Head of the Male and Female, who may speak; and the Church is called a Royal Priesthood, so the Woman must offer as well as the Man," Rev. 22.17.[24]

Her argument goes on to suggest that the priests who speak against women are really speaking against Christ. There are two churches. There is a Church that belongs to Christ and a church of the serpent:

[T]he Church of Christ is a woman, and those that speak against the womans speaking, speak against the Church of Christ, and the Seed of the woman, which Seed is Christ; that is to say, Those that speak against the Power of the Lord, and the Spirit of the Lord speaking in a Woman, not regarding the Seed, and Spirit, and Power that speaks in her; such speak against Christ, and his Church, and are of the Seed of the Serpent; wherein lodgeth the enmity.[25]

The true Church recognizes and learns from stories about women who were important models of effective leadership throughout the history of Christianity. Jesus himself relished the love and care of women: "Thus we see that Jesus owned the Love and Grace that appeared in Women, and did not despise it, and by what is recorded in the Scriptures, he received as much love, kindness, compassion, and tender dealing towards him from Women, as he did from any others, both in his life time, and also after they exercised their cruelty upon him."[26]

Margaret lists examples of female models from the New Testament including the Woman of Samaria, Mary and Martha, the Woman with the Alabaster Jar, the Women who provided means for Jesus out of their own substance, the Women at the tomb, and Anna. Men listened to women and found their judgment to be helpful as in the story of Priscilla and Apollos.[27] Would there be a church today if the apostles had not listened to the women who told them about the resurrection? "Mark this, you that despise and oppose the Message of the Lord God that he sends by women, what had become of the Redemption of the whole body of Mankind, if they had not believed the Message that the Lord Jesus sent by these women, of and concerning his Resurrection?"[28]

SUMMARY

Margaret's work was groundbreaking. After the death of the judge, she ran her own house, managed her children, chose her own religion and a new husband. She also dared to write a tract defending the God-given biblical rights of herself as well as all women to speak in public.

Her animosity toward the religious structure which imprisoned her led her to identify it with evil, the serpent. She warned her opposers not to speak against women because they have been foundational to the very church they administer. Their importance exceeds the pope's. Women are central and will always be central to the message of the true God, so let them speak!

SARAH MOORE GRIMKÉ (1792–1873)

I have suffered too keenly from the teaching of man,
to lead any one to him for instruction. . . .[1]

Now if God ordained man the governor of woman, he must
be able to save her, and to answer in her stead for all those
sins which she commits by his direction.
Awful responsibility.[2]

BIOGRAPHY

Sarah and her sister Angelina Grimké[3] were two of the first publicly outspoken Charleston-born females who challenged the South to abandon slavery on grounds that it was immoral and against Christianity. Angelina, a younger sister, received abrasive public treatment because of her public speeches against slavery.[4] In 1837, Sarah wrote "Letters on the Province of Woman" for the *New England Spectator* in response to the abuse her sister received for speaking out against slavery.[5] Those letters were collected and printed in a book entitled *Letters on the Equality of the Sexes and the Condition of Women.* Her letters are addressed to Mary S. Parker, president of the Boston Female Anti-Slavery Society.[6]

Sarah was a sensitive child who early in life understood the restrictiveness of slavery and the position of women in a southern home. She witnessed a slave being whipped and promptly at the age of five attempted to board passage on a steamliner to a place where slavery did not exist. She taught her own attendant to read, thus breaking a South Carolina law prohibiting the teaching of black children to read or write. At her attendant's death she refused to take on another personal slave.

Sarah had an excellent mind and hoped to someday become an attorney and perhaps follow in the steps of her father who was chief judge of the Supreme Court of South Carolina. She studied day and night and planned to attend college with her older brother Thomas. When her parents discovered her plan she was forbidden to study Thomas' books or any of the languages. There were no colleges for women in the North or the South and it was thought to be frivolous for her to spend her time training to do something that was not available to her. Her father supposedly remarked, "that if she [Sarah] had not been a woman she would have made the greatest jurist in the land."[7]

John Grimké, her wealthy father, owned hundreds of slaves, fathered at least fourteen children, and was a strong advocate of slavery and the subordinate position of women: "So long as she is nervous, fickle, capricious, delicate, diffident, and dependent, man will worship and adore her. . . . Woman, like children, has but one right and that is the right to protection. The right to protection also involves the obligation to obey a husband, a lord and and master designed for every woman."[8]

Sarah wasted her life away in South Carolina for twenty-six years. Her father's sudden undiagnosed illness led him to seek medical help in Philadelphia. He took only Sarah with him and Sarah buried him in a small grave in New Jersey not long after the beginning of their journey. In Philadelphia she discovered the Quakers, who opened her eyes to the possibility of fulfilling a desire to use her academic skills and life in a meaningful way.

Returning home to South Carolina, she soon migrated north and began many years of study with the Quakers. Her sister Angelina followed her when she was in her early twenties. Together they began a crusade for the abolition of slavery and soon discovered that they were also preaching for the freedom of women, too. Angelina joined the Female Anti-Slavery Society of Philadelphia and later guest lectured for the American Anti-Slavery Society.[9] Their careers were remarkable.[10] During a six month period between 1837 and 1838, they held eighty-eight meetings in sixty-seven towns with attendance of as many as 40,000 people.[11]

Logically their careers should have flourished, but instead they chose to abandon public life. Angelina married Theodore Weld, a leading and outspoken abolitionist, who believed that a woman should take care of the home. Sarah, even though mortally wounded by Weld's highly critical remarks about her speaking style, chose to live with them for most of the rest of her life.[12] She never married although offers had come her way. Suggestions have been made that Angelina, after the birth of her first child, had a complete break-down. Sarah died in 1873 after a very long life of over eighty years.

While Sarah may have retired from public life, her letters did not. They continued to influence the women's movement during the remainder of the nineteenth century.

> They posed the basic questions of human equality for most of the century. In 1850 when Lucretia Mott was asked to respond to Richard Henry Dana's attack on women's equality, she took many of her arguments, including exact phrases, from Sarah Grimké's *Letters*. At the end of the nineteenth century, when Elizabeth Cady Stanton decided that a refutation of the Bible's subordination of the female was finally in order, she too returned to Sarah Grimké's biblical analysis before writing her own *Woman's Bible* in 1898.[13]

THE PROBLEM AND THE TIMES

In many states and counties on the eastern seaboard, women were prohibited from speaking in public by law.[14] Women went to great lengths to find a man to open their meetings with prayer. Sarah found this situation intolerable: "The idea is inconceivable to me, that Christian women can be engaged in doing God's work, and yet cannot ask his blessing on their efforts, except through the lips of a man. I have known a whole town scoured to obtain a minister to open a female meeting, and their refusal to do so spoken of as quite a misfortune."[15]

Sarah said that power "is now vested solely in the hands of men"[16] which was usurped from women.[17] Men had cornered the market on power in the church. They had created laws based upon misin-terpreted scriptural passages, and they presumed that Scripture teaches a distinction between men and women. That opinion is unscriptural and "perverted."[18] Their logic is culturally conditioned and has created a "corrupt public opinion."[19]

According to Sarah, the political reality was that, "Woman has no political existence."[20] In 1837 a woman, if she was married, had no independent legal status of her own. She was "absorbed in her master."[21] A wife could not take legal action against anyone,[22] her property at marriage becomes her husband's,[23] and the husband is in absolute control of any profits made by his wife.[24]

These political laws were framed by men who also created laws within "ecclesiastical bodies."[25] Both of these excluded women from the decision-making process yet both governed and punished her:[26] "These same men use women to promote themselves . . . woman has more or less been made a means to promote the welfare of men, without due regard for her own happiness."[27]

Sarah believed that men had been in control of society for thousands of years and the only way that women could find freedom was by males relinquishing their power.[28] Men did not allow women to be educated in the ancient languages or at educational levels available to themselves:[29] "[I]t seems to me man might be satisfied with the dominion he has claimed and exercised for nearly six thousand years, and that more true nobility would be manifested by endeavoring to raise the fallen and invigorate the weak, than by keeping woman in subjection."[30]

Yet they continue to treat women as dolls:[31] "[T]hey have dressed them like dolls, and used them like toys to amuse their hours of recreation."[32] "Ah! how many of my sex feel in the dominion, thus unrighteously exercised over them, under the gentle appellation of protection, that what they have leaned upon has proved a broken reed at best, and oft a spear."[33]

Christianity was not the only religion nor was America the only place where women were enslaved and used by men for their own benefit. In letters five through eleven in *Letters on the Equality of the Sexes*, Sarah summarized the abuse of women from the perspective of a world culture.[34]

VIEW OF SCRIPTURE

Sarah was careful to point out that she believed that the Bible was inspired in the original but all of the translations were corrupted.[35] She suggested that those who lean heavily upon the King James Version have a "superstitious reverence" for that translation. It is a sacred record, including both the Old Testament and New Testament, that contains historically accurate information which has been misinterpreted:[36] "My mind is entirely delivered from the superstitious reverence which is attached to the English version of the Bible. King James's translators certainly were not inspired. I therefore claim the original as my standard, believing that to have been inspired, and I also claim to judge for myself what is the meaning of the inspired writers. . . ."[37]

INTERPRETATIVE STRATEGY

Sarah's approach was complex and diverse in making her case for the equality of the sexes. She used retranslation,[38] redefinition of words,[39] quotations from biblical authorities,[40] and declared that terms such as "man" and "brethren" were inclusive by claiming that they also refer to women.[41]

In addition she employs what might be considered proto-historical, literary, textual, and canonical criticisms.[42] She asserts that the Scriptures developed within a historical time period and should be understood or interpreted within that time period.[43] For example, the Israelites sold women into slavery but that was during a different time period, so those Scriptures did not apply to people in her time period.

Most ancient commentators employ the use of allegory or symbolism in their interpretation of texts from the Hebrew Bible or Old Testament without realizing that they are employing a method of interpretation. The New Testament should also be interpreted as "allegorical" or containing "metaphor" yet it should be consistent and logical:[44] "Now I must understand the sacred Scriptures as harmonizing with themselves, or I cannot receive them as the word of God."[45] Sarah was aware of the authorship of the text, of the immediate and larger context of a passage of Scripture,[46] and often used passages within the Bible to interpret other passages. She questioned the authority of Paul and the commentaries who interpret his words.[47] He was only human and was probably heavily influenced by Jewish cultural forces.[48] She cited her own male authorities to prove her points; among them are John Gurney, Adam Clarke, John Locke,

John Newton, and others identified only by their last names, Scott, Stratton, Henry, and Blackwell.[49]

SUMMARY OF HER INTERPRETATIONS

THE SCRIPTURES: THE PRINCIPLE OF EQUALITY

While Sarah rehearsed a litany of accusations against males, ecclesiastical bodies, and cultures both at home and around the world, she appeared to argue for equality as a principal that is taught in Scriptures. It should be the foundation for marriage and also for women who want to lead the same lives and function in the same roles as men, especially preaching.

GENESIS 1

Sarah begins where so many others begin, in Genesis. "So God created man. . . ." "Man" is a generic term and includes woman; there is no hierarchy:[50] "They were both made in the image of God; dominion was given to both over every other creature, but not over each other. Created in perfect equality, they were expected to exercise the vicegerence intrusted to them by their Maker, in harmony and love."[51]

Male and female are completely equal: "It was to give him a companion, in all respects his equal; one who was like himself a free agent, gifted with intellect and endowed with immortality; not a partaker merely of his animal gratifications, but able to enter into all his feelings as a moral and responsible being."[52]

In analyzing the story of the fall she emphasized that Eve was tempted by a supernatural being, and Adam was tempted by his equal. She hinted that the woman did not have experience in understanding "satanic intelligence." Her world contained only her beloved Adam and God,[53] while Adam was not tempted by "the instrumentality of a supernatural agent, but through that of an equal.":[54] "Had Adam tenderly reproved his wife, and endeavored to lead her to repentance instead of sharing in her guilt, I should be much more ready to accord to man that superiority which he claims; but as the facts stand disclosed by the sacred historian, it appears to me that to say the least, there was as much weakness exhibited by Adam as by Eve."[55] She concluded that the pair fell from innocence and happiness "but not from equality."[56]

Sarah maintained that the curse was not a command but a prophecy. Using retranslation, observation of the context, and comparison with similar scriptures Sarah concluded that the phrase "Thou wilt be subject unto thy husband, and he will rule over thee. . . ."[57] is the result of a struggle for political power over dominion that was prophesied from the beginning: "Our translators having been accustomed to exercize lordship over their wives, and seeing only through the medium of a perverted judgement . . . translated it shall instead of will. . . ."[58]

Woman and man are equal and women should only be in subjection to God and "to him alone is she accountable for the use of her talents."[59] Eve and Adam are symbols or representatives of the entire human race. Both fell and sinned and both were guilty. She accepted this awesome responsibility and used Romans 5:12 as a prooftext, ". . . as by one man sin entered the world."[60] Adam seems to be a bit more guilty again because he was fully aware of the consequences of his actions. Eve was not. I Timothy 2:4 states that Adam was not deceived and 2 Corinthians 11:3 mentions that Eve was beguiled.

These prooftexts were used as a springboard for a sermon on the reasons why women should be ministers. "My present object is to show, that as woman is charged with all the sin that exists in the world, it is her solemn duty to labor for its extinction. . . ."[61]

EQUALITY IN MARRIAGE

People view each other primarily as sexual beings. Men and women cannot forget that they are a different sex which generally excites "the low propensities of our nature."[62] Man always approaches and seeks to communicate with a woman through her sexual nature: "[H]e seeks access to her heart; and when he has gained her affections, he uses her as an instrument of his pleasure. . . ."[63]

The man gains a housekeeper and a chef while the woman takes care of household duties in the cloistered existence of the home. Sarah acknowledged that woman was designed as a "helpmeet" but she cannot fulfill her role unless she is an equal. That equality is based upon a reading of Galatians 3:38. There should be no distinction between male and female.[64]

Equality of the sexes is found throughout the Old and New Testaments. Sarah ranged back and forth between the testaments using isolated stories and prooftexts to prove her thesis. The laws of the Israelites were addressed to both men and women and in "the decalogue, there is no direction given to women to obey their masters." This is also true of Jesus; no such command is found in the sermon on the mount.[65] Even on the controversial subject of divorce, Jesus and Paul placed men and women "on the same ground."[66] (Mark 16:11, 12 and I Cor. 7:12 and 13). She concluded, if there is no equality and "man is constituted the governor of woman, he must be her God. . . ."[67]

> The idea that man, as man is superior to woman, involves an absurdity so gross, that I really wonder how any man of reflection can receive it as of divine origin; and I can only account for it, by that passion for supremacy which characterizes man as a corrupt and fallen creature. If it be true that he is more excellent that she, as man, independent of his moral and intellectual powers, then every man is superior by virtue of his manship, to every woman.[68]

OBEDIENCE OF WIVES
(EPHESIANS 5:22; COLOSSIANS 3:18; I PETER 3:2)

In arguing for the equality of woman Sarah pointed out that the terms "weaker vessel" in I Peter 3:7 do not refer to intellect but to physical strength.[69] All of the passages listed above call for the subjection of women but they also have stipulations attached to the males. Sarah referred to the context of Ephesians 5 which reads "submitting yourselves one another in the fear of God."[70] Her conclusion was that the accepted interpretation that women should submit to men violates the intention of the texts: "According to the generally received meaning of the passages I have quoted, they directly contravene the laws of God, as given in various parts of the Bible."[71]

Continuing her discussion of the epistles, Sarah admitted that they contain the metaphor of Christ and his church which is viewed through the relationship of a male and female. She disclaimed any authority that males may derive from this comparison: "Now if God ordained man the governor of woman, he must be able to save her, and to answer in her stead for all those sins which she commits by his direction. Awful responsibility."[72]

EQUALITY IN THE MINISTRY

Early in her letters, Sarah asserted that women have a duty to minister to others and that ministry to the helpless makes a woman a better wife and mother.[73] Her conclusions were based upon no particular scripture. Letter XIV entitled "The Ministry of Women" is the high point of her writings. She employed most of her interpretative tools in this section in order to prove "that woman is bound to preach the gospel."[74]

Her first argument began with prophets in the Old Testament. Prophets function differently that priests. "The prophets prophesy falsely, and the priests bear rule by their means."[75] It is an error to assume that present-day Christian ministers are in the line of the ancient priests. The only person that is in the line of the priests is Christ and when he died he abolished the priesthood.[76]

Huldah, Miriam, and Deborah[77] were numbered among the prophets in the Old Testament. She argued that since male ministers followed in the line of the prophets then women of her day should be prophets or ministers. She added that women also have the spirit and possess the gifts the same as males do.[78]

It is often triumphantly inquired, why, if men and women are on an equality, are not women as conspicuous in the Bible as Men? I do not intend to assign a reason, but I think one may readily be found in the fact, that from the days of Eve to the present time, the aim of man has been to crush her. He has accomplished this work in various ways; sometimes by brute force, sometimes by making her subservient to his worst passions, sometimes by treating her as a doll, and while he exluded from her mind the light of knowledge, decked her person with gewgaws and frippery which he scorned for himself, thus endeavoring to render her like unto a painted sepulchre.[79]

Continuing her case for equality in the ministry, Sarah cited stories about women prophets in the New Testament "dispensation"[80] such as Philip's daughters, Priscilla, and Phoebe.[81] In passing she turned to historical evidence supporting the existence of female ministers in the founding days of the church. Female ministers were martyred for their faith in the early church.[82]

She tackled I Corinthians 11 and 14 by arguing from context, culture, and personal experience, while citing noted opinions of authorities such as John Locke and Adam Clarke. Two testimonies from women ministers Rebecca Collier and Rachel Brachen plus the account of Mary Sewall interpret and apply these verses from the point of experience.

Sarah concluded that the Corinthian letters were written to correct problems within the Christian communities. On the issue of silence in the church she pointed to the verse that commands men to be silent "as well as the women."[83] Both men and women were guilty of speaking at the same time, so both were charged with silence. An Adam Clarke quotation concluded that I Corinthians 14 has nothing to do with preaching. "It is evident from the context, that the apostle refers here to asking questions, and what we call dictating in the assemblies."[84]

In attempting to interpret I Timothy she avoided some of the major problem verses in favor of establishing equality in I Timothy 2:8,9. She concluded that the verse has been misinterpreted and suggested that both men and women should pray everywhere. The remainder of the chapter describes how female ministers should dress and the phrase "learning in silence" refers to learning and not to preaching.

Her final argument appealed to consistency in the biblical documents. Either Paul contradicts himself and the fulfillment of the daughters prophesying in Joel and Acts is "a shameful infringement of decency and order"[85] or the above verses are only meant to be interpreted within a certain time period and meant to solve problems with local customs and in local congregations.

SUMMARY OF HER WORK

Sarah produced a well-written, logical interpretation of the Bible considering her lack of formal education. She took a monumental step toward a critical understanding of the historical situation, context, and translation of the Bible. Sarah hit at the heart of discrimination by the clergy—they have cornered the market on the translation of the Bible. Their interpretations bolster their own power over woman. Why should they rethink or reevaluate their foregone conclusions when they stand to lose so much?

LUCRETIA COFFIN MOTT (1793–1880)

The veneration of man has been misdirected,
the pulpit has been prostituted,
the Bible has been ill-used.[1]

The law had crushed woman;
and the Church, supporting the law,
had assumed that the Bible forbade woman from using her rights.[2]

BIOGRAPHY

Lucretia Coffin Mott has been credited with the advancement of equality for all women in the United States.[3] Her life and work became a link between the early abolitionist efforts and the feminist movement of the nineteenth century.[4] Early in her career, as first a teacher and then a minister within the Quaker faith, she argued for the prohibition of slavery and the full equality of both blacks ("coloreds") and women: "Ultimately the liberation of all the oppressed became Mott's self-chosen mission."[5] Some labeled her the "black man's goddess."[6] Later in life she fought desperately for the right of women to vote. Answering a man who claimed that a woman ought to listen to her husband, she retorted, "If he lay stress on his Scripture argument, that the wife must obey the husband, it may in some cases come to cut the other way; as in mine, for example, because my husband wishes me to vote, and therefore, according to the Scripture, the gentleman must, even in his own reasoning, allow me the right to vote."[7]

Mott received a nontraditional education in New York at Nine Partners, a Quaker boarding school. After completion of her degree, she was offered a position at the school but declined to take it because of the issue of pay equity with her male colleagues.[8]

At twenty-eight she became a minister within Quakerism. Her community emphasized withdrawal from politics and encouraged its members to help their own parishioners rather than strangers. Lucretia's career began to blossom and so did her ideas about changing unjust laws and cultural norms. Admiring the rational works of the Unitarians and the Transcendentalists which taught independence of thought and the discovery of the Divine within one's self, she ultimately joined a splinter group within Quakerism known as the Hicksites.[9] The Hicksites were a throwback to old Quakerism which taught reliance upon the "inner light" from God as personal truth and a commitment to change society's oppressive structures.

Some of her great accomplishments included helping to establish Swarthmore College in 1864. She was foundational to the American Anti-Slavery Society (1833), the Philadelphia Anti-Slavery Society, and the Anti-Slavery Convention of American Women (1837). Chosen as a delegate to the World's Anti-Slavery Convention in London in 1840, she was not allowed to speak because she was a woman. In 1866 she became the president of the American Equal Rights Association.

Among her closest friends and associates were Elizabeth Cady Stanton, Susan B. Anthony, and Julia Howard Ward. Other friends such as Rabbi Isaac M. Wise and Ralph Waldo Emerson stood hand and hand with her when the Free Religious Association of religious liberals was constituted in 1867.

Lucretia devoted her life to helping others achieve a measure of equality that she had found in her marriage and within her Quaker faith. In spite of her social activism, Lucretia also lead a traditional life as a mother of four, having given birth to six children. Her marriage in 1811 to fellow teacher (and some say one of her first teachers) James Mott lasted fifty-seven years. James was a constant companion and supporter in her egalitarian endeavors.

THE PROBLEM

Lucretia preached that public law and Christianity cooperated in the subjugation of women. Both had taught men to believe that the subservience of women was a divine sanction. According to Dana Greene, "In Mott's eyes the contemporary state of religion was deplorable. It was characterized by sectarianism and dogmatism, emphasized priestcraft, theology, ritual and ceremony, condoned injustice and inequality."[10]

Women were conditioned to believe that they needed to be secluded and protected from the arduous tasks of public life. She observed that culture produced a woman who was incapable of desiring her own freedom. She often became a caricature of a doll, a plaything for men. In a speech entitled "The Laws in Relation to Women," she said, "Has the slave been oppressed so long that he cannot appreciate the blessings of Liberty? and has women been so long crushed, enervated, paralyzed, prostrated by the influences by which she has been surrounded, that she too is ready to say she would not have any more rights if she could?"[11]

During her lifetime, men viciously attacked her philosophy of coequality in speeches and through the press. Many women politely declined to support her efforts to gain suffrage and equal access to the pulpit. She often engaged her male opponents by logically refuting their arguments with demeaning or self-effacing sarcastic rhetoric. Here are two quotes from some of her well-known speeches at Woman's Rights conventions: "Such dupes are men to custom, that even servitude, the worst of ills come to be thought as a good, till down from sire to son it is kept and guarded as a sacred thing."[12] She sardonically retorts to one of her opponents in a speech entitled, "The Principles of the Co-Equality of Woman and Man," "He must remember it is hard for weak women to answer such solid arguments, and he must pity us if we do not come up to his standard of excellence."[13]

Lucretia's 1849 historic address, "Discourse on Woman"[14] at the Assembly Building in Philadelphia, was given in response to the remarks made by Richard Henry Dana, a lecturer who ridiculed women seeking equal civil rights. Contained in her response are brief references to how the Bible might be interpreted in order to bolster equality. Mr. Dana's musings were never published but a news story summarizing his arguments appeared in the *Literary World* in 1850. Here is an excerpt from that story,

> Mr. Dana is not at all of the modern school, who affect to make Woman what she is not, never has been, and never can be, man and woman, both, or perhaps we should rather say, simply man for the the unsexing philosophy ignores the woman altogether. . . .
>
> Mr. Dana is old-fashioned enough to believe in essential differences of sex, mental and moral marked as the physical; . . . There has been some cavil at Mr. Dana's lecture, as it has been delivered on other occasions, but we are convinced that the heart of every woman present responded to its beauty and truth; its harmonious position of woman in the scale of creation, not the inferior of man, but his divinely constituted complement, the other half of a perfect whole.[15]

While the newswriter above enjoyed Dana's lofty musings, Mott countered that his speech contained "vulgar epithets"[16] which retarded the progress of women. Dana saw no reason to change the restricted role of women within society. After all, everyone was happy with the way things were. Mott answered that charge and worried that women will continue to be only a "mere plaything or toy of society."[17] "So with woman. She has so long been subject to the disabilities and restrictions, with which her progress has been embarrassed, that she has become enervated, her mind to some extent paralyzed; and, like those still more degraded by personal bondage, she hugs her chains. Liberty is often presented in its true light, but it is liberty for man."[18]

Dana accused women of stepping out of their appropriate roles in society.[19] He claimed that they act like men.[20] Mott agreed to some of these charges. Women, according to Mott, cannot depend upon men to help them make progress. Men are responsible for limiting their present liberties.[21] Take for example preaching in the pulpit: "In religious society her disabilities, as already pointed out, have greatly retarded her progress. Her exclusion from the pulpit or ministry— her duties marked out for her by her equal brother man, subject to creeds, rules, and disciplines made for her by him—this is unworthy her true dignity."[22]

Lucretia maintained that this exclusion from the pulpit is based upon perverted interpretations of the Bible which have been used as political weapons against women. These biblical misinterpretations of the clergy had become the foundation of civil or political discrimination against women in the pulpit, education, taxation, the vote, marriage, and property rights.

VIEW OF SCRIPTURE

Lucretia was a Quaker who believed in the Divine Light above all else. Scripture was important, but for her the Divine Light was the authoritative source to which she turned. In her second speech at the 1853 National Women's Rights Convention she said, "I am not troubled with difficulties about the Bible. My education has been such, that I look to the Source whence all the inspiration of the Bible comes. I love the truths of the Bible. I love the Bible because it contains so many truths; but I never was educated to love the errors of the Bible. . . ."[23]

The Bible is authoritative and relevant for her and everyone in her audience.[24] Laws found in the Old Testament and words from Jesus teach equality.[25] Although she always referred to God as a "He," she insisted that the Scriptures exclude no one who wants to help her fellow neighbor.[26]

INTERPRETATIVE STRATEGY: THE EVE STORY

Following in the footsteps of her Quaker ancestors, Lucretia did not lay the blame for evil upon women, nor did she recognize the curse of submission to man in her "Discourse on Woman."[27] If a woman has received the light then she is restored to her rightful plane of equality described in Genesis 1:27. In quoting the verse from Genesis, she took liberties with the text and combined the name of Adam from chapter 2 with the verse in 1:27 in order to make her point stronger: "Male and female created he them, and blessed them, and called their name Adam." And she adds, "He gave dominion to both over the lower animals, but not to one over the other."[28] Genesis 1:27 in the Old King James Version reads: "So God created man in his own image; in the image of God created he him; male and female created he them."

EQUALITY IN THE OLD TESTAMENT NARRATIVES

In her historic speech on woman, Mott proceeded to argue for the equality of women based upon Scripture passages in both testaments. No distinction is made between men and women in the giving of the law by Moses; both sexes must follow the laws.[29] Indeed, "in the early ages . . ." there were great women who were leaders of the tribe of Israel and worked with men by their side. There was Deborah and Barak, and Miriam and Aaron. She also remembers Jael and Huldah while pointing out for her audience that women also can be corrupted by power. Take for example the women in Ezekiel 13:17 and 18: "There were also false prophetesses as well as true. The denunciations of Ezekiel were upon those women who would prophesy out of their own heart, and sew pillows to all armholes."[30]

Ezekiel 13:17–18 in the *Revised Standard Version* reads: "And you, son of man, set your face against the daughters of your people, who prophesy out of their own minds; prophesy against them and say, Thus says the Lord God: Woe to the women who sew magic bands upon all wrists, and make veils for the heads of persons of every stature, in the hunt for souls."

FEMALE MODELS OF LEADERSHIP

Lucretia lists a host of female role models including Anna the prophetess, women who were companions of Jesus, Philip and his four prophesying daughters, Tryphena and Tryphosa, whom she claims were coworkers of Paul, Priscilla, and Phoebe.[31]

WOMEN AS MINISTERS

Women were ministers, too, yet male ministers ignored that fact.
Even during Lucretia's lifetime, if a woman "asked to be a religious
teacher, the perversion of the words of Paul was presented to keep
her back."[32] Historically, translators have ignored the references that
suggest that women did indeed minister or preach. Lucretia correctly
observed that when a male is mentioned in the Scriptures he is
referred to as a minister. When a female is mentioned she is referred
to as a servant, even though the same word is used in both instances.
Translators are so biased that even when the Scriptures do relate a
story about a woman preaching, they attempt to deny it by mis-
translating the passage of Scripture. The following quotation seems
to be a short-hand version of major statements that she made concerning women and preaching: "Phebe is mentioned as a servant of
Christ, and commended as such to the brethren. It is worthy of note,
that the word *servant,* when applied to Tychicus, is rendered *minister.*
Women *professing* godliness, should be translated *preaching . . .*"[33]

Her astute observations and conclusions are probably drawn from
Ephesians 6:21 and Colossians 4:7 and I Timothy 2:10. The word "to
profess" in I Timothy 2:10 does mean "to announce" and could be
translated "preaching."

In taking on the prohibition against preaching in the church she
questioned the "supposed apostolic prohibition." Quoting from Joel
2:28 and Acts 2:17, Lucretia emphasized that the spirit was poured
out on both daughters and sons and "they should prophesy." If this is
true then why should there be a problem with passages that might
suggest otherwise?[34]

She wondered whether speaking and asking questions in I Corinthians 14:34 can be equated with a prohibition against preaching.
She noted correctly that Paul does not use the word preach or
prophesy in this passage.[35] In her remarks delivered at the seventh
National Woman's Rights Convention in 1856 she agreed that Paul's
words have hindered women.[36] But those words also recognize the
essential worth of woman, too: "And even Paul, though he is quoted
so much as an authority for bringing women under subjection, even
he gave special directions to woman how she should attire herself
when she did publically pray or prophesy; and in the seeming prohibi-

tion of woman's speaking in church, there is no mention of preaching, of praying, or prophesying."[37]

MARRIAGE

The passages in the Bible which deal with the issue of the subjection of woman in marriage must not be interpreted literally. These passages must be understood as a metaphor of the Church. It is a great mystery.

> In the metaphors of that age you know there is great liberty taken on other subjects; why not on that? Even though Paul should approve of many things, being himself under the influence of the Jewish customs of that age, with regard to woman, I would ask of those who religiously bind themselves to the authority of Scripture, whether they find any Scripture text from the beginning to the end of the Bible that makes it incumbent upon them to receive any recommendation given by Paul to the women of the Church of this day. . . . for, if the recommendations of Paul were applied now, no woman would be allowed to enter into a second marriage after having lost her first husband.[38]

The present cultural myth that when two marry they become one may be rooted in the misapplication of these "subjection" Scriptures. When a woman marries the man becomes her ruler. This is "despotism:"[39] "When she became a wife, the Church stepped in, and asserted the authority of the husband, and made the wife acknowledge her inferiority and promise obedience to him."[40]

Finally in her "Discourse on Woman," she urged her listeners to look back in history to female ministers who suffered martyrdom for their faith. History and experience suggest that the way that the Scriptures have been interpreted is incorrect. The verse silencing women was meant only for that group of Christians: "Where is the Scripture authority for the advice given to the early church, under peculiar circumstances, being binding on the church of the present day?"[41]

She makes similar observations during the National Women's Rights convention in 1853: "All Bible commentators agree that the

Church of Corinth, when the Apostle wrote, was in a state of great confusion. They fell into discussion and controversy; and in order to quiet this state of things, and being the Church to greater propriety, the command was given out that women should keep silence. . . ."[42]

CONCLUSION

Lucretia owed much of her interpretative strategy to earlier Quakers. She added her own ideas on marriage, female ministers, and the equality of the sexes throughout the biblical narratives. She recognized that the Scriptures have been mistranslated and misinterpreted. These male activities had prohibited her from preaching in church and speaking her mind in public: "It is important that we be familiar with these facts, because woman has been so long circumscribed in her influence by the perverted application of the text, rendering it improper for her to speak in the assemblies, of the people, to 'edification, to exhortation, and to comfort.' "[43]

PHOEBE WORRALL PALMER (1807–1874)

God has, in all ages of the church,
called a few of his handmaids
to eminent publicity
and
usefulness. . . .[1]

They [Women] were the strength of the early church,
as they are the strength of the church today.
They did more to extend it,
to hallow it,
and adorn it,
and immeasurably less to mutilate and disgrace it,
than men did;
and to this day the love of Christ glows in their hearts
with a steadier and purer
power than the harder and coarser nature of man can exhibit.[2]

BIOGRAPHY

Phoebe Palmer made an important contribution to improving the status of women within Methodist and Holiness circles in the nineteenth century. While living the life of a privileged lady whose charm and femininity were well known, she also advocated the right and responsibility of woman to speak publicly on behalf of her religious convictions. She avoided political issues in favor of working within her own religious tradition. While a mother and wife, she was also an evangelist, author, editor, and volunteer social worker in New York City. According to W. J. McCutcheon,

> [S]he and her Methodist associates followed a policy of public neutrality on the slavery question. She also eschewed the cause of woman's rights and sought to avoid public prominence; . . . Although her modesty, personal charm, and lack of feminist fanaticism saved her from conservative criticism, her very example did signalize and popularize the larger role for women that was a feature of the holiness movement.[3]

Phoebe Palmer was a dedicated Holiness preacher and author who attempted to live what she preached. She founded the Five Points Mission in New York City which included a school, a place of worship, and houses for twenty indigent people. Palmer also played a significant role in the New York Female Assistance Society for the Relief and Instruction of the Poor. This organization was run by women who were interested in saving children from street gangs. In the midst of attempting to educate and save lives, many women became trained in administrative tasks, politics, and preaching.[4]

Some say that Phoebe influenced the lives of at least twenty-five thousand people through her ministry and afternoon meetings at the Allen Street and Mulberry Street Methodist churches. These meetings became so popular that pastors and ministers from several congregations attended. Among the lives touched by Phoebe were Frances Willard, Bishop L. Hamline, John Dempster, Bishop Edmund S. James, and Nathan Bangs.[5]

Her marriage to Walter Clark Palmer, a physician, in 1827 at the age of nineteen, produced six children. Only three of the children survived infancy. During those early years she wrote several books including, *The Way of Holiness* (1843), *Pioneer Experiences* (1868), *Faith and Its Effects* (1849); *Devotion to God* (1853), and *The Promise of the Father* (1859). Several of these publications gave opportunities for women to tell their own stories of religious experiences and problems. In 1862, Phoebe became editor of the journal the *Guide* after her husband purchased it.

Walter Palmer was an ardent supporter of Phoebe and often traveled with her on evangelistic treks. Both were dedicated to lecturing on the topic of holiness in a person's life. Many years were spent abroad in England preaching and teaching. In the United States they often visited Methodist camp meetings teaching people about the second work of grace, perfection and sanctification.[6]

Phoebe answered the questions,

> What is Gospel Holiness, or Sanctification? and How may we enter into the enjoyment of holiness?" in one of her essays: "Holiness is a state of soul in which all the powers of the body and mind are consciously given up to God; and the witness of holiness is that testimony which the Holy Spirit bears with our spirit that the offering is accepted through Christ. The work is accomplished the moment we lay our all upon the altar.[7]

VIEW OF THE BIBLE

Liberation for Phoebe came through reading her Bible. It was the standard by which she judged everything else in her life. This highly individualistic approach to the Bible helped Phoebe maintain her independent status within religious circles during her entire life. Although she preached, wrote, and held revivals, she was never ordained by any denomination. For her, the Bible was a book of "eternal remembrance"[8] which helped people find their way to holiness.

She believed that "all Scripture, whether historical or otherwise, is given by inspiration" and was the Word of God:[9]

> "Not Wesley . . . . but the Bible, the holy bible, is the first and last, and in the midst always. The Bible is the standard, the groundwork, the platform, the creed."[10]

THE PROBLEM

Women were receiving the "power of God" in their lives and wanted to share their experiences with others. Pastors were humiliating women by refusing to allow them to speak in the churches: "Hundreds of ministers in the present day are standing in an attitude of open resistance to the use of the gift of prophecy in women. Let a female member of their charge attempt to open her lips in prayer or in speaking of the revelations of infinite grace to her soul. . . . She would at once be branded as a fanatic, and regarded as a subject of public animadversion and church discipline."[11]

In a strident voice, Phoebe alarmed the world that this practice continued in the Roman Catholic Church and the Church of England.

> The Church of Rome has made her insidious approaches in the form of Puseyism, and not a few have been deluded by her sophistries, and proportionately as the deceptive principles of this fall church prevail, will nunneries be multiplied. Yes, nunneries, though not confining their sad and worse than useless victims within walls, "By vows and grates confined," will debar them, by church dogmas, from yielding to the dictates of the Spirit, and engaging in the holy activities which Scriptural Christianity inculcates.[12]

The misinterpretation by clergy of the verses from I Timothy by the men in power have imposed a "cruel seal of silence" upon women, placing women in bondage:[13]

> "Whence has the idea obtained that she may not even open her lips for God in the assembly of the pious, without being looked upon repulsively, as though she were unwomanly in her aims and predilections."[14]

Some people were even saying that women were losing their femininity because they were speaking in public. Phoebe declared them to be in error: "As far as our observations have aided us, the effect has been diametrically opposite. Religion does not despoil woman of her refined sensibilities, but only turns them into a finer mould, and brings out to the charmed beholder everything that is pure, lovely, and of good report."[15]

INTERPRETATIVE STRATEGY

Phoebe's strategy was complicated and multifaceted. She cited role models of women who were leaders in the Old Testament and within the New Testament. Individual words were very important to her. She reinterpreted and redefined them, using at least sixteen male scholarly references including Chrysostom, Justin Martyr, Grotius, and Drs. Clarke, Marsh, Wayland[16] in the book *Promise of the Father* to support her conclusions. She even followed the word "prophesy" through the entire Bible which was a common practice of Bible scholars termed "word study." She reinterpreted the subordination passages in Genesis, Ephesians 5, I Corinthians 11, 14, I Timothy 2, and the "weaker vessel" problem in I Peter by appealing to ancient custom, specificity of the case, and then to clarification of the words or context.

While stating her case, Palmer used whatever passage in the Bible she thought would help clarify the meaning of the text. In her own words, she believed that the Bible should interpret itself: "The Scriptural way of arriving at right Bible conclusions is by comparing Scripture with Scripture."[17] Some would label her approach, "Canonical Criticism."

EXTRAORDINARY WOMEN

Phoebe began her famous *Promise of the Father* by assuring her readers that she is not one of those women in the "movement." She is not going to discuss the rights of women nor even the issue of ordination or preaching: "It is not our aim in this work to suggest, in behalf of woman, a change in the social or domestic relation."[18]

> We believe woman has her legitimate sphere of action, which differs in most cases materially from that of man; and in this legitimate sphere she is both happy and useful. . . . But we have never conceived that it would be subservient to the happiness, usefulness, or true dignity of woman, were she permitted to occupy a prominent part in legislative halls, or take a leading position in the orderings of church conven-

tions. Ordinarily, these are not the circumstances where woman can best serve her generation according to the will of God.[19]

In the midst of this conservative-traditional rhetoric Phoebe placed the word "ordinarily." And with that one word she began to slowly open the mind of the reader to consider the extraordinary women in the Bible, in history, and in their own lives.

WOMEN AS ROLE MODELS AND LEADERS

According to Phoebe, God had chosen notable women in special circumstances throughout history in order to fulfill His design. Daughters are prophesying now.[20] The prophetic verses in Joel 2:28 and Acts 2:18 were being fulfilled in her lifetime. But daughters or women prophesied much earlier, too. There was Miriam, Huldah, Anna, Philip's four daughters, Mary, the Woman of Samaria, Deborah, and Priscilla. Apollos "was not ashamed to be indebted to the instruction of a Christian woman."[21] And the Woman of Samaria "was the first Apostle for Christ in Samaria."[22]

Women should be allowed to preach and give their testimony in church because women go about doing "good" for others when men do not have the time, courage, or ability. Women may be physically inferior to men (I Peter) but they are stronger reasoners.[23] Witness the lives of Deborah and Barak, Manorah and his wife, Abigail and David, Huldah and Josiah, and the Wise Woman and Joab.[24] The word "preach" means so much more than speaking pious words from a pulpit: ". . . [W]e believe all Christ's disciples, whether male or female, should covet to be endued with the gift of prophecy; then will they proclaim, or, in other words, preach Christ crucified, as far as in them lies, under all possible circumstances; and it is thus only that the command of the Head of the church can be obeyed, 'Preach the gospel to every creature.' "[25]

Women were the strength of the early church. What if the disciples had chosen to ignore Mary's message about the risen Jesus, just because she was a woman?[26] God has chosen great women of today and yesterday such as Deborah and Huldah "not because there were no men in Israel."[27] Barak's faith and courage could not lead Israel, so God chose a woman. No male prophet of Israel could help Josiah, the King of Israel, so God chose a woman: "And when, in the order of God, woman has from time to time been called to sustain positions of momentous trust, involving the destinies of her country, facts show that she has not been wanting in ability to meet the demands of her station in such a manner, as to command the respect of her constituents or the homage of her subjects."[28]

Quoting Grotius, Palmer found that the gift of prophecy was also given to women long before the advent of the New Testament. She quoted his translation of Psalm 68:11 and claimed that women were publishers and evangelists: "The Lord shall give the word, that is, plentiful matter of speaking; so that he would call those which follow the great army of preaching women, viz., victories or female conquerors.[29] Both Dr. A. Clarke and Rev. J. Benson support this translation of the Hebrew word *hambaseroth*. Dr. A. Clarke quoted the original text, and followed it with the literal rendering, of the female preachers there was a great host."[30]

PROBLEM PASSAGES OF SCRIPTURE

Palmer accepted the story of creation literally. Adam was created first and so women must acknowledge that males were created first. But first in creation does not mean that all females must be subordinate to males. Both Galatians 3:28 and Ephesians 5 teach mutuality and equality. Only Christianity placed women on an "equal footing" with men.[31] Accordingly, the supposed subordination of women in Paul's letters to the Corinthians and to Timothy were intended for only those churches. If women are to be silent, then that means that they cannot sing or participate in any way in the service.

Paul's letters contradict themselves.[32] In discussing the texts in I Corinthians 11, 14 and I Timothy 2, she assumed that the readers were familiar with the texts, so she only alluded to them, taking small phrases from each passage to illustrate her points. In I Corinthians 11, Paul admits that women are prophesying in public.[33] How could he tell the same women to be silent in the church, to go home and ask their husbands about the contents of the service, and to not ursurp authority from a male?[34] She concluded that these verses "can have no special bearing on the present day."[35] I Corinthians 14:34 must have been intended only for married women who were asking too many contentious questions; it has nothing to do with preaching.[36]

Palmer's strategy when interpreting in I Timothy 2 was to push the logic of the "supposed" subordination law to its ultimate meaning for women. On the issue of teaching and usurping authority over males she continued,

> Most persons opposed to the praying or prophesying of females understand from this passage that no woman is to teach, and that all teaching by women is usurping authority over the man. But this grants too much, inasmuch as it involves the following difficulties: No woman is to teach her children to sew, or cook, or read, or write &c. No woman is to keep a school. No woman is to write books; for this is one excellent method of teaching. . . .[37]

Women who preach in public have no special authority over males, they are merely instruments of God.[38]

SUMMARY

This analysis of Palmer's work has concentrated on her use of Scripture, but her argument is strengthened by giving historic examples of ancient and modern women who have gained political or religious power. Most of her book rehearses stories about women during her own lifetime who had made a difference within society or the church because they were not afraid to step outside their prescribed role.

Phoebe Palmer knew that if she took a direct approach to attempting to prove the equality of women that she would be met with very strong opposition. Throughout her book, *Promise of the Father*, she claimed that she was only arguing for a few special females and not the whole human race, when in reality she was arguing for the recognition of the leadership abilities of every woman who would aspire to a position within a church or society. (What would life be like without all of these courageous women?) She gave ample evidence to prove that women have succeeded in such positions and will do so in the future.

BARBARA KELLISON (1867?)

You might as well try to convince me that I have no soul
as to persuade me that
God never called me to preach His Gospel.[1]

You might as well say, the woman has no flesh,
as to say she has no right to preach.[2]

BIOGRAPHY

After a thorough search of all the resources of the university library, interlibrary loan, and databases, nothing was discovered on the life of Barbara Kellison.[3] Who was she? The pamphlet *The Rights of Women in the Church* published in 1867 (1862) in Dayton, Ohio, lists her as an authoress and claims that she was a member of the Des Moines Christian Conference in Iowa and lived in Wintersett, Madison County, Iowa. Her husband was Elder Kellison. Yet no records are found in this county.

The manuscript reveals that Kellison was a very strong woman who had the support of her husband in her work. She had faced enormous criticism both from ministers and a number of female societies which had varying reasons for their rejection of her position on female preaching. She appears to have been well-educated and knowledgeable of both the Bible and commentaries in the area. She had read books by Emma Ockerman, Miss Barrett, and she knew about the history of the Quakers, including the works of Margaret and George Fox. She was probably a minister or traveling evangelist.[4]

THE PROBLEM

Barbara was faced with prejudice[5] from both males and females concerning the right of a woman to preach in church to a congregation. Not only did the scholars[6] within Christianity argue against equality but she said, "some of my own sex are opposed to women preaching."[7] She was determined to create a document that would help her sisters because she believed that no other documents existed to support their claims to equality: "That this pamphlet may be productive of good and advance the cause of truth, and especially aid and encourage my Christian sisters in their pilgrimage journey, is the sincere desire of the writer."[8]

Kellison said that ruling males are in control and, thus, are responsible for the social plight of females which had kept them ignorant and uneducated:[9] "There are a great many in the present century who profess Christianity, that will say, 'Let the rules of their Churches be burned before they will admit the female to have equal rights with the male.' "[10]

Her short treatise examined and attempted to refute arguments against women preaching in the church. They included,

1. Women were not chosen Apostles.[11]
2. Paul will not allow women to preach.[12]
3. Paul silenced women.[13]
4. Paul saw the preaching of women as something shameful.[14]
5. Women should consider their appearance: "It does not look well for her to go into the pulpit with the men."[15]
6. Women should not preach because she is weaker.[16]
7. Women do not have souls.[17]
8. Women should not preach to men.[18]

She also presented the plight of the female who felt called by God to preach but feared the men who would stand in her way: "But, Oh! the trembling female that feels it her duty to preach the gospel, what trials she has to undergo. The ministers will preach against it and say it is wrong and she has been taught that it was not right, yet those words roll through her mind, 'Woe is me if I preach not the gospel.' "[19]

PRESUPPOSITIONS REGARDING SCRIPTURE

The Bible which is the Word of God[20] is inspired from cover to cover and the precepts and stories which are found within this volume should be used to govern life in the nineteenth century: "I have offered the testimony of Christ and his apostles, the inspired Prophets and Patriarchs of Old . . ."[21]

She believed that she was quoting the actual words of Jesus and the evangelists.[22] Yet she also argued that women such as Deborah were "the mouth of God."[23]

INTERPRETATIVE STRATEGY

Ms. Kellison used a literal word by word study of the Bible to refute her enemies. One by one she took her opponents' objections and demonstrated reasons why a woman should preach in the church. The lines between the Old Testament or Hebrew Bible and the New Testament blurred as she began her explanations.[24] She pointed to missed verses and the ignored context of certain other verses. Occasionally she instructed the reader as to what the verse did *not* mean. She built her irrefutable case upon numerous similar citations which supported her general theses.

THE CREATION STORY

She admitted that Eve did make a mistake by arguing long and hard with the serpent. But it was not her fault that she failed. First of all, Adam knew all the rules and regulations of the garden and Eve did not. Secondly, if Adam had not been away from home at the time "she would not have been deceived"[25] and Adam was deceived much easier than Eve.[26]

She did not admit that Adam had a right to rule over Eve. Neither one of them wanted to rule over the other in the garden. Yet, the need for males to govern females is an indication of his sin: "There is so much sinfulness in the world that man desires to oppress the female; but God never designed that he should rule her with such power that she could not worship God according to the dictates of her conscience. . . ."[27]

PROPHETESSES

Kellison wrote, "The prophetess is a woman who foretells future events; which is the highest and most divine order of heaven."[28] Women did prophesy in times past "which is the highest and most divine order in heaven."[29] "By searching the word of God we find that women have rights as well as men, and that by the authority of God."[30] Among those prophetesses should be listed Deborah, who became an important "helpmeet" to her husband by leading troops into battle.[31] Other prophetesses included Miriam,[32] Huldah,[33] Nodiah, Ruth, Anna, and the four daughters of Philip.[34] "Those ancient Priests were not so fearful of the woman being in office as some in the present day. . . ."[35]

PRAYING, SINGING, AND PREACHING

Kellison ought to establish that women have been heard throughout the ages and in the church. Miriam, the forty-five singers in Nehemiah, and Ezra's songmakers were women.[36] Paul speaks to the issue of woman praying or prophesying in I Corinthians 11:45: "If man here has the privilege to pray in the congregation so as to be heard, the woman has the same; and no person can deny this with a good conscience, in the sight of God, for the inspired Apostle gives the same privilege to one as the other. . . ."[37]

In discussing the opinions of such learned men as Henry, Burkitt, Clark, and Scott, and others who would limit a woman's participation in church, Kellison became somewhat sarcastic: "I presume that he would prefer a female Heaven, or have them in one corner by themselves, as he will not permit them to worship as the men, of course, he would not have them in the same place; but, perhaps he might admit them long enough to sing."[38]

In chapter 4, Kellison attempted to directly refute objections to women preaching in the church. She took each argument and listed verse after verse to prove that women should have the same rights as men. Her strategy involved redefining commonly understood terms and accepted interpretations of verses. The word "disciple" has no "distinction of sex."[39] There were many women who labored with

Jesus and with Paul; there was Tabitha, and the women who followed Jesus in Luke 8:1–3, Phoebe,[40] Priscilla, and the husband-wife team of Andronicus and Junia,[41] Tryphena and Tryphosa,[42] and the four daughters of Philip,[43] or the four Holy Women.[44] In each story or listing of the above people, Kellison argued that they worked in much the same manner as Paul.

She vehemously attacked myths that silenced woman in the church, maintaining that she is not fit to preach, and that claim that woman has no soul. Kellison pointed to the context of I Corinthians 14:28 which silences both men and women:[45] "Says one, 'I never knew the word of God silenced a man.' No, for you always read that place with your green spectacles on, i.e., prejudice against woman's preaching."[46]

I PETER 3:1

I Peter 3:1 claims that women are weaker vessels. Yet even though some women may not be as physically strong as men, the verse says nothing about mental ability or oratory skill. "God never said she had the weaker mind, but he has chosen the weak things of this world to confound the mighty." And some women are "more robust" in preaching than men.[47]

In a very literal interpretation of the story of Noah and the Ark, Kellison refuted the myth that women have no souls by pointing to Old Testament or Hebrew Bible passages: "[F]or eight souls were saved in Noah's Ark; there were only four men and four women,"[48] and a woman's soul is mentioned eleven times in Numbers 30.[49] If a man denies the right to preach to woman then he is denying God who has put that need in her heart or soul.

Finally, she listed women in the New Testament who did preach, even to men.[50] Women were persecuted because they preached. Among the biblical stories are the Samaritan woman,[51] the women at the tomb,[52] the two on the road to Emmaus, women who followed Jesus in Luke,[53] and the elect lady in 2 John.[54] Her strategy consistently involved quoting from a commentary and then refuting it. Here is an example of her method.

> The Savior refers to the promise that God made to Joel in his prophecy, when he said it should come to pass that he would pour his spirit

upon all flesh, and the sons and daughters shall prophesy; and when we turn to Acts 2:17, we find the promise fulfilling and both man and women prophesying, or preaching; therefore God is not slack concerning his promises. But says the objector, I believe that women did preach in the apostles' day, but they have no right now. But this argument will not bear investigation, for on the same ground of reasoning we may say with propriety, the men have no right to preach, but we have no account in the word of God, that either will cease until the end of time, and that is as long, as I wish to preach.[55]

Jesus and Paul approved of women preaching[56] and so did her husband Elder Kellison.[57] The resurrected Jesus told the women, "Go tell my brethren."[58] and the Philippian women worked with Paul and he did not object to their ministry.[59]

Kellison ended on a defiant note warning men of the day of judgment when they will be found guilty of preventing women from working for God: ". . . [A]nd I believe if men will not permit her to improve her talent in the Church, they will be accountable at the Day of Judgment for her and the souls that are lost. . . ."[60] "[A]nd I thank God, all that man can do against female preaching has not stopped it, nor never will, for it is the work of God; and he will chose such instruments to promote his cause as he sees best."[61]

SUMMARY

Kellison, although speaking within the context of the church, longed for a time when women would have the same "male rights" in society.[62] Her arguments for the equality of women were born out of a deep belief that women are essential to the Divine purpose. Men are thwarting that purpose and so must be ignored: "I say to you, dear sisters in Christ, receive the truth of God's word, and do your duty, regardless of the sayings of men. . . .[63]

Kellison recognized that there is very little support for women who want to preach within the church, from either men or women. Therefore, women must abandon all the traditions of men and follow their own hearts and minds, creating a virtual rebellion or revolution. It is the only thing they can do if they are to follow the call of God in their lives.

Notes

GEORGE FOX

1. Barry Reay, *The Quakers and the English Revolution* (New York: St. Martin's Press, 1985), 51.
2. "Quakers," *The Encyclopedia of Religion*, Mircea Eliade, ed. (New York: Macmillan, 1987), 5:404–405.
3. Barry Reay, *The Quakers and the English Revolution*, 43–56.
4. Ibid., 58.
5. George Fox, *A Collection of Many Select and Christian Epistles and Testimonies. Written on Sundry Occasions, by that Ancient, Eminent, and Faithful Friend and Minister of Christ Jesus.* Second Edition. (London: T. Soble, 1698), 358.
6. George Fox, *Gospel Truth Demonstrated in a Collection of Doctrinal Books, Given forth by that Faithful Minister of Jesus Christ, George Fox: Containing Principles Essential to Christianity and Salvation, held Among the People called Quakers.* 3 vols. A reprint of the 1706 edition. (New York: Isaac T. Hopper, 1831), 1:107.
7. George Fox, *Gospel Truth Demonstrated*, vol. 1:184.
8. William C. Braithwaite, *The Beginnings of Quakerism.* Second Edition edited by Henry J. Cadbury (Cambridge: The University Press, 1912), 28. Footnoted by the editor from George M. Trevelyan, *England under the Stuarts*, 312.
9. William C. Braithwaite, *The Beginnings of Quakerism*, 28–30.
10. Ibid., 31.
11. Catherine L. Albanese, *America Religions and Religion.* Second Edition (Belmont: Wadsworth, 1992), 118–119.
12. William C. Braithwaite, *The Beginnings of Quakerism*, 12.
13. "Quakers," *The Encyclopedia of Religion*, Mircea Eliade, ed. (New York: Macmillan, 1987), 5:404–405.
14. William C. Braithwaite, *The Beginnings of Quakerism*, 66.
15. Ibid., 53.
16. George Fox, *Gospel Truth Demonstrated*, 1:191.
17. William C. Braithwaite, *The Beginnings of Quakerism*, 53–54.
18. Samuel Macauley Jackson, ed., *The New Schaff-Herzog Encyclopedia of Religious Knowledge* (New York: Funk and Wagnals, 1909), 4:348.
19. Mary Agnes Best, *Rebel Saints.* Reprint of 1925 edition. (New York: Books for Libraries Press, 1968), 65.
20. Ibid., 66.
21. Susan Mosher Stuard, "Women's Witnessing: A New Departure," in *Witnesses for Change: Quaker Women over Three Centuries.* Elisabeth Potts Brown and Susan Mosher Stuart, eds. (London: Rutgers University Press, 1989), 14.
22. George Fox, *Gospel Truth Demonstrated*, 1:105–109.
23. George Fox, *A Collection of Many Select and Christian Epistles and Testimonies*, 370.
24. Ibid., 373.
25. Ibid., 369.
26. George Fox, *Gospel Truth Demonstrated*, 1:104.
27. George Fox, *A Collection of Many Select and Christian Epistles and Testimonies*, 369.
28. George Fox, *Gospel Truth Demonstrated*, 1:104.

29. George Fox, *A Collection of Many Select and Christian Epistles and Testimonies*, 370.
30. Ibid.
31. George Fox, *Gospel Truth Demonstrated*, 1:349, 383.
32. George Fox, *A Collection of Many Select and Christian Epistles and Testimonies*, 384.
33. Ibid., 411.
34. Ibid., 373–380.
35. Ibid., 375.
36. Ibid., 377.
37. Ibid., 380–381.
38. Ibid., 324.
39. See Margaret Hope Bacon, *Mothers of Feminism* (San Francisco: Harper and Row, 1986).
40. George Fox, *A Collection of Many Select and Christian Epistles and Testimonies*, 349.
41. Ibid., 385.
42. Ibid., 373.
43. Ibid., 369.
44. Ibid., 387.
45. Ibid., 383.
46. Ibid., 323.
47. Ibid., 349.
48. Ibid., 385.
49. Ibid., 386.
50. George Fox, *Gospel Truth Demonstrated*, 1:105.
51. George Fox, *A Collection of Many Select and Christian Epistles and Testimonies*, 385.
52. George Fox, *Gospel Truth Demonstrated*, 1:110.
53. George Fox, *A Collection of Many Select and Christian Epistles and Testimonies*, 385.
54. See Phyllis Mack, "Gender and Spirituality in Early English Quakerism, 1650–1665," in *Witnesses for Change: Quaker Women Over Three Centuries*. Elisabeth Potts Brown and Susan Mosher Stuard, eds. (London: Rutgers University Press, 1989), 31–64.
55. George Fox, *A Collection of Many Select and Christian Epistles and Testimonies*, 388.
56. Ibid.
57. George Fox, *Gospel Truth Demonstrated*, 1:109.
58. Henry J. Cadbury, "George Fox and Women's Liberation," *The Friends Quarterly* (October 1974): 270–376 concludes that Fox was kind to women but was not progressive. He supported women and claimed to have initiated their separate meetings as a way of utilizing all the sources available in order to sustain the movement. In other words, Fox's view of women was utilitarian.

MARGARET ASKEW FELL FOX

1. Mary Maples Dunn, "Saints and Sisters: Congregational and Quaker Women in the Early Colonial Period," *American Quarterly* 30 (1978): 597. See also Elisabeth Potts Brown and Susan Mosher Stuard, eds., *Witnesses for Change: Quaker Women over Three Centuries* (London: Rutgers Press, 1989).

2. Isabel Ross, *Margaret Fell: Mother of Quakerism* (London: Longmans and Green, 1949), 408–412.

3. William C. Braithwaite, *The Beginnings of Quakerism.* Second Edition, Henry J. Cadbury, ed. (Cambridge: The University Press, 1912), p. 28. Footnoted by the editor from George M. Trevelyan, *England under the Stuarts*, 99. See also Phyllis Mack, *Visionary Women: Ecstatic Prophecy in Seventeenth-Century England* (Los Angeles: University of California Press, 1992).

4. William C. Brathwaite, *The Beginnings of Quakerism*, 134.

5. Ibid., 104.

6. Margaret Fell Fox, *Women's Speaking Justified, Proved and Allowed by the Scriptures* (1688). First printed in 1666, reprinted by William Andrews Clark Memorial Library, 1979. Introduction by David J. Latt, iv. For accessible copies of her pamphlet consult: Moira Ferguson, ed., *First Feminists: British Women Writers 1578–1799* (New York: The Feminist Press, 1985), 114–127. An abbreviated version may be found in Barbara J. MacHaffie, *Readings in Her Story: Women in Christian Tradition* (Minneapolis: Fortress Press, 1992), 109–112.

7. Isabel Ross, *Margaret Fell: Mother of Quakerism*, 407.

8. Margaret Fell Fox, *Women's Speaking Justified*, 4.

9. Ibid., 10.

10. Ibid., 7.

11. Ibid., 12.

12. Ibid., 10.

13. Ibid., 18.

14. Ibid., 17.

15. Ibid., 1.

16. Ibid., 4.

17. Ibid., 5.

18. Ibid., 18.

19. Ibid., 8.

20. Ibid., 13.

21. Ibid., 10.

22. Ibid., 4.

23. Ibid., 4.

24. Ibid., 17.

25. Ibid., 5.

26. Ibid., 6.

27. Ibid., 12–14.

28. Ibid., 7.

SARAH MOORE GRIMKÉ

1. Sarah M. Grimké, *Letters on the Equality of the Sexes and the Conditions of Woman. Addressed to Mary S. Parker, President of the Boston Female Anti-Slavery Society* (New York: Burt Franklin, 1838), 21.

2. Ibid., 97.

3. See Gerda Lerner, *The Grimké Sisters from South Carolina: Rebels Against Slavery*

(Boston: Houghton Mifflin Company, 1967 and *The Grimké Sisters from South Carolina: Pioneers for Woman's Rights and Abolition* (New York: Schocken Books, 1971); Ellen Reid Gold, "The Grimké Sisters and the Emergence of the Woman's Rights Movement," *The Southern Speech Communication Journal* 46 (Summer, 1981): 341–360.

4. Margaret Hope Brown, *Mothers of Feminism: The Story of Quaker Women in America* (New York: Harper and Row, 1982), 105.
5. Nancy A. Hardesty, *Women Called to Witness: Evangelical Feminism in the Nineteenth Century* (Nashville: Abingdon, 1984), 121.
6. Sarah M. Grimké, *Letters on the Equality of the Sexes,* preface.
7. Judith Nies, *Seven Women: Portraits from the American Radical Tradition* (New York: Penguin Books, 1977), 10.
8. Ibid., 12–13.
9. Nancy A. Hardesty, *Evangelical Feminism in the Nineteenth Century,* 18–19.
10. Alice S. Rossi, *The Feminist Papers: From Adams to de Beauvoir* (New York: Columbia University Press, 1973), 282–296.
11. Nancy A. Hardesty, *Evangelical Feminism in the Nineteenth Century,* 122.
12. Judith Nies, *Seven Women,* 26–27.
13. Judith Nies, *Seven Women,* 24. See also Elizabeth Ann Bartlett, ed., *Sarah Grimké: Letters on the Equality of the Sexes and Other Essays* (New Haven: Yale University Press, 1988), 1–29.
14. Sarah M. Grimké, *Letters on the Equality of the Sexes,* 19, 21.
15. Ibid., 125.
16. Ibid., 119.
17. Ibid., 27.
18. Ibid., 7, 122.
19. Ibid., 3.
20. Ibid., 74.
21. Ibid., 75.
22. Ibid., 76.
23. Ibid., 79.
24. Ibid., 80.
25. Ibid., 83.
26. Ibid., 83.
27. Ibid., 12.
28. Ibid., 10.
29. Ibid., 119.
30. Ibid., 10.
31. Ibid., 27.
32. Ibid., 27.
33. Ibid., 21.
34. Ibid., 27–73.
35. Ibid., 104.
36. Ibid., 103.
37. Ibid., 4.
38. Ibid., 7, 108, 113,
39. Ibid., 95.

40. Ibid., 104.
41. Ibid., 111, 4.
42. Ibid., 104.
43. Ibid., 12, 89.
44. Ibid., 97.
45. Ibid., 96.
46. Ibid., 2, 118.
47. Ibid., 91.
48. Ibid., 91.
49. Ibid., 104–108.
50. Ibid., 4.
51. Ibid., 4–5.
52. Ibid., 5.
53. Ibid., 6.
54. Ibid., 6.
55. Ibid., 7.
56. Ibid., 7.
57. Ibid., 7.
58. Ibid., 7.
59. Ibid., 8.
60. Ibid., 116.
61. Ibid., 116.
62. Ibid., 22.
63. Ibid., 23.
64. Ibid., 23.
65. Ibid., 89.
66. Ibid., 89.
67. Ibid., 90.
68. Ibid., 68.
69. Ibid., 95.
70. Ibid., 95.
71. Ibid., 96.
72. Ibid., 97.
73. Ibid., 25.
74. Ibid., 99.
75. Ibid., 101.
76. Ibid., 100.
77. Ibid., 102.
78. Ibid., 103.
79. Ibid., 102.
80. Ibid., 107.
81. Ibid., 108.
82. Ibid., 107.
83. Ibid., 111.
84. Ibid., 112.
85. Ibid., 114.

LUCRETIA COFFIN MOTT

1. Lucretia Coffin Mott, "The Laws in Relation to Woman: Remarks, Delivered at the National Women's Rights Convention, Cleveland, Ohio, 1853," *National Women's Rights Convention Proceedings.* (Cleveland: Gray Beardsley, Spear and Co., 1854). Also found in Dana Greene, ed., *Lucretia Mott: Her Complete Speeches and Sermons* (New York: Edwin Mellen Press, 1980): 215.
2. Lucretia Coffin Mott, "The Argument that Women do not Want to Vote. Address, Delivered to the American Equal Rights Association, New York, May 9–10, 1867," in *Proceedings of the First Anniversary of the American Equal Rights Association* (New York: Robert J. Johnston, 1867). Also found in Dana Greene, ed., *Lucretia Mott: Her Complete Speeches and Sermons* (New York: Edwin Mellen Press, 1980): 287.
3. See the following for additional information: "Mott, Lucretia Coffin," *Notable American Women 1607–1950: A Biographical Dictionary* (Cambridge, MA: The Belknap Press of Harvard University Press, 1971): vol. 2: 592–595 and "Mott, Mrs. Lucretia," in *American Women: Fifteen Hundred Biographies with over 1,400 Portraits* (New York: Mast, Crowell, & Kirkpatrick, 1973): 526. See also Margaret H. Bacon, *Liberating Woman: The Life of Lucretia Coffin Mott* (New York: Walker and Company, 1980).
4. Greene, *Lucretia Mott: Her Complete Speeches and Sermons,* 17.
5. Ibid., 15.
6. Ibid., 20.
7. Lucretia Coffin Mott, "The Principles of the Co-Equality of Woman with Man. Remarks, Delivered at the Woman's Rights Convention, New York, September 6–7, 1853." Also found in Dana Greene, ed., *Lucretia Mott: Her Complete Speeches and Sermons* (New York: Edwin Mellen Press, 1980): 209.
8. Greene, *Lucretia Mott: Her Complete Speeches and Sermons,* 4.
9. Ibid., 9.
10. Ibid., 15.
11. Lucretia Coffin Mott, "The Laws in Relation to Woman. Remarks, Delivered at the National Women's Rights Convention, Cleveland, Ohio, 1853," *National Women's Rights Convention Proceedings.* (Cleveland: Gray Beardsley, Spear and Co., 1854). Also found in Dana Greene, ed., *Lucretia Mott: Her Complete Speeches and Sermons* (New York: Edwin Mellen Press, 1980): 213.
12. Greene, *Lucretia Mott: Her Complete Speeches and Sermons,* 215.
13. Ibid., 209.
14. Lucretia Coffin Mott, *Discourse on Woman.* A speech delivered at the Assembly buildings, December 17, 1849. Being a full phonographic report, revised by the author (Philadelphia: T. B. Peterson, 1850).
15. Lucretia Coffin Mott. "Discourse on Woman, 1849," in vol. 1. *Man Cannot Speak for Her: A Critical Study of Early Feminist Rhetoric,* Karlyn Kohrs Campbell, ed. (New York: Greenwood Press, 1989): 72–73.
16. Lucretia Coffin Mott. *Discourse on Woman,* 4.
17. Ibid., 8.
18. Ibid., 14.

19. Ibid., 6.
20. Ibid., 8.
21. Ibid., 12.
22. Ibid., 13.
23. Greene, *Lucretia Mott: Her Complete Speeches and Sermons*, 224.
24. Lucretia Coffin Mott. *Discourse on Woman*, 4.
25. Ibid., 5.
26. Ibid., 6.
27. Ibid., 5.
28. Ibid., 4.
29. Ibid., 5.
30. Ibid., 5.
31. Ibid., 5–6.
32. Greene, *Lucretia Mott: Her Complete Speeches and Sermons*, 287.
33. Lucretia Coffin Mott. *Discourse on Woman*, 6.
34. Ibid., 6.
35. Ibid., 6
36. Greene, *Lucretia Mott: Her Complete Speeches and Sermons*, 229.
37. Ibid., 231.
38. Ibid., 231.
39. Ibid., 287.
40. Ibid., 288.
41. Lucretia Coffin Mott. *Discourse on Woman*, 6.
42. Greene, *Lucretia Mott: Her Complete Speeches and Sermons*, 17.
43. Lucretia Coffin Mott. *Discourse on Woman*, 6.

PHOEBE PALMER

1. Phoebe Palmer, *Promise of the Father* (Boston: H. Degen, 1859) (Reprint: New York: Garland Publishing, 1985), 51.
2. Phoebe Palmer, *Promise of the Father*, 99.
3. Edward T. James, *Notable American Women 1607–1950* (Cambridge: Harvard University Press, 1971), 3:14. See Charles Edward White, "The Beauty of Holiness: The Career and Influence of Phoebe Palmer," *Methodist History* 25 (1987): 75–76 who says, "I believe that Mrs. Palmer's contribution to American religion has been ignored because she was a female, pious, and Methodist," p. 74.
4. Nancy A. Hardesty, *Evangelical Feminism in the Nineteenth Century: Women Called to Witness* (Nashville: Angdon, 1984), 133.
5. Edward T. James, *Notable American Women 1607–1950*, 3:14.
6. Edward T. James, *Notable American Women 1607–1950*, 3:13–15. See J. A. Rocke, "Mrs. Phoebe Palmer," *The Ladies Repository* (February, 1866): 65–70 for an early biography.
7. Amy Oden, ed., *In Her Words: Women's Writings in the History of Christian Thought* (Nashville: Abingdon Press, 1994), 290.
8. Phoebe Palmer, *Promise of the Father*, 3.
9. Phoebe Palmer, *Promise of the Father*, 237, and see Nancy A. Hardesty, *Evangelical Feminism in the Nineteenth Century*, 58.

10. Phoebe Palmer, *Promise of the Father*, 227.
11. Ibid., 46.
12. Ibid., 35.
13. Ibid., 152, 4, 5, 13.
14. Ibid., 4.
15. Phoebe Palmer, *Promise of the Father*, 9–10. See also a speech by Palmer included in Rosemary Radford Ruether and Rosemary Skinner Keller, eds., *Women and Religion in America, vol. 1: The Nineteenth Century, a Documentary History* (New York: Harper and Row, 1981), 217–218.
16. Phoebe Palmer, *Promise of the Father*, 10, 24, 25, 26, 27, 28, 36, 37, 40, 44, 46, 48, 97–99.
17. Ibid., 50.
18. Ibid., 13.
19. Ibid., 1 and 19.
20. Ibid., 51.
21. Ibid., 31–40; 11, 46.
22. Ibid., 12.
23. Ibid., 96–97.
24. Ibid., 96.
25. Ibid., 37.
26. Ibid., 143, 151.
27. Ibid., 2.
28. Ibid., 3.
29. Ibid., 27–28.
30. Ibid., 325.
31. Ibid., 10, 8, 99.
32. Ibid., 7.
33. Ibid., 8.
34. Ibid., 7–8.
35. Ibid., 9.
36. Ibid., 47.
37. Ibid., 48.
38. Ibid., 9.

BARBARA KELLISON

1. Barbara Kellison, *The Rights of Women in the Church* (Dayton: Herald and Hanner Office, 1862, Reprint 1867), 20.
2. Ibid., 27.
3. Several works on women and religion include references to Kellison's work or excerpts, yet no one has discovered her identity. Records in Madison County were thoroughly researched but none could be found. See Nancy Hardesty, *Evangelical Feminism in the Nineteenth Century: Women called to Witness* (Nashville: Abingdon, 1984), 163; Rosemary Radford Ruether and Rosemary Skinner Keller, eds., *Women and Religion in America*, vol. 1, *The Nineteenth Century, A Documentary History* (New York: Harper and Row, 1981), 219–223.

4. Barbara Kellison, *The Rights of Women in the Church*, 37–44.
5. Ibid., 17.
6. Ibid., 20.
7. Ibid., 44.
8. Ibid., iii–iv.
9. Ibid., 41–42.
10. Ibid., 42.
11. Ibid., 15.
12. Ibid., 15.
13. Ibid., 16.
14. Ibid., 17.
15. Ibid., 16.
16. Ibid., 18.
17. Ibid., 18.
18. Ibid., 19.
19. Ibid., 35.
20. Ibid., 10.
21. Ibid., iii.
22. Ibid., 36.
23. Ibid., 8.
24. Ibid., 10.
25. Ibid., 6.
26. Ibid., 7.
27. Ibid., 5.
28. Ibid., 7.
29. Ibid.
30. Ibid., 9.
31. Ibid., 8–9.
32. Ibid., 7.
33. Ibid., 9.
34. Ibid., 10.
35. Ibid.
36. Ibid., 11.
37. Ibid., 14.
38. Ibid., 20.
39. Ibid., 15.
40. Ibid., 21.
41. Ibid., 24.
42. Ibid., 23.
43. Ibid., 25.
44. Ibid., 28.
45. Ibid., 16.
46. Ibid., 17.
47. Ibid., 18.
48. Ibid.
49. Ibid., 19.
50. Ibid., 32.

51. Ibid., 31.
52. Ibid., 33.
53. Ibid., 35.
54. Ibid., 36.
55. Ibid., 34.
56. Ibid., 36.
57. Ibid., 44.
58. Ibid., 36.
59. Ibid., 25.
60. Ibid., 42.
61. Ibid., 41.
62. Ibid., 44.
63. Ibid., 43.

Chapter 3

GYNOCENTRISM: WOMAN AT THE CENTER

INTRODUCTION

While Elizabeth Cady Stanton and Antoinette Louisa Brown Black-well used some of the same strategies in interpreting the Bible as those listed in chapter 1, they, and Mary Hays, placed woman squarely in the center of their quest. They no longer wanted equality; they saw something different within women and they want something more out of life.

Mary Hays, a Unitarian who lived in the eighteenth and early nineteenth centuries in England, described the frivolous lifestyles of women of means. She described women as the slaves of men, who rarely receive an education. This made them worthless for most occupations or tasks. She pretended to claim that women are weaker in some areas that require physical strength, such as carpentry, or the pursuit of long education, such as the profession of law. Ignoring the story of Eve and Adam as a mere myth that has nothing to do with reality, she pointed to the example of Jesus who recognized the worth of women. If women were given a chance to improve and were allowed their independence in decision making, such as Jesus did, they would make life better for everyone. Men and women would learn to love each other in a very different way.

The Woman's Bible, created and edited by Elizabeth Cady Stanton, stands as a beacon to all women who would challenge the traditional approach and interpretation of the Bible. Enlisting the help of women from all over the world, she hoped to create a book that would interpret the Bible from a woman's point of view. They attempted to choose passages within the Bible that contained stories or references only to women. The task was extremely difficult and the project produced many political problems for its interpreters.

Interpretations in *The Woman's Bible* are as varied as the interpreters who created them. They draw on resources from historical critical commentaries and works, the Occult, Theosophy, Astrology, and more. They linked specific Scriptures with social problems in their cultures. They placed the blame for the oppression and subjugation of women on the Bible, not merely the interpretation of the Bible. Some of the stories about women were positive but most of them could not be salvaged for use by the new woman of the emerging twentieth century. In a way, the interpreters in this volume were announcing to the world that they were indeed considering the merits of the Bible for their lives, but they no longer needed the Bible to guide them in their journeys. They could create the journey for themselves.

And lastly, Antoinette Louisa Brown Blackwell, the first ordained minister in the United States, was also one of those people who declared that she would create her own journey. That journey included entering a seminary and becoming a minister. During her time of study at Oberlin, she authored an article which attempted to prove that women should be allowed to teach publicly, and to preach publicly. The entire article focuses on the status and opportunities that should be available to women. A later speech, written when she was much older, places the blame for women's subjugation on herself: she has the power to be free, if only she will recognize it within herself and use it.

All three of these women believed that women had the power of change within them and the Bible had something to do with allowing them to change. Mary hoped for a better family life and better marriages. Elizabeth believed that women were better interpreters and could lead people in a direction that would not be alienating or subjugating. And finally, Antoinette refused to believe that women had to live a life of submission to men. Women had the power and the will to break the chains and free themselves.

MARY HAYS (1759/60–1843)

What Women Are.

Thus many a good head is stuffed with ribbons, gauze,
fringes, flounces, and furbelows,
that might have received and communicated, far other and
more noble impressions.

What Men Are.

. . . the high priest of authority,
—the selfish egotist,—
with arbitrary opinions.

We only mean to infer from all that has been said on this subject, that men are
much more guided by their fancies, and by the complexion of the times, in their
ideas about women; than by reason, or any other settle standard whatever.

Oh man! that you vainly and arrogantly presume to dictate to her, and to point out
the road to happiness and perfection, as lying only through the medium of
submission and obedience to you?[1]

BIOGRAPHY

England in the eighteenth and nineteenth centuries presented many obstacles for the woman who wanted to be "free." Mary Hays was one of those women. She wanted complete control of her body as well as her mind. Mary could never have known what price she would have to pay for her dreams. While England offered no formal educational institutions for women, Mary disciplined herself to study alone. One evening at a meeting of dissenters she discovered John Eccles, who shared her consuming love for learning. Unfortunately, following their engagement, he died shortly before their marriage.

Mary Hays was a middle-class Unitarian, dissenter, and authoress who grew up in Southwark, England. Very little is known about her childhood and family. Her friends included Mary Wollenstonecraft, authoress of *A Vindication of the Rights of Woman* (1792), and people such as George Dyer, William Frend, Thomas Paine, and Anna Laetitia.[2]

Her passion for self-sufficiency and knowledge kept her from marrying anyone else and often placed her in awkward economic situations. She wanted it all but could have none of it, so on the advice of her friend and mentor, William Godwin, she wrote novels and lived her life through the characters.[3]

Her most famous book, *Appeal to the Men of Great Britain in Behalf of Women,* is not a novel but a treatise containing arguments, among others, for the education of women based upon a reinterpretation of the Bible. The book was written anonymously in order to avoid a backlash, which had, after publishing her second novel, caused her to go into hiding.

In 1800, after Charles Lloyd accused Mary of "offering herself to him in the manner of Emma Courtney," Samuel Taylor Coleridge described Mary this way, ". . . 'a thing, ugly & petticulted' who seeks to 'ex-syllogize a God with cold-blooded Precision, & . . . Religioun thro' with an Icicle.' "[4]

Most of Mary's fiction featured women interwoven with feminist and political themes which created hostile reactions from conservatives. Her heroines were brassy and creative, throwing themselves at the men they loved. Titles of her novels include *Victim of Prejudice* (1799) and *Memoirs of Emma Courtney* (1796). She also contributed regularly to the *Monthly Magazine*[5] and reviewed novels for Wollenstonecraft. Among her many nonfiction books is a six-volume set of *Female Biography; or Memoirs of Illustrious and Celebrated Women of all Ages and Countries, Alphabetically arranged (1803).*[6]

THE PROBLEM

> For it is very clear, that they [women] are not what they ought to be, that they are not what men would have them to be, and to finish the portrait, that they are not what they appear to be.
>
> Petty treacheries—mean subterfuge—whining and flattery—feigned submission—and all the dirty attendants, which compose the endless train of low cunning; if not commendable, cannot with justice be severly censured, when practiced by women. Since alas—THE WEAK

HAVE NO OTHER ARMS AGAINST THE STRONG! Since alas!
NECESSITY ACKNOWLEDGES NO LAW, BUT HER OWN![7]

Women are not what they should be because men are in control.[8]
And women are unhappy because of the control over their lives. As
lovers, men are friends, as husbands they are tyrants.[9] Men are
guided by "fancies" instead of reason,[10] perceive women to be inferior,[11] are selfish and indulgent,[12] and have created a slave class of
people that are either necessary drudges in the lower classes or
"ornaments of society" in the upper classes:[13]: "In plain language,
women are in all situations rendered merely the humble companions
of men,—the tools of their necessities,—or the sport of their authority, of their prejudices, and of their passions."[14]

UNEDUCATED WOMEN ARE THE SLAVES OF MEN

Women receive a miserable education, if any, which has produced a
degenerated, pitiful, and frivolous class of women.[15]

> In the first place then, I hold it as an infallible truth, and a truth that
> few will attempt to deny; that any race of people, or I should rather say
> any class of rational beings,—though by no means inferior originally
> in intellectual endowments,—may be held in a state of subjection and
> dependence from generation to generation, by another party, who, by
> a variety of circumstances, none of them depending on actual, original
> superiority of mind, may have established an authority over them. And
> it must be acknowledged a truth equally infallible, that any class so
> held in a state of subjection and dependence, will degenerate both in
> body and mind.[16]

> Driven and excluded from what are commonly esteemed the conse-
> quential offices of life;—denied, and perhaps with reason and pro-
> priety too, any political existence;—and literary talents and acquire-
> ments, nay genius itself, being in them generally regarded rather with
> contempt or jealousy, than meeting with encouragement and
> applause;—nothing in short being left for them, but domestic duties,
> and superficial accomplishments and vanities.[17]

MASCULINE WOMEN

Some suggest that women who are educated are masculinized and this will harm their relationships with men. Not so, said Mary; education will to some extent masculinize a woman but it will only help her "smooth the rugged paths of life"[18] with family and husband.[19] Ignorance can make matters worse for the husband:[20]

> If then my reasoning is well founded it appears, that if we use the term masculine woman, for characters such as I have been describing, it is undeniably true, that knowledge does naturally produce such.[21]

> Thus we see that from various accomplishments which do really render women masculine, in the only objectionable points of view, men seem by no means averse, but much otherwise. We therefore fairly deduce from this, what we have before advanced; that women may be, and often, are, masculine, and yet are not consequently disagreeable to the men.[22]

WOMEN ARE WEAKER

In an odd twist of logic or reasoning, Mary also admitted that women are indeed physically weaker (profound exaggeration?) which excludes them from numerous careers including law and divinity. Yet they may have some talent in the areas of "physic and surgery."[23]

> Nature has decidedly likewise denied to women the bodily strength, the abilities, and the inclination for being masons, carpenters, blacksmiths, farriers, and a thousand other occupations which so readily occur, . . .

> Again, common sense, in which propriety of conduct and character are necessarily included, certainly excludes women from the professions of law and divinity.[24]

WOMEN AND PERSONAL FREEDOMS

Yet Mary called for changes in laws allowing women the right to govern herself, to have some power over her own life, as the men do through voting.[25]

> In forming the laws by which women are governed, and in the arbitrary opinions which have been taken up and encouraged with regard to them, and which have nailed the fetters of the law down, ... have not men in forming these ..., consulted more their own conveniency, comfort, and dignity, ..., than that of women; though they are as nearly concerned, and much more likely to be sufferers, as having no hand in forming them?[26]

This situation and attitude has never been supported by Christianity or reason and must change if people are ever going to find happiness.[27]

VIEW OF SCRIPTURE

The Bible, as the foundation of "all the laws of Christians and polished countries," is a book that is venerated and respected. Mary did not claim to be a master interpreter of this book, but claimed to approach it with "common sense."[28] Her common sense criticized what she terms as "Jewish ideas" (legalistic) she finds in the Old Testament that were taken over by unreflective Christians.[29]

She accepted the divine Mosaic authorship of Genesis but concluded that the Ten Commandments could not have been written by males because they do not take advantage of women: "If proofs were wanting of the divinity of their origin this were one; for had they been fabricated by mere man, he undoubtedly would have introduced, some tyrannical, some unjust, some vexatious clauses against poor defenceless woman."[30]

Using the same logic, she did not venerate the words of the "disciples' [she does not specify] because they speak to the inferiority of women. Thus, Jesus' words which include and praise women are Divine. They are the only words which can lead people to happiness.[31]

INTERPRETATIVE STRATEGY

Mary was a novelist and therefore understood literary forms and creative interpretative methods. She discussed figurative, literal, and analogous ways of interpreting the Bible. She also warned the reader about those who would explain passages of Scripture based upon "opinion" or "system advanced." Constantly calling her audience back to reason and logic rather than "fancy" or "opinion," she used the Bible to defend her belief in equality. While quoting a few passages, she generally drew conclusions based upon a summary of the texts or stories.

CREATION: REMYTHOLOGIZED

Unlike many other interpreters, Mary readily admitted that Eve was at fault in the Creation story. Her submission was only natural under the circumstances. After all, she loved Adam.

> When she saw her husband daily toiling for her support and that of her offspring; when she saw that by the order of the Almighty thorns and thistles were produced by the earth, if he on his part were not a slave for her sake; when added to this she felt the humiliating consciousness of guilt, and the still more dreadful consciousness of having seduced her husband, and involved him in her guilt . . . , was it possible that she on her's should not look up to him, with a mixture of gratitude, affection, respect and pity, which made this command [submission], now deemed so hard, the sweetest part of her duty?[32]
>
> While admitting Eve's guilt she contended that this story is only an allegory which had nothing to do with people who live in the eighteenth century. The punishment that was given to the pair was for them only.[33] If the story was meant to be interpreted as law for the whole human race then, ". . . the men are as much bound to perpetual toil and hard labor, as the women to perpetual and undistinquished obedience. And that men, by breaking through laws of equal authority, with those by which they endeavour to enslave the other sex; with all their boasted superiority, set women a very bad example, both in principle and practice."[34]

JESUS TAUGHT AND LIVED EQUALITY

The ten commandments demonstrate equality and so does the life of Jesus. Jesus talks to and heals women[35] and never speaks against them.[36] His conduct and speech always respected and supported women: "Accordingly, after the strtictest examination it will appear, that not a word is attributed to him, that even glances at their inferiority in spiritual concerns; and if any thing can be of more importance in heaven or on earth, Judge ye!"[37]

Mary used the examples of divorce and the story of the woman caught in adultery to prove her case of equality. She quoted Matthew 19:3: "The Pharisees also came unto him, tempting him, and saying unto him,—Is it lawful for a man to put away his wife for every cause?—And he answered and said unto them, Have ye not read, that he which made them at the beginning, made male and female?"[38]

Jesus' answer to the question suggests that men may not divorce their wives for any reason. Mary contended that this proves that men do not have authority over women in all areas and that women and men have been equal from the beginning of time. Even when the woman of adultery was caught in the act, Jesus forgave her:

> For, when this very crime was actually proved against woman, and she brought before him to be judged; does he not put all her accusers to shame and to flight by a simple, and unexpected appeal to their own consciences; by bidding him who is free cast the first stone? And does not this as clearly as words can express it, place woman on a footing of equality, where she could least of all perhaps expect it. . . .[39]

Mary appealed to the "spirit of justice" found in Jesus to invade the hardened hearts of men so that they won't use authority over their wives.[40] Mary concluded, ". . . [T]here is not I believe I may boldly say, a single sentence [of Jesus'] that even can be tortured into a meaning, against the liberty, equality, or consequence of Woman; I shall endeavour next to convince myself, as much as I am myself convinced, that reason goes hand in hand with religion in opposing the claims of the one sex, to a right of subjecting the other."[41]

Mary boldly claimed equality for women based upon the words of Jesus. This equality, if given to women by men, would ultimately mean that both of them would find happiness.[42]

SUMMARY

Mary's hope was for a more peaceful, equitable personal life without the hostilities experienced between males and females: "Women then . . . ought to be considered as the companions and equals, not as inferiors."[43] While many would contend that the Bible places women in a subordinate position, Mary demonstrated that those scholars were in error. They ignored all of the wonderful words and actions of Jesus. God has ordained equality.[44] They have taken the Bible too literally and have ignored the truth.

The Bible, Nature, and Reason walk hand in hand when it comes to the concerns for the freedoms and happiness of women. All three declare that women have minds, and therefore rights to control their own lives. Women have a right to be selfish, to pursue their own happiness. They can be more than nurses or household drudges.

Similar to Mary Astell's plea, Hays did not call for complete freedom for women in society. They, obviously, can't do all the tasks that men do (with tongue in cheek). She conceded that there are differences between the sexes. This strategy may have kept her critics at arm's length and her more conservative readers interested. But one wonders if Mary was, on the other hand, playing with her audience by pretending to agree with them. After all, Eve loved Adam, didn't she?

ELIZABETH CADY STANTON
(1815–1902)

Henry sides with my friends, who oppose me in all that is dearest to my heart. They are not willing that I should write even on the woman question. But I will both write and speak.[1]

BIOGRAPHY

Elizabeth was an extraordinarily gifted social reformer, politician, mother, homeopathic nurse, budding child psychologist, editor, and writer. By the time she had written her memoirs, *Eighty Years and More: 1815–1897* at the age of eighty-three, she had witnessed almost an entire decade of substantial change for women in the United States.

Born into a Scotch Presbyterian family of six children, Elizabeth learned early from her mother, Margaret Livingstone, how to manipulate and lobby to get her way. Her father, Judge Daniel Cady, taught her organizational skills and introduced her to the law. Schooled at the Troy Female Seminary in New York, the only college available for women, Elizabeth wished to fulfill the dreams of her father and become the son he had lost. Her dreams remained only a faint hope because she was unable to secure a graduate education in law and her father later disinherited her because of her work in the women's movement.[2] In fact, most of her family repudiated her efforts at social change and reform.

After a torrid love affair with her brother-in-law, in her mid-twenties she married Henry Brewster Stanton, an executive with the men-only American Anti-Slavery Society, who later became an attorney and politician. She became the mother of seven children. Lois W. Banner says, "The lack of power over her reproductive life increased Cady Stanton's sense of subordination and eventurally contributed to the centrality of the birth control message in her feminist theory and activism."[3]

She often complained that she did not understand birth control early in her marriage. She spent most of her life wavering between political life and domestic responsibilities. She missed many of her speeches and appointments due to giving birth or to illnesses relating to pregnancies. And her life at home was at times overwhelming because of the almost constant absence of her activist husband.

> I suffered with mental hunger, which, like an empty stomach is very depressing. . . . The general discontent I felt with woman's portion as wife, mother, housekeeper, physician and spiritual guide, the chaotic conditions into which everything fell without her constant supervision, and the wearied, anxious look of the majority of women impressed me with a strong feeling that some active measures should be taken to remedy the wrongs of society in general and of women in particular. I could not see what to do or where to begin—my only thought was a public meeting for protest and discussion.[4]

In spite of her domestic duties, Elizabeth made time for such people as Lucretia Mott, Angelina Grimké and Sarah Grimké, Frederick

Douglass, Matilda Joslyn Gage, and her best friend, Susan B. Anthony. Her career was filled with travel, the lecture circuit, and the organizing of several organizations, such as the Woman's State Temperance Society, and conferences on women. She ran for Congress in 1866 and received twenty-four votes.[5] Her goal was to demonstrate that women could legally hold office but could not vote. Her most famous success, at the age of thirty-three, was organizing the First Women's Rights Convention in 1848 in Seneca Falls, New York, which demanded equal rights for women.

Toward the end of her life, she committed herself to creating the *The Woman's Bible*[6] which attempted to draw upon female scholarship from around the world. While *The Woman's Bible* (*WB*) is a product of several women, it was Elizabeth's brainchild and she remained its editor, responsible for its production and editing. The entries are varied and betray several approaches to theology, philosophy, and biblical interpretation. Unfortunately this critical approach to the Bible caused so much negative criticism that it was never taken seriously by any of the societies within the women's movement.[7]

ORGANIZATIONAL AND INTERPRETATIVE STRATEGY

Several women were chosen to comment upon Scriptures that included references to women.[8] They began by clipping out verses of the Bible which mentioned women and then listed their comments under the verses. The committee's aim was to study the languages, biblical history, manuscripts, and commentaries on the passages. This cut and paste approach to the theme of woman in the Scriptures produced volumes that are at best uneven in interpretation and interpretative strategy.

THE PROBLEM

Males are in control of the church, its documents, and the structures of society. At the heart of this control are religious traditions which uphold the power of men over women. Males are hostile to the notion of equality for females. In their most recent translation of the

Bible in 1888, they do "not exalt and dignify woman."[9] They have produced a translation that is riddled with errors. Women must have a voice and *The Woman's Bible* will be that voice.

Elizabeth said that all religions degrade women[10] and that the worst enemies of women are the leaders within the Protestant religion who have used the Bible to silence women.[11]

> Woman's influence is most clearly set forth by all the Apostles in meek submission to their husbands and to all the church ordinances and discipline. A reverent silence, a respectful observance of rules and authorities was their power. They could not aid in spreading the gospel and in coverting their husbands to the true faith by teaching, by personal attraction, by braided hair or ornaments.[12]

Elizabeth feared that if women did not soon rebel against the male authority dominating them that "he will make her a slave, a subject, the mere reflection of another's will."[13]

Elizabeth and the committee also had many public relations problems. *The Woman's Bible* committee had been unsuccessful in recruiting female language scholars or other capable educated women because some feared retribution because of their association with them. Other capable women lacked the self-confidence needed to engage in the project and so they declined their offer to participate in the commentary.

PRESUPPOSITIONS REGARDING SCRIPTURE:
THE SACRED FABULIST

Elizabeth and the committee believed that the the Bible had become a "fetish" that was worshipped uncritically by too many people. It was written by a sacred fabulist.[14] It is no longer the Word of God but an instrument used by people to subjugate others. Some of the pages within the Old Testament contain such violent and repulsive stories that no one could consider them to be written by God. Those stories may even teach people to falsify their testimonies.[15]

Their outlook on the New Testament changed little even though the Gospels contain the direct recorded words of Jesus.[16] Luke is the only Gospel that recognizes the importance of women and their ministries.[17] Dorcas,[18] Priscilla, and Phoebe[19] highlight the possibilities for women. Their canon includes the Apocrypha and Kabbalah which are held in the highest esteem because of references to woman as Deity.[20]

> Does any one seriously believe that the great spirit of all good talked with these Jews, and really said the extraordinary things they report? It was, however, a very cunning way for the Patriarchs to enforce their own authority, to do whatever they desired, and say the Lord commanded them to do and say thus and so. Many pulpits even in our day enforce their lessons of subjection for woman with the same authority, "Thus saith the Lord," "Thou shalt," and "Thou shall not."[21]

They reiterated later in the book that the Bible is not inspired, although it contains worthy passages of literature.

> We have no fault to find with the Bible as a mere history of an ignorant, undeveloped people, but when special inspiration is claimed for the historian, we must judge of its merits by the moral standard of today. . . .[22]

> Does any one at this stage of civilization think that the Bible was written by the finger of God, that the Old and New Testaments emanated from the highest divine thought in the universe? Do they think that all men who write the different books were specially inspired. . . ? Parts of the Bible are so true, so grand, so beautiful, that it is a pity it should have been bound in the same volume with sentiments and descriptions so gross and immoral.[23]

INTERPRETATIVE STRATEGIES: ALLEGORY, THE OCCULT,
AND HIGHER CRITICISM

The conclusions in the *WB* are consistent but methodologies vary. They recognize the problem of interpreting a verse without its context yet contend that the book of Revelation should be interpreted within the highly unusual context of astrology.[24] In another odd twist of interpretation, the stories of Sarah and Hagar became allegories based upon the sayings of Paul "the prince of Occult philosophers" in Hebrews.[25] They used social customs of their day to explain the veiling of women in I Corinthians 11,[26] and throughout the book there were many attempts to relate the discoveries of "higher criticism."[27] They recognized date, authorship, development of canon, and historical as well as geographical problems. In the midst of their attempt to cover the entire Bible, the committee often concentrated more on peripheral issues than on the topic of "woman" alone.

In general, the committee took a systematic approach in the creation of *The Woman's Bible* by beginning with the Old Testament or Hebrew Bible and following it through to the New Testament. They chose to make personal comments after each selected text. Occasionally, they made a point by referring to a mistranslated word or manuscript tradition, preferring their own translation and choice of readings.[28] They consulted primarily male theologians or historians and an occasional woman. Among those listed are Adam Clarke, German scholars Graef and Meinhold, Lecky, Eusebius, Professor Moore of Andover Theological Seminary, Dr. Abott, Confucius, Bishop Doane, Dr. Edwin Hatch, Madam Blavatsky, Goldwin Smith, and some unknown scientists.[29] Julia Smith is mentioned as a translator of a Bible but the committee chose to use varying translations.[30]

THE NEGATIVE VIEW OF WOMAN IN THE BIBLE

Unlike other interpreters who were interested in presenting the most positive examples of women leaders, the committee readily admitted that in general, the stories in the Old or New Testaments do not characterize appropriate role models for the modern nineteenth-century woman.

> If Sarah and Rebekah are the types of womanhood the Patriarchs admired, Jacob need not have gone far to find their equal. In woman's struggle for freedom during the last half century, men have been continually pointing her to the women of the Bible for examples worthy imitation, but we fail to see the merits of their character, their position, the laws and sentiments concerning them. The only significance of dwelling on these women and this period of woman's history, is to show the absurdity of pointing the women of the nineteenth century to these as examples of virtue.[31]

Their main strategy was to demonstrate how the Bible from cover to cover degrades women. It preserved only a few references that recognize the importance, equality, and occasional superiority of women. For instance, female animals are not accepted as the most appropriate sacrifices in Exodus.[32] Women go nameless in the Old Testament. They are wives, daughters, and sisters of the male.[33] They do not have their own personhood. The phrase "Sons of God and daughters of men" correctly captures the attitude of the writers toward women.[34]

When Moses received the Law, the males were told not to have a conversation with a woman.[35] Only one woman is mentioned in Leviticus, in 24:10.[36] The genealogies which she termed census tables recognize primarily males.[37] A woman's word was worthless.[38] In Deuteronomy, "Though the women were ignored in all the civil affairs and religious observances of the Jews, yet in making war on other tribes they thought them too dangerous to be allowed to live. . . ."[39]

The story of Rahab demonstrates that men are willing to use women for their own advantage.[40] Although Isaac, a male, was spared the sacrificial knife, the unnamed daughter of Jephthah in Judges did not fair so well.[41] The rite of circumcision, performed only on males and members of the cult, "means a disparagement of all female life, unfit for offerings, and unfit to take part in religious services, incapable of consecration."[42] "In the midst of such teachings and examples of subjection and degradation of all woman kind, a mere command [in Exodus] to honor the mother has no significance."[43]

THE CREATION ACCOUNT

Genesis 1:26–28, so long seen as a banner of equality for women, becomes the first assertion of the "ideal Heavenly Mother."[44] She was there with "He" from the beginning. Both female and male were evolved by the "Let us," the "He," and the "She." Man was not prior nor superior; both were equal.[45] The name "Elohim," which is really feminine,[46] begins a "polytheistic fable of creation." Recognizing that Genesis contains two Creation stories[47] the *WB* asserts, "It cannot be maintained that woman was inferior to man even if, as asserted in chapter ii, she was created after him without at once admitting that man is inferior to the creeping things, because [he was] created after them."[48]

Chapter 2 of Genesis is an allegory. Reality therapy suggests that it is man who comes from woman and not visa versa. Some "wily writer" or "highly imaginative editor" added this story in order to "prove her inferiority."[49] Yet even in this Creation story about the fall of humans, woman is not the originator of sin because it existed before she did.[50]

I CORINTHIANS 11; 14:34 AND I TIMOTHY 2:9

Little attempt is made to give a new interpretation to these verses. On the issue of the "veil" in I Corinthians 11,[51] they point to the custom of wearing hats and say this about the verses in I Corinthians 14, "There is such a wide difference on this point among wise men, that perhaps it would be as safe to leave women to be guided by their own assisted common sense."[52] And about I Timothy they write, "It appears very trifling for men, commissioned to do so great a work on earth, to give so much thought to the toilets of women."[53]

Recognizing the inconsistency in Paul's view of woman and whether or not she may preach, another writer laments Paul's prejudice.

> If it is contrary to the perfect operation of human development that woman should teach, the infinite and all wise directing power of the universe has blundered. It cannot be admitted that Paul was inspired by infinite wisdom in this utterance. . . . The doctrine of woman the origin of sin, and her subjection in consequence, planted in the early Christian Church by Paul, has been a poisonous stream in Church and State.[54]

In the New Testament, a direct attempt was made to "reduce women to silent submission" by Paul:[55] "While there are grand types of women presented under both religions, there is no difference in the general estimate of the sex. In fact, her inferior position is more clearly and emphatically set forth by the Apostles than by the Prophets and the Patriarchs."[56]

WOMEN AS ROLE MODELS

Occasionally, they recognized positive stories about women such as the story about the property rights of Zelophehad in Numbers,[57] that the ass of Balaam was a "she,"[58] and that Moses was indebted to several women.[59] Heroines such as Miriam,[60] Deborah,[61] Esther, Huldah, and Vashti merit a second look:[62]

> Look at Deborah!

> We never hear sermons pointing women to the heroic virtues of Deborah as worthy of their imitation. Nothing is said in the pulpit to rouse them from the apathy of ages, to inspire them to do and dare great things, to intellectual and spiritual achievements, in real communion with the Great Spirit of the Universe.[63]

> Women as queenly, as nobel and as self-sacrificing as was Esther, as self-respecting and as brave as was Vashti, are hampered in their creative office by the unjust statutes of men. . . .[64]

> Look at Huldah and Vashti!

> . . . Huldah and Vashti added new glory to their day and generation—one by her learning and the other by her disobedience; for Resistance to tyrants is obedience to God.[65]

> Vashti was the prototype of the higher unfoldment of woman beyond her time. She stands for the point in human development when womanliness asserts itself and begins to revolt and to throw off the yoke of sensualism and of tyranny.[66]

> Vashti stands out a sublime representative of self-centered womanhood. Rising to the heights of self-consciousness and of self-respect, she takes her soul into her own keeping, and though her position both as wife and as queen are jeopardized, she is true to the Divine inspirations of her nature.[67]

Their strategies took them to esoteric writings such as the Kabbalah,[68] the Polychrome Bible,[69] and astrological forecasts.[70] In a very strange strategy, the writer of the Gospel of Matthew is accused of falsifying the story of Herodias.[71] The conclusion is based upon a reading from Josephus:

> Says Josephus: When others came in crowds about him (John the Baptist), for they were greatly moved by hearing his words, Herod, who feared lest the great influence John had over the people might put into

his power and inclination to raise a rebellion (for they seemed ready to do anything he should advise), thought it best, by putting him to death, to prevent any mischief he might cause. . . . Accordingly he was sent a prisoner, out of Herod's suspicious tempter, to Macherus, the castle I before mentioned, and was there put to death.[72]

SOCIAL COMMENTARY

Finally, when Elizabeth or one of the committee members were at a loss to understand a scriptural passage, they resorted to social commentary or theologizing: "If Deborah way back in ancient Judaism, was considered wise enough to advise her people in time of need and distress, why is it that at the end of the nineteenth century, woman had to contend for equal rights and fight to regain every inch of ground she has lost since then."[73]

In several instances, they recognized violence toward animals and humans while questioning whether a just God could author the command to annihilate another culture. When the issue of marriage or legal ownership is central to the narrative, they usually commented upon the prevailing ethic of the day or on the laws handed down by the English law, an example being primogeniture.[74] Rather than affirming the fulfillment of bearing children, Elizabeth related the death of Rachel in childbirth[75] with the ambition of women to bear children for their own benefit.

MALE-BASHING

Male-bashing occurs throughout the book. An especially good example is her rendering of the golden calf story in Exodus 32: "It was just so in the American Revolution, in 1776, the first delicacy the men threw overboard in Boston harbor was the tea, woman's favorite beverage. The tobacco and whiskey, though heavily taxed, they clung to with the tenacity of the devil-fish."[76]

Another example may be implied in Elizabeth's answer as to whether or not a woman has a soul. The reader is pointed to Genesis 46 which speaks of seventy souls, and two women are mentioned:

"Here it is plainly asserted that all the souls that came out of the loins of Jacob were seventy in number. The meaning conveyed may be that the man supplies the spirit and intellect of the race, and the woman the body only. Some late writers take this ground."[77] Elizabeth rebuffs this idea by sarcastically pointing to two areas of males where women may have originated: "If so, the phraseology would have been more in harmony with the idea, if the seventy souls had emanated, Minerva-like, from the brain of father Jacob, rather than from his loins."[78]

SUMMARY

The Woman's Bible was revolutionary; it dared to put in written form many of the comments made by women in the nineteenth century. It was a valiant attempt to demonstrate the biased nature of interpretation and its social-psychological effects upon women. In the process of uncovering the patriarchal bias, the committee revealed their own propensities to the Occult, Theosophy, and Astrology. Christianity had been their seed-bed, but they found that it held little sustenance as they attempted to grow and produce. In fact, instead of helping them to find themselves and discover new possibilities in life, it became the killer of their souls. Parts of the Bible are useful but the majority of its words only serve to alienate and subjugate woman. God could not have written this book if He really loved women.

ANTOINETTE LOUISA BROWN BLACKWELL
(1825–1921)

I told her [Lucy Stone] of my intention to become a minister.
Her protest was most emphatic. She said, "You will never be allowed to do this.
You will never be allowed to stand in a pulpit, nor to preach in a church, and
certainly you can never be ordained." [1]

Resolved, that every women is morally obligated to maintain her
equality in human rights in all her relations in life,
and that if she consents to her own subjugation,

either in the family,
Church or State,
she is as guilty as the slave is in consenting to be a slave. [2]

BIOGRAPHY

The Reverend Antoinette Blackwell's long life of ninety-six years was filled with accomplishments of which most people could only dream. Born into a successful farming family which relocated from upstate New York to the edge of the wilderness in western New York, Antoinette was fortunate to have received an excellent education. She graduated from the district school in 1838 when she was thirteen and began work at the first secondary school in the county, Monroe County Academy.[3] By the time she was sixteen years old, she was teaching school herself. Looking for a worthy and challenging career, and being a member of a liberal Congregational church, Antoinette decided that she wanted to be a minister: "I have felt unwilling to go to most of our Seminaries, where the great object is to make mere butterflies of females. I wish to go where not only the intellect, but the moral principle will be cultivated, disciplined and trained for active service in the vineyard of the Lord."[4]

It took her several years before she finally made it, but in 1846 she entered Oberlin Collegiate Institute in Ohio. Oberlin was accepting females and even granting them bachelor's degrees in a classical course. Vassar and other women's colleges would not be founded for at least two more decades. Yet Oberlin was not the mecca of which Antoinette had dreamed: "Despite Oberlin's radical reputation and its interest in social reform, the college shared common prejudices about women's roles. Female education, according to this traditional view, should be geared toward moral and religious self-improvement, which would contribute to women's preordained roles as wives, mothers, and moral teachers."[5]

Early in her career, the faculty encouraged her to study for the ministry and complete a theological studies program, but then refused ordination and graduation in 1850 on the grounds that she was not a male.[6] In order to pacify Antoinette, they published her famous essay on I Corinthians and I Timothy while a student in 1849.

Antoinette did not abandon her dream. She began lecturing all along the East Coast. By the spring of 1853 she was called to pastor a Congregational church in South Butler, New York. Shortly after her ordination, she attempted to address the "Whole World's Temperance Convention," and was hissed off the stage. Horace Greeley summarized the response of the crowd to her in the *Tribune.*

> First Day—Crowding a woman off the platform.
> Second Day—Gagging her.
> Third Day—Voting that she shall stay gagged.[7]

She remembered that day,

> I feel calm and strong again and sit down until [their] anger has way. "Do you think," says a voice in my ear, "that Christ would have done so?" "I think he would," spoken with a positive emphasis . . . I arise, turning away from them all, and feeling a power which may perhaps never come to me again. There were many angry men confronting me and I caught the flashing of defiant eyes, but above me and within me, there was a spirit stronger than them all. At that moment not the combined powers of earth and hell could have tempted me to do other wise than stand firm.[8]

The following autumn, at the age of twenty-eight, under great protest, she was ordained at the Butler church. Yet within a year, possibly due to the loneliness and isolation of her new job and the pressures of a pastorate, she nearly collapsed. She left her job for the solace of her family and friends. After a period of recuperation, Antoinette resumed the lecture circuit and wrote articles for the *New York Tribune.* When she was thirty-one, in 1856, after much soul-searching, she married Samuel Blackwell.

Marrying Mr. Blackwell changed her literary, social, and ideological courses forever. Within the next eighteen years, she would give birth to seven children, of which two died. It was not until later in her life, 1878, when her husband had financial problems that she decided to preach once again. During her "domestic" time she also worked diligently for the American Woman Suffrage Association and the Association for the Advancement of Women, finally voting in 1920. In addition, Antoinette had the privilege in the late nineteenth century of ordaining two women, Marian Murdock and Florence Buck.[9]

Later in life, her literary achievements drifted away from biblical issues as she grappled with evolutionary theory. Some of her books include *Studies in General Science* (1869); *The Sexes throughout Nature* (1875); *The Physical Basis of Immortality* (1876); *The Philosophy of Individuality* (1893); and others.[10]

THE PROBLEM
BIBLICAL POLITICS: OLD SCHOOL, LIBERAL, NEW SCHOOL

In 1849, "old school" interpreters maintained that the Bible prohibited women from teaching or preaching in public. Some even asserted that women should not be allowed to teach in a public school. They used passages in I Corinthians and I Timothy as prooftexts in order to prove their arguments.[11] According to Antoinette, other "liberal theorists" also interpreted these passages inconsistently and illogically.[12] Some "new school interpreters of these passages" claim that while women did not speak in the church during Paul's time that "it has become . . . entirely proper, right, and even necessary" for women to preach during her life time because it is in "the best interests of society."[13] Antoinette rejected all of these political arguments:[14] "To assume, that the apostle commanded those women to abstain from public teaching, lest it should prove a stumbling block on account of the Jewish and Gentile prejudices, is entirely unwarrantable. . . . If it is wrong for them to teach in public, it is wrong for us; and if it was right for them . . . it is right for us."[15]

Brown, similar to others, engaged in what may be termed "double-speech" at the beginning of her article. She claimed that she was not addressing the problem of ordination or women preaching in the church directly. Her only and main purpose was to study the passages under consideration. (One wonders if a faculty member had a hand in some of the editing of the text?) Yet, she really did undermine the position taken by those who support the subordination of women. She argued for the right of a woman to be ordained and to pastor a church.[16]

VIEW OF SCRIPTURE: INFALLIBLE DIRECTION TO MEN

Early writers who penned the sacred writings[17] received words or commandments from God which were given for the benefit of all people throughout time.[18] "They often received truth direct from the lips of the most High, and they knew the doctrine where of they affirmed was infallible."[19] Therefore, the Bible must be logical (not contradicting) and consistent in its message.[20] She assumes that most, if not all of the words, were directed to men and women who had the experience of the Spirit.[21]

INTERPRETATIVE STRATEGY

Antoinette's goal (supposedly) was to answer the question of whether or not the Bible prohibits women from speaking in public or public school teaching. She posed the dilemma, if it is natural for women to keep silent then how does one account for "ancient prophetesses . . . called of the Lord to become teachers of Israel."[22] Circumstances may require a woman to be a public teacher if she is to follow the dictates of her God.

In a meticulous, systematic, word by word study, Brown began with interpreting the silence passages of I Corinthians 14:34–35 and I Timothy 2:11–12 separately because she contended that the contexts are different. In the past, the passage in I Timothy had been used to interpret verses about women who speak in I Corinthians, thus corroborating the silence of all women in church. She asked and then answered this question, "[W]ere they designed alone for the Corinthian women, and for those females who were under the pastoral charge of Timothy, or were they given as universal principles, binding upon all nations, in all ages?"[23]

Antoinette's research and argumentation generally followed these steps in her lengthy discussion of I Corinthians 14:34,35:

1. Suggested that the passages in I Timothy and I Corinthians must be considered separately, thereby implicitly denying that the "doctrine" being taught in both passages is the same.[24]

2. Considered the immediate context of the letter and its "real purpose" for the Corinthians.[25]
3. Identified key vocabulary which she used to build her own interpretation of the passage. Her research referred to trans-literated Greek words. When discussing the passage in I Timothy she wrote, "Look at the connection in which it is found, and since words in all languages have various significations, see what particular meaning is here required."[26]
4. Consulted a Greek lexicon and quoted classical Greek writers on the meaning of words.
5. Supported her conclusions with quotations from noted scholars.
6. Studied the vocabulary within the Pauline corpus—the larger context. "Let us now refer to a few passages, as examples of St. Paul's method of using this word [to speak] . . ."[27]
7. Added support from scholars and references passages in the Gospels which used the same terms under consideration.
8. Consulted the context of "the external circumstances" within the Corinthian church by discussing the status of Greek and Jewish females during the proposed "age."[28]
9. Consulted the immediate context of the verses.[29]
10. Drew conclusions and made applications while consulting cultural peculiarities of the time period.

THE BIBLICAL CONTEXT: I CORINTHIANS 14:34–35

". . . for it is not permitted unto them to speak."[30]

Antoinette studied the word "to speak" or *laleo* within several contexts. What does it really mean? Obviously, women did speak as prophetesses in Israel and within the early church.[31] After consulting a *Liddell and Scott's Lexicon* and other writings, she concluded that the exact meaning of the word depends upon the context in which it is used. In general, it refers mainly to plain speech.[32] Paul used the word in several cases, suggesting that it can mean "to be loquacious, prattle, talk unwisely, inconsiderately."[33] After further study she drew this conclusion: "Again, if the connection plainly shows that the word here means simply to speak, to use the voice, without any reference to the word: spoken, then all the vocal exercises of the church must be unlawful to females, and a manifest violation of this precept."[34]

CULTURAL CONTEXT

Before continuing her quest of understanding the true meaning of the word "to speak," Antoinette digressed into hypothesizing about females in the first century. Women were "the more ignorant and degraded class."[35] Jewish women were not allowed to study the Torah and knew nothing of their faith. Gentile women were in "abject degradation to which heathenism has always subjected its female victims."[36] When they were "quickened" by the Spirit and became Christians, they would often become very zealous and sometimes tended toward "disorderly conduct."[37] This was a common problem.

IMMEDIATE CONTEXT OF THE CHAPTER

In interpreting I Corinthians 14, she noted that it is a chapter about spiritual gifts for the whole church. All of the precepts "apply equally to all mankind. . . ."—"The apostle is not talking about teaching at all."[38] He was talking about the misuse of spiritual gifts. She suggested that if you take the passage literally it means that women throughout the church could not utter a sound in public. They could not sing, pray, or teach little children.[39] This interpretation is impossible. A better interpretation would be that silence should come from those who are making speech "which was not profitable to the church."[40] "Whatever was not calculated to instruct and benefit the congregation, had no right to a place in their public assemblies, and it must be given up by all who would be the disciples of Him. . . ."[41]

APPLICATION OF INTERPRETATION

This exegesis makes the passage have nothing whatever to do with the question of public teaching. The females were not forbidden to take part in the work of instructing the church. . . . and moreover, as we have already seen, being taught by the Spirit of the mighty God, they did actually take part in these exercises.[42]

THE BIBLICAL CONTEXT: I TIMOTHY 2:11–12

Brown challenged the interpretation of this passage: "Let the woman learn in silence with all subjection. But I suffer not a woman to teach, nor usurp authority over the man, but to be in silence."[43] Antoinette's strategy was, again, to use context as a way of interpreting the passage. This particular passage does not specify whether teaching is a "public" or "private" event.[44] Brown drew the same logical conclusion with "to teach," *didaskein*, as she did earlier with "to speak." These verses, if taken to their logical conclusion, suggest that women should never teach anyone of any age at any time (370). To her this was an absurd interpretation. The "silence," *esuchia*, in these verses cannot mean total silence. It must mean "a quiet, teachable spirit."[45] Her argument and definition is based upon other verses found in 2 Thessalonians 3: 11, 12 and Acts 12:2, where the word is used to mean "tranquil." Since women cannot be required to cease teaching her own children, *didaskein* must refer to something negative. Brown suggested, "It is connected with usurping authority, and evidently includes a dictatorial, self-important, over-bearing manner of teaching, which was far from salutary in its influence."[46]

CULTURAL CONTEXT

Once again Antoinette reverted to her argument about the degraded state of women during this time period, the cultural context.

> Here we may again appeal to the united testimony of history and human nature, to substantiate the fact that the females of the primitive church were greatly faulty in this respect; and that their inordinate love of power and want of meekness, was entirely at variance with the great law of love, and was worthy of the severe rebuke which it every where receives from the inspired penman. Now because women of that, or of

any other age of the church, who had been kept in an ignorant, degraded and un-christian subjection, when placed suddenly upon the gospel platform of equality, should be led into the snare of the adversary, and attempt to teach over man, and usurp authority over him, thus deserving the reproof and exhortation of their instructors; therefore to infer that woman may not teach at all, even though she might have truths to deliver which would be for the edification of the church, is certainly illogical.[47]

APPLICATION OF INTERPRETATION

Brown's ultimate answer to the silence question was that the verses should be applied equally to all "mankind" because no one should speak while having such an attitude. In the end it is up to the individual whether or not he or she should speak. Thus, this passage should never prohibit a woman from teaching "a message worth communicating."[48]

VIEW ON WOMAN AND EQUALITY: THE CREATION ACCOUNT

In a speech made to the National Women's Rights Convention Debate in New York City in 1860, Brown tackled another sticky problem: Did the Bible ordain the subordination of women from the beginning of time? Based upon an interpretation of the creation account in Genesis, Antoinette developed a philosophy of equality of woman and man in the church, home, and society. Woman becomes the one responsible for her own subjection.

This view differs remarkably from her earlier view in the above article on I Timothy and I Corinthians, where she assumed that women were kept in a degraded state by men. Here are a few of her statements on divorce which were voiced eleven years after her first article. She began the address with thirteen resolutions. Number eleven and following read,

Resolved, That every woman is morally obligated to maintain her equality in human rights in all her relations in life, and that if she consents to her own subjugation, either in the family, Church or State, she is as guilty as the slave is in consenting to be a slave.[49]

I believe that God has so made man and woman, that it is not good for them to be alone, that they each need a co-worker.[50]

She need not absorb herself in her home, and God never intended that she should; . . . .[51]

It is a shame for our women to have no steady purpose or pursuit, and to make the mere fact of womanhood a valid plea for indolence, it is a greater shame that they should be instructed thus to throw all the responsibility of working for the general good upon the other sex. God has not intended it. But as long as you make women helpless, ineffi-cient beings, who never expect to earn a farthing in their lives, who never expect to do any thing . . . you cannot have true marriages. . . .[52]

Antoinette advocated giving woman her own independence or "self-sovereignty" so that she can take care of herself financially:[53] "So long as society is constituted in such a way that woman is expected to do nothing if she have a father, brother, or husband, able to support her, there is no salvation for her, in or out of marriage."[54]

COMMENTS AND CONCLUSION

Brown did everything she was supposed to do to be successful. She listened to her mentors at Oberlin, and even interpreted the Bible based upon systematic exegetical procedures. She didn't give up and she won. And when she had won, she discovered that the prize may not have been worth all of the effort. She won equal standing and a place to preach, but she was never accepted as one of the "group." The isolation, the rigid parishioners, and thankless attitude by a religious hierarchy proved to be more effective in keeping her away from the ministry than their hostile words and actions.

As all people have a right to do, Brown Blackwell changed her views about women and the reasons for their secondary position in society. In her earlier article, written while a student at Oberlin in 1849, she assumed that the "degraded" state of early Christian women in an-cient times was rooted in their own experience of oppression in other religious traditions and cultures. Yet in her speech made in 1860, she vacillated among the reasons given for the oppression of women. Within Christianity, women should not consent to be used as a slave. If she does consent, it is her own fault if she is treated like a slave. But Brown also recognized that society is to blame for the way it socializes women to be helpless. The ideal within a Christian marriage and home is equality.

Brown also changed her approach and relationship to Scripture, perhaps in the same way that her life moved away from Congregationalism to Unitarianism. Instead of being dominated by a book, method, or a theology, she stepped aside and created her own philosophy of women. In her earlier years, she refuted her adversaries by interpreting the Bible line by line in order to make her point about the freedoms women must have to express themselves. In her speech above, she merely alluded to the Bible and used it as a springboard to give her own opinions about what should be done and not done with regard to women in society.

Notes

MARY HAYS

1. Mary Hays, *Appeal to the Men of Great Britain in Behalf of Women*. With an Introduction by Gina Luria (London: J. Johnson, 1798. Reprinted by New York: Garland Publishing, 1974), 67, 79, 155, 158, 187, 149.
2. Anne Crawford, ed., *The Europa Biographical Dictionary of British Women* (Detroit: Gale Research Company, 1983) 194. See also Katharine M. Rogers, "The Contribution of Mary Hays," *Prose Studies* 10(2, 1987): 131–142, who compares her work with Mary Wollstonecraft's works.
3. Gina M. Luria, "Mary Hays's Letters and Manuscripts," *Signs* 3(2, 1977):525.
4. Mary Hays, *Appeal to the Men of Great Britain in Behalf of Women*, 13.
5. Ibid., 11.
6. Anne Crawford, ed., *The Europa Biographical Dictionary of British Women* (Detroit: Gale Research Company, 1983), 194.
7. Mary Hays, *Appeal to the Men of Great Britain in Behalf of Women*, 67, 91.
8. Ibid., 130.
9. Ibid., 86.
10. Ibid., 187.
11. Ibid., 135.
12. Ibid., 159.
13. Ibid., 67, 160.
14. Ibid., 160.
15. Ibid., 82, 171.
16. Ibid., 69. See also: 75, 79.

17. Ibid., 82.
18. Ibid., 177.
19. Ibid., 191.
20. Ibid., 192.
21. Ibid., 179.
22. Ibid., 191.
23. Ibid., 196.
24. Ibid., 194.
25. Ibid., 150.
26. Ibid., 159.
27. Ibid., 156.
28. Ibid., 2.
29. Ibid., 12.
30. Ibid., 13.
31. Ibid., 21, 14.
32. Ibid., 4–5, 17–19, 21.
33. Ibid., 6.
34. Ibid., 7.
35. Ibid., 17.
36. Ibid., 16.
37. Ibid., 18.
38. Ibid., 19.
39. Ibid., 22.
40. Ibid., 24.
41. Ibid., 25.
42. Ibid., 88.
43. Ibid., 127.
44. Ibid., 146.

ELIZABETH CADY STANTON

1. Judith Nies, *Seven Women. Portraits From the American Radical Tradition* (New York: Penguin Books, 1977), 86.
2. Ibid., 65.
3. Lois W. Banner, *Elizabeth Cady Stanton: A Radical for Women's Rights* (Boston: Little, Brown, and Co., 1980), 35.
4. Judith Nies, *Seven Women,* 79.
5. Judith Nies, *Seven Women,* 87. See also Amy Oden, *In Her Words. Women's Writings in the History of Christian Thought* (Nashville: Abingdon, 1994), 314–320.
6. Elizabeth Cady Stanton, *The Original Feminist Attack on the Bible.* Introduction by Barbara Welter (New York: Arno Press, 1974); see also Elizabeth Cady Stanton, *The Woman's Bible* (Seattle: Jane T. Walker, 1974.) 2 vols.
7. Carol DuBois, *Elizabeth Cady Stanton and Susan B. Anthony* (New York: Schocken Books, 1981); Lois W. Banner, *Elizabeth Cady Stanton,* 1–53, and *Notable American Women 1607–1950: A Biographical Dictionary* (Cambridge, MA: Harvard University Press, 1971): 344–346.
8. The people on the revising committee of Part I and II were: Elizabeth Cady

Stanton, Phebe A. Hanaford, Clara Bewick Colby, Rev. Augusta Chapin, Ursula N. Gestefeld, Mary Seymour Howell, Josephine K. Henry, Mrs. Robert G. Ingersoll, Sarah A. Underwood, Ellen Battelle Dietrick, Lillie Devereux Blake, Matilda Joslyn Gage, Rev. Olympia Brown, Frances Ellen Burr, Clara B. Neyman, Helen H. Gardener, Charlotte Beebe Wilbour, Lucinda B. Chandler, Catharine F. Stebbins, Louis Southworth, Baroness Alexandra Gripenberg, Ursula M. Bright, Irma von Troll-Borostyani, Priscilla Bright McLaren, and Isabelle Bogelot. Suzan E. Hill, "The Woman's Bible: Reformulating Tradition," *Radical Religion* 3(2, 1977): 23–30 writes an interesting article describing backgrounds of some of the authoresses. She also suggests that evolutionary theory, New Thought or New Religions, and the historical critical method influenced the making of the commentary.

 9. *The Woman's Bible*, 1:12.
10. Ibid.
11. Ibid., 1:13.
12. Ibid., 2:174.
13. Ibid., 2:175.
14. Ibid., 1:12.
15. Ibid., 1:65.
16. Ibid., 2:143.
17. Ibid., 2:13.
18. Ibid., 2:146.
19. Ibid., 2:154.
20. Ibid., 1:17.
21. Ibid., 1:40.
22. Ibid., 1:60.
23. Ibid., 1:61.
24. The strategies are as varied as the members on the committee. While some of the opinions contained in the *WB* are written by others, since Stanton was the editor and to make things a little easier to read, we will not refer to the multiple authors in the text. *The Woman's Bible*, 1:37 and 2:176.
25. *The Woman's Bible*, 1:43.
26. Ibid., 2:49.
27. Ibid., 2:8.
28. Ibid., 1:17
29. Ibid., 1: 56, 80, 103; 2: 16, 35, 115, 149, 182, 179, 122.
30. Julia E. Smith, *The Holy Bible containing the Old and New Testaments. Translated Literally from the Original Tongues* (Hartford, CT: American Publishing Company, 1876).
31. *The Woman's Bible*, 1:53.
32. Ibid., 1:78.
33. Ibid., 1:79.
34. Ibid., 2:26.
35. Ibid., 1:80.
36. Ibid., 1:94.
37. Ibid., 1:98.
38. Ibid., 1:118.

39. Ibid., 1:126.
40. Ibid., 2:12.
41. Ibid., 2:25.
42. 1:75.
43. Ibid., 1:83.
44. Ibid., 1:14.
45. Ibid., 1:15.
46. Ibid., 1:17.
47. Ibid., 1:18.
48. Ibid., 1:19.
49. Ibid., 1:20–21.
50. Ibid., 2:21.
51. Ibid., 2:158.
52. Ibid., 2:159.
53. Ibid., 2:162.
54. Ibid., 2:163.
55. Ibid., 2:150.
56. Ibid., 2:113.
57. Ibid., 1:108.
58. Ibid., 1:112.
59. Ibid., 1:88.
60. Ibid., 1:81; 2:102.
61. Ibid., 2:19.
62. Ibid., 2:92.
63. Ibid., 2:20.
64. Ibid., 2:92.
65. Ibid., 2:83.
66. Ibid., 2:88.
67. Ibid., 2:88.
68. Ibid., 2:106.
69. Ibid., 2:111.
70. Ibid., 2:176.
71. Ibid., 2:120.
72. Ibid.
73. Ibid., 2:22.
74. Ibid., 1:133; 135.
75. Ibid., 1:63.
76. Ibid., 1:84.
77. Ibid., 1:69.
78. Ibid.

BROWN BLACKWELL

1. Elizabeth Cazden, *Antoinette Brown Blackwell: A Biography.* (New York: The Feminist Press, 1983), 30. See also Nancy A. Hardesy, *Evangelical Feminism in the Nineteenth Century: Women Called to Witness* (Nashville: Abingdon, 1984), 45–169.
2. Antoinette Louisa Brown, "Speech of Rev. Antoinette Brown [Blackwell]," in

Karlyn Kohrs Campbell, ed., *Man Cannot Speak for Her: Key Texts of the Early Feminists* (New York: Greenwood Press, 1989), 2:204.

3. Elizabeth Cazden, *Antoinette Brown Blackwell*, 12.
4. Ibid., 16.
5. Ibid., 27.
6. Edward T. James, ed., *Notable American Women 1607–1950* (Cambridge, MA: Harvard University Press, 1971), 1:159.
7. Elizabeth Cazden, *Antoinette Brown Blackwell*, 80.
8. Ibid., 80. Luther Lee preached her ordination sermon. See Barbara J. Mac-Haffie, *Readings in Her Story: Women in Christian Tradition* (Minneapolis: Fortress Press, 1992), 139–142 for an example of Luther's preaching.
9. Edward T. James, ed., *Notable American Women 1607–1950*, 159.
10. Ibid., 160.
11. Antoinette Louisa Brown, "Exegesis of I Corinthian XIV., 34, 35 and I Timothy II, 11,12," 4(1849): *Oberlin Quarterly*, 369.
12. Antoinette Louisa Brown, "Exegesis of I Corinthian XIV," 366, 370.
13. Ibid., 360.
14. Ibid.
15. Ibid.
16. Ibid., 358.
17. Ibid., 362.
18. Ibid., 372.
19. Ibid., 363.
20. Ibid., 366.
21. Ibid., 359, 368.
22. Ibid., 358.
23. Ibid., 359.
24. Ibid., 362.
25. Ibid., 361.
26. Ibid., 370.
27. Ibid., 362.
28. Ibid., 363, 364.
29. Ibid., 365.
30. Ibid., 358.
31. Ibid., 359.
32. Ibid., 362.
33. Ibid., 363.
34. Ibid.
35. Ibid., 364.
36. Ibid.
37. Ibid.
38. Ibid., 365.
39. Ibid.
40. Ibid., 367.
41. Ibid., 368.
42. Ibid.
43. Ibid., 369.

44. Ibid.
45. Ibid., 370.
46. Ibid., 372.
47. Ibid.
48. Ibid., 373.
49. Antoinette Louisa Brown, "Speech of Rev. Antoinette Brown [Blackwell]," in Karlyn Kohrs Campbell, ed., *Man Cannot Speak for Her. Key Texts of the Early Feminists* (New York: Greenwood Press, 1989), 2:204.
50. Ibid., 2:211.
51. Ibid., 2:213.
52. Ibid., 2:213.
53. Ibid., 2:214.
54. Ibid., 2:24.

Chapter Four

THE SUPERIOR
FEMALE:
MATRIARCHAL
READINGS

INTRODUCTION

Our society is so thoroughly androcentric or patriarchal that to even suggest that females are superior is to offend almost everyone. Men don't like it because they have been taught that they are the privileged sex. Women don't like it because it detracts from the males with whom they have relationships. It is no secret that Judeo-Christian hierarchies, even after thousands of years of evolution, still peddle a male point of view on just about everything.

Surprisingly, even as early as the middle of the sixteenth century in Europe, one male recognized this problem and wrote about its affect upon females. Heinrich Cornelius Agrippa von Nettesheim, lawyer, physician, and defender of witches, wrote a treatise addressed to the Queen of the Austrians and Burgundians, defending and lauding the opposite sex as the superior sex. Central to the control of women is the use of the Bible, which he feriously refutes. Men take the Bible and make it into laws that imprison women. They ignore the narratives that prove that women have been in control, and that they are stronger and more intelligent than men. And besides all of this, the women are more beautiful, keep themselves cleaner, and have a natural protection against diseases.

Living in England during the late seventeenth century and the beginning of the eighteenth century, Mary Astell deplored the state of women. They lead empty lives because their heads are empty. Women, during her lifetime, were not admitted to educational institutions, and so were often not taught how to read and write properly. She proposed a female institution where women would study the Bible. This study of the Bible would help them to improve their relationships with their husbands and families and help them to gain freedom in society. She hints that this freedom could lead to dominance over the males.

Judith Sargent Murray, who lived during the Revolutionary War period in America, actually visited with George and Mary Washington. Raised by a wealthy family in Massachusetts, Judith was fortunate to obtain an excellent private education through studying with friends, relatives, and tutors. Women during those early years were not admitted to colleges or seminaries.

She authored many articles for the *Massachusetts Magazine*, wrote and helped to produce her own plays, as well as kept avid notes of everything she did. Her article, "On the Equality of the Sexes," published in 1790, reinterprets the Eve and Adam tragedy, infering that the Divine may be a She and that Eve was in control of Adam. While her main complaint was the need for a proper education for women, she warned her readers that the power Eve had over Adam could surface again at any moment.

Writing at the end of the nineteenth century in America, Matilda Joslyn Gage created a masterpiece entitled *Woman, Church, and State* which surveys the ways in which men have subjugated and abused women. Refuting passages of the Bible thought to dictate the submission of women, Gage pointed to other passages in the Bible where men brutalize women and children. Her answer to this dilemma is to create a matriarchate and to worship the feminine element in God. This is the only way that the violence can be subdued. Her hope is for a total cultural revolution.

Frances Willard, one of the most popular speakers in the nineteenth century, dedicated her life to the advancement of women. She is the only woman to be placed in the statuary hall in Washington, D.C. Among her many works is a book entitled *Woman in the Pulpit*, in which she criticized the male religious hierarchies for incompetencies, prejudice, and an inadequate interpretation of the Bible, which had handicapped women. Her work attacked the traditional passages of Scripture used to oppress women, then suggested that women are better and superior by citing the accomplishments of women mentioned in the New Testament.

Finally, this chapter ends with the work of Charlotte Perkins Gilman, a social philosopher and feminist, and a woman whose thoughts touch the twenty-first century. She saw the need for communal kitchens and child-raising facilities over a hundred years ago. These institutions would help to free women to accomplish other tasks in life. Her works, both fiction and prose, challenged the reader to think about living in matriarchal space. Christianity is a death-based religion, whereas a religion centered in the worship of a female would be birth-based. Condemning the Pauline attitude toward women, and the malicious interpretation of the Eve and Adam story, she like so many other writers found solace in the words of Jesus, who never oppressed women.

HEINRICUS CORNELIUS AGRIPPA VON NETTESHEIM (1486?–1535)

But the woman was the best work of God,
brought in of God into this world,
as the Queen of it into a palace prepared for her. . . .
being the end,
so the glory, and perfection.[1]

I shall freely therefore declare the glory of women,
and their accomplishments I
shall not hide; in doing which,
far be it from me that I should be ashamed
of the argument taken in hand that
I prefer women before men. . .[2]

THE SIXTEENTH CENTURY, C.E.—ITALY, FRANCE, ENGLAND

Social and political structures in Europe crumbled during the sixteenth century. Times were turbulent and people lost their lives in the pursuit of freedom of conscience and an adequate livelihood. In 1517, Luther penned his ninety-five theses and changed forever the relationship of many with the Roman Catholic Church. The Peasant's Revolt was in full swing in Germany by 1525. In 1523 in Switzerland, Zwingli broke away from Rome and the papacy punished such reform leaders (heretics) by taking their lives. Henry VIII of England waged his own crusade for personal freedom by breaking with the mother church in 1534 and creating the Church of England.[3]

Faced with a dwindling empire, the Roman Catholic Church launched a world-wide missionary effort through the newly ordained Jesuits. And while the Inquisition, i.e., a movement against those suspected of heresy against the present ruling religious powers, was inaugurated by the Roman Catholic Church in 1542, witch hunts and trials had been happening all over Europe for hundreds of years.[4]

Agrippa von Nettesheim lived during these stormy times. He was an unusual man who in spite of the political cost, chose to support the equality and importance of women. It is reported that in Cologne in 1520, when he was in his mid-thirties, he risked his life and career by denouncing the Inquisition and defending an alleged witch in public.[5]

According to Anne Lleywellyn Barstow, the witch hunts in Germany were particularly violent: "In one town, Rottenberg, for example, by 1590 at least 150 women had been executed, and worse was to come." By the end of the century as many as 26,000 to 30,000 women may have been put to death for witchcraft by the Germans.[6]

Barstow blames the deaths on changing economical, political, and social situations. "Reforming Puritanism combined with princely greed to make the average person's life more onerous."[7] "[H]apless peasants, discovering that no matter how hard they worked they ended up with less, blamed their poverty on the witchery of neighbors."[8]

After defending the woman accused of witchcraft, Agrippa was driven away by the clergy. It appears that he wandered from job to job perhaps because of his liberal positions on religion and women. He became a medical practitioner in Switzerland and in 1524 was found working as a physician in Lyon to the Queen-dowager of France. In Antwerp, he was accused of sorcery and labeled an occult philosopher because of the publication of *De Incertitude et Vanitate Scientarium* (1530) and *De Occult Philosophia* (1531–33). Some would argue that these books place him on the cutting edge of both science (alchemy), and metaphysics. Ultimately, he paid the ultimate price for his support of women and independent thinking. He was imprisoned at Lyon and died in Grenable in 1535.[9]

Agrippa accomplished much in his lifetime. He was reportedly a knight, a magistrate, and held teaching positions in England and France. A practicing physician to Charles V of Spain, he also held the Doctor of Law.[10] He wrote *The Glory of Women: or, A Treatise Declaring the Excellency and Preheminence of Women above Men which is proved both by Scripture, Law, Reason, and Authority, Divine and Humane.*[11] The book is addressed to "Margaret Augusta, Queen of the Austrians and Burgundians," about whom he wishes, "[T]hat the lustre of your Sex may shine forth in you, as in a Sun, who hath ascended to the highest degree, because you have exceeded whatsoever hath bin blazed abroad concerning the praises of the Female Sex, both in Life and manners be a present example, and a most faithful witness of the same Sex." (*The Epistle Dedicatory*)[12]

VIEW OF SCRIPTURE

Agrippa claimed a divine origin for his words and interpretations concerning women. He said it was "decreed to me from above, which hither to the multitude of learned men seem utterly to have neglected."[13] Having the ultimate respect for the Bible, he described it as "holy Writ,"[14] "holy Scriptures,"[15] "holy Bible"[16] and quotes passages from the Hebrew Bible, Apocrypha, and the New Testament. All of the works in the canon were equally important, citing also from Judith,[17] and the Maccabees.[18] Yet proofs for the excellency of woman were also drawn from Kabbalistic literatures, ancient writers such as Augustine,[19] Pliny,[20] classical poets[21] and playwrights,[22] Aristotle,[23] Averros,[24] Origen,[25] Bernard,[26] and Eusebius,[27] to name only a few.

In his arguments it appears that he gave equal weight to all of these resources. He would quote the Bible using a verse that says "God said" and then also quote a poet, historian, or a character in the Bible to prove his point. He mustered all the evidence in his reading to prove that women were indeed the superior creature.

THE PROBLEM

Agrippa admitted that males dominate society. While he never used the word "patriarchal," he described how women were tyrannized by males.[28] He criticized their power and proceeded to condemn them for their violence. He charged, "the rising of all evils is of man, none of the woman."[29] "We read of some men worst than the worst of women." He cited Judas and the Antichrist.

THE EVIL NATURE OF MALES

Men have a brutish nature. They were the first enviers in the Bible, the first manslayers, and the first to have two wives. Lamech was a drunkard and Ham saw the nakedness of his father. Nimrod was a tyrant and idolater. Men committed adultery, incest, made covenants with the devil, and engaged in the profane arts.[30] Cane, Esau, Uzzah, and Saul were failures.[31] Men betrayed, sold, bought, accused, condemned, crucified, and killed Christ.[32] Agrippa challenged his audience to prove that the "wickedness of man is better than a woman's well doing."[33]

THE CONTROL OF WOMEN IN SOCIETY AND THE CHURCH

Men controlled women's existence from birth until the grave. They were responsible for the repressed state of women in society.

> But you will say, that liberty and priviledge which was given to Women, is restrained by the Lawes of men (whose tyranny usurpes against God and Natures Lawes) abolished by use and custome, and extinguished by the manner of their education; for a woman by and by as soon as she is borne, and from the first beginning of her years is detained in sloth at home, and as uncapable of another Province, she is permitted to think of nothing besides her Needle or the like; when afterwards she reacheth to ripeness of age, she is delivered up to the jealous rule of her husband, or else shut up in the perpretual Bridewell of Nuns; also

publicke Offices are forbidden them by Lawes, it is not permitted that any one plead in judgement, be she never so wife.[34]

Men limited women's educations, by forbidding them to "learn letters."[35] Treated as pawns in war, men humor themselves by enforcing their privileged place over women.[36] The religious may be even more guilty than others because they use the Bible to subjugate women: "There are moreover which assume Authority to themselves over Women by vertue of Religion, and doe prove their Tyranny out of holy Writ; who have that curse of Eve continually in their mouths; under the power of man thous shalt be, and hee shall rule over thee."[37]

They also taught women that it is against the laws of God to preach in the churches.

Also it is not lawfull for them to preach the word of God; which is against expresse Scripture, in which the holy spirit promiseth to women by the Prophet Joel saying, And your daughters shall prophesy; . . . So great is the wickednesse of all late Law-makers, that they have made voide the commandments of God by their owne traditions; because, Women, otherwise by the preerogative of Nature, and excellency in dignity most noble, they pronounce more vile by condition, and inferiour to all men. By their Lawes, women are compelled to give place to men. . . .[38]

Agrippa deplored their state within the church and argued that there was plenty of evidence to suggest that women had excelled within his own religion, Roman Catholicism: "In our Religion, although the office of Priest-hood be forbidden women, we known notwithstanding, that Histories declare, that women sometimes concealing their Sex have ascended to the top of the High Priest's office."[39]

INTERPRETATIVE STRATEGY

Agrippa explained the strategy taken in his treatise both at the beginning and the end of the work. In the dedication, he claimed that his work was not created with the intentional flattery or rhetoric or praise. He used "Reason, Authority, Examples, and by the testimony of the Holy Writ, and of both Lawes:"[40] "I have shewed the excellency of the Female Sexe by many Arguments, (viz.) by Name, by Order, by Place, by Matter: And what dignity the Woman hath acquired (above the Man) from God. Afterwards we have demonstrated by Religion, Reason, Nature, Humane Lawes, by various Authority, Reasons, and Examples."[41]

Agrippa's approach to interpreting the Scriptures employed no single method. When necessary he substantiated his arguments by appealing to Greek mythological characters, philosophy, fantasy, legends, or successful females in ancient history. He also cited noted philosophers or historians. His interpretation began with the literal or straightforward approach and then branched into analogy, allegory, or a symbolic interpretation if it fit the passage. Often he took a text from the Hebrew Bible and matched it with a text from the New Testament to prove his point. He reinterpreted words such as "Eve" claiming that he was doing an etymological study which may have been aligned closer to numerology.

FEMALES ARE EQUAL

Agrippa argued for equality based upon the first chapter in Genesis. Men and women both have souls which makes them equal. They are different only because their bodies have differing parts.

> God the Creator of all things, in whom the plenitude of both Sexes hath made Man like himselfe: Male and Female Created he them: It is manifest that the difference of the Sexes consists only in the different Situation of the parts of the Body, which the office of generation did necessarily require. But certain it is, he gave one and the same indifferent soule to Male and Female, in which undoubtedly there is no distinction of Sex:. . . . Therefore there is no preheminence of Nobility (between man and woman, by the offence of the Soule) of one about the other, but an equal inbred dignity to both.[42]

FEMALES ARE SUPERIOR—ETYMOLOGY OF NAME: EVE

In an odd etymological study of the translation of words, Agrippa concluded that the name "Adam" means "earth" and "Eve" means "life." In God's great wisdom He gave names which "expresse the Nature, Property and Use of things."[43] Von Nettesheim suggested that "the name of woman hath more affinity with that unspeakable four-letter'd name of the divine omnipotency, than the name of man, which agreeth with the divine name, neither in characters, neither in figure, neither in number."[44]

In the Genesis creation story, the female was created last and therefore is the highest creation of God. Woman was formed in paradise by God alone and made of a purified substance; man was made in an ordinary field out of mud. Man is even missing a rib. Woman is the artifice of God and capable of divine splendor. To Agrippa, God shines through her—man is only vile clay.

In refuting the curse of Eve, Agrippa argued that it was Adam who caused the first sin. The command not to eat was given to Adam, not to Eve. He says, "The man was forbid to eate of the fruite of the tree, the woman not so." She was ignorant and manipulated by the devil. "We have drawn original sin, not from the Mother the female, but from the Father, the Male." And he proved quite aptly that males are the founders and creators of sin. That is why males are circumcised and females are not. The circumcision is a sign of sinfulness. Christ came as a man because males were more humbler creatures than females.[45]

FEMALES ARE MORE BEAUTIFUL, STRONGER, AND INTELLIGENT

The remainder of the book argued for the superiority of woman. Women were more beautiful because they were the glory of God. Examples of beauty can be found in Sarah, the daughters of men, Abigal, Vashti, Abishag, Susanna, and the Virgin Mary.[46] Women are more modest, more compassionate, and their body heat could revive an old man like David. He quoted from Proverbs on finding a good woman and concluded that she was the consummation and glory of man.

Agrippa rehearsed stories of heroines who were stronger and more intelligent than their male companions. He recognized the age-old mythological stories about the wiles of a woman, but rather than condemn a woman, he saluted their efforts in defeating our outwitting the males. A woman humbled Samson, and provoked Lot to

incest. A woman deceived Solomon and the woman of Canaan provided keen insight for Jesus.[47] Rachel deluded her father about the
household idols. Rebecca and Rahab both used deception to win
their cause. Women excel in conjugal love and chastity and protected
their virtue in spite of death threats: "Doe not you think, if it might be
Lawful for women to make Lawes, write Histories, but they could
write tragedies concerning the unmeasurable malice of men."[48]

Men may have run the religious institutions of the day, but the holy
and honest people were the women: "Let us search the holy scriptures, and we shall see the constancey of women in faith and holy
duties far above men."[49] Look at Judith, Ruth, Esther, Sarah, Rebecca, Elizabeth, Anna, Philip's four daughters, the woman of Samaria, and the woman with the issue. Martha's confession was equal
to Peter's. Priscilla, Anna, and the four daughters of Philip were
prophetesses.[50] Priscilla even instructed Apollos "an Apostolicall
man, most learned in the Law, the Bishop of the Corinthians."[51] He
concludes "neither was it an unseemly thing for an Apostle to learne
of a woman, which could teach in a church." There was nothing
throughout history that had been done by men "which may not as
excellently be done by women."[52]

CONCLUSION

Agrippa idealized woman. He placed her on that effervescent pedes-
tal. His arguments to prove her superiority stretched the meaning
and logical limits of some of the passages, yet he gave ample reasons
and evidence for women to be treated as equals. He hoped that those
in power would learn to appreciate the treasures within women as he
did, and to recognize their tyranny over such beautiful jewels.

MARY ASTELL
(1666–1731)

For since GOD has given Women as well as Men
intelligent Souls,
why should they be forbidden to improve them? [1]

... [S]uch an Institution as this would be the most
probable method to amend the
present, and improve the future age. [2]

BIOGRAPHY

Mary Astell was born into a polite family that maintained "traditions of loyalty to the church and to the King"[3] during the end of the seventeenth and the beginning of the eighteenth century. Her father was a clerk for George Dawson in Newcastle, and there are records suggesting that other close family members may have been a lawyer and a vicar.[4] Mary lived among the educated and wealthy class in London and Chelsea all of her life, although she possessed little financial support of her own.

After the death of her mother, she maintained a modest residence and later lived with female friends until her death. Apparently, even her house on Swan Walk was a gift from a Mr. Blount.[5] She never married and proclaimed in *A Serious Proposal to the Ladies* that she was a "Lover of her Sex," although some suggest that she was celibate.[6]

Her academic career is unknown. Claiming ignorance of the "Sacred Languages," she possessed a smattering of ability in French and knew enough about ancient philosophers and historians to mention their names.[7] Among her most noted books are *Letters Concerning the Love of God, Some Reflections upon Marriage,* and *The Christian Religion as Profess'd by a Daughter of the Church of England.* An *Essay in Defense of the Female Sex* is attributed to her but recent scholarship disputes her authorship.[8]

It appears that her "progressive" attitudes, sometimes labeled "proto-feminist" were met with derision within her society.[9] Much of her spare time was spent in writing political and social pamphlets refuting and attacking claims against her educational proposals and philosophical views.

THE PROBLEM

According to Astell, females and males lived empty, diseased lives pursuing frivolity.[10] She deplored the pomp and the flattery at court. Mary observed, "When she sees the vain and the gay, making Parade in the World and attended with the Courtship and admiration of the gazing herd, no wonder that her tender Eyes are dazzled with the Pageantry, and wanting Judgment to pass a due Estimate on them and their Admirers, longs to be such a fine and celebrated thing as they?"[11]

This meaningless existence led to personal and financial problems within marriage as well as infidelity. It may even have led to financial ruin as the woman followed the herd. Some women followed the dictates only of their bodily desires because they had not cultivated their minds or good judgment.[12]

Women seemed to have nothing on their minds. To Astell, that was because women did not have the opportunities to study. They were told what to think and believe by the men. Mary suggested that they would be better women if they could be educated in ways similar to men. They would be able to choose better mates and keep themselves from temptations. She also criticized men for their display of vain knowledge, which seemed worthless.

The knowledge she proposed to attain or impart was from the Bible and therefore on sturdy, eternal ground. Women had not been allowed to study it and it was time that they took care of their souls. If they took care of themselves they would be better caretakers of their families.

VIEW OF SCRIPTURE

Astell read her Bible and saw the influence of Christianity or religion upon the lives of women. They were religious but they did not know why they were religious. They believed but they did not know exactly what and why they believed. The Bible was the foundation of knowledge—it must be studied in order to build a strong rational foundation for one's faith. But, for Astell, it was not the ultimate source of revelation. Personal and independent reason must be used when studying the Scriptures. Only then will the truth be uncovered.

> [H]ow we shall come to the knowledge of it? the Answer is ready, that the Eternal Word and Wisdom of GOD declares his Father's Will unto us, by *Reason* which is that Natural and Ordinary Revelation by which he speaks to every one; and by that which is call'd Revelation in a stricter Sense, which is nothing else but a more perfect and infallible way of Reasoning, wherefore we are Clearly and Fully instructed in so much of God's will as is fit for us to know. We must therefore Improve our Reason as much as our Circumstances in the World permit, and to supply its deficiency Seriously, Devoutly and Diligently study the Holy Scriptures. . . .[13]

INTERPRETATIVE STRATEGY

While the Bible was foundational to Mary, she did not quote it. She indirectly referred to its myths and laws which everyone would have known and which would have influenced her own life. She addressed the issue of teaching in the church but did not refer to I Timothy or to the submission texts in Ephesians or Colossians.[14] She knew of characters in the Bible such as Priscilla but did not refer to the book in which they were found, Acts of the Apostles.[15] Paul aspired to perfection "who was Crucified to the World and the World to Him."[16]

Mary believed that the study of Scripture would bring about equality in society although she did not argue for the right of women to enter politics or to preach or to administer the Church of England. She accepted the cultural prohibition that women should not speak in church: "We pretend not that Women shou'd teach in the Church, or usurp Authority where it is now allow'd them; permit us only to understand our own duty, and not be forc'd to take it upon trust from others. . . ."[17]

Her argument, on the surface, upheld the submission of women yet throughout her works she argued for the equality of men and women. Woman was also made in the image of God and "she is God's Workmanship, endow'd by him with many excellent Qualities and only God. . . ."[18] Presently, she believed her inferior status stemmed from her lack of a formal education.

This lack of education placed women in a vulnerable position. Men used them. In the following attack she belittled men who used women for sexual purposes.

> As for those who think so Contemptibly of such a considerable part of GOD'S Creation, as to suppose that we were made for nothing else but to Admire and do them Service, and to make provision for the low concerns of an Animal Life, we pity their mistake, and can calmly bear their Scoffs, for they do not express so much Contempt of us as they of our Maker; and therefore the reproach of such incompetent Judges is not an Injury but an Honor to us.[19]

For her, this prejudice and contempt for women was really an action against God. Mary would not have numbered herself among the dissenters, such as the Ranters who talked of revolution. Yet in her own sophisticated way Mary advocated a revolutionary approach to solving inequality.[20]

EDUCATIONAL RETREAT: FOR WOMEN ONLY

Mary advocated a school for women modeled on the style of a convent but without the vows associated with celibate communities. She envisioned this retreat as an image of heaven where women would magnify God, love each other, and communicate with useful knowledge: "Happy Retreat! which will be the introducing you into such a Paradise as your Mother *Eve* forfeited. . . ."[21]

Women must understand why they believe. Belief without knowledge was faulty. This knowledge would prevent them from falling into sin and living silly, decadent, unproductive lives. Women would learn how to manage their families, educate their children, and have intelligent conversations with their neighbors.[22]

> Now as to the Proposal, it is to erect a *Monastery*, or if you will . . . we will call it a *Religious Retirement*, and such as shall have a double aspect, being not only a Retreat from the World for those who desire that advantage, but likewise, an Institution and previous discipline, to fit us to do the greatest good in it; such an Institution as this . . . would be

the most probable method to amend the present, and improve the future Age.[23]

In this monastery women would live together temporarily and study the Bible, but not the Bible only. The Bible was a complicated book and before anyone could understand its pages she must study numerous other books: ". . . [A] Christian needs understand no other Book to know the duty of his Faith and Life, tho indeed to understand it well, 'tis ordinarily requisite that a pretty number of other Books be understood."[24]

She supported her proposal by appealing to the stories of strong, intelligent, and educated women such as Priscilla. And remember that it is the mothers who teach the sons. The more education a mother has, the more education she can impart to her sons.[25]

> But they "must excuse me, if I be as partial to my own Sex as they are to theirs, and think Women as capable of Learning as Men are, and that it becomes them as well. For I cannot imagine wherein the hurt lies, if instead of doing mischief to one another, by an uncharitable and vain Conversation, Women be enabled to inform and instruct those of their own Sex at least; the Holy Ghost having left it on record, that Priscilla as well as her Husband, catechiz'd the eloquent Apollos and the great Apostle found no fault with her.[26]

Astell's goal was to educate women so that they could be in control of their own lives. She predicted problems arising when an educated woman lived with a man who was less educated: "The only danger is that the Wife be more knowing than the Husband; but if she be 'tis his own fault, since he wants no opportunities of improvement; unless he be a natural *Block-head*, and then such an one will need a wise Woman to govern him; whose prudence will conceal it from publick Observation, and at once both cover and supply his defects."[27]

For centuries, the Bible was used to subjugate women and Mary claimed that it would enlighten and free them from the bonds of a society that they did not understand. Appealing to Scriptures as the ground for the educational enlightenment and intellectual strength of women was an innovative idea in her age.

Mary sought individual freedom for self-improvement. Underlying her appeal to the men was a criticism of their educational foundation. She hinted that if women had only a fraction of the education of the men they would be better communicators.

The Men therefore may still enjoy their Prerogatives for us, we mean not to intrench on any of their Lawful Privileges, our only Contention shall be that they may not out-do us in promoting his Glory who is Lord both of them and us; And by all that appears the generality will not oppose us in this matter, we shall not provoke them by striving to be better Christians. They may busy their Heads with Affairs of State, and spend their Time and Strength in recommending themselves to an uncertain Master, or a more giddy Multitude, our only endeavour shall be to be absolute Monarchs in our own Bosoms. They shall still if they please dispute about Religion, let 'em only give us leave to Understand and Practise it. And whilst they have unrival'd the Glory of speaking as *many* Languages as *Babel* afforded, we only desire to express ourselves Pertinently and Judiciously in One.[28]

SUMMARY AND OBSERVATIONS

How could a woman who hated men, hated their power over women, and hated their access to education, actually propose a monastery that would teach women to be in complete submission to men? If we read Mary's words literally we may draw the conclusion that her main concern was founded upon her sympathies with society as a whole and not with the women in particular.

J. K. Kinnaird suggests that Mary spoke against the "tyranny of ignorance" and cared little for the social advancement of women:[29] "In a *Serious Proposal* she makes no plea that the universities should admit women as well as men; she never argues that women have as much right as men to enter the professions and take part in the public life of the nation."[30] And again, "She preached not women's rights but women's duties, not personal fulfillment or self-expression but corporate responsibility, not a secular but a religious way of life."[31]

Ruth Perry characterizes education for women in England in the seventeenth and eighteen centuries this way: "The universities were open to the male offspring of brewsters and haberdashers, but closed to the daughters of the oldest and noble families in England."[32] "England had never had a tradition for women's scholarship, as on the Continent, and there had never been learned orders for women in England."[33]

Throughout history, women have had to create strategies of deceit

and manipulation in order to survive. Astell's works could be read as a tongue-in-cheek rhetoric. Her real message was education, liberating education.

A confrontation against a monolithic force could mean self-annihiliation. To directly argue for women's rights may have gone unnoticed, or worse, she could have been considered an enemy of the state. To have suggested a women's academy may have been a brilliant idea. In an age when many were criticizing the lack of female education, her theories contained the ammunition needed to defeat and conquer the enemy.

Mary did not call for mere equality, she called for a hopeful superiority. Women were to create their own institution, free from the powers of men. The academy was designed so as not to offend or threaten men. It would not be celibate. It would not be a place where women would be totally away from the responsibilities of family and especially husband. It would be a retreat.

Mary made a special note of explaining that the education offered would not be at the level of the males. Nor would the women have competed intellectually with them: "We will not vie with them in thumbing over Authors, nor pretend to be walking Libraries, provided they'll but allow us a competent Knowledge of the Books of God."[34]

She even argued that the results of the school on the lives of the women would make the lives of the men better. They would have better wives and mothers because of it. Society would be better for their education and the men's lives would be richer.[35]

Civil wars could be fought for equality, but after the dust settles would society change? In order to change a culture there must be a system that will survive one regime after another, one generation after another. What better place to begin change than in a school? If women did indeed become educated they could eventually supersede and bypass the "blockheads" (Mary's word) in control of society and the church. And when they did, they would take over the leadership and change the world. After all, if the women gain control over themselves, haven't they gained control over their masters?

JUDITH SARGENT MURRAY
(1751–1820)

. . . [A]fter we have from early youth been adorned with ribbons, and
other gewgaws, dressed out like the ancient victims previous to a sacrifice,
being taught by the care of our parents in collecting the most showy materials
that the ornamenting our exteriour ought to be the principal object of our attention;
after, I say, fifteen years thus spent,
we are introduced into the world,
amid the united adulation of every beholder . . .
It is expected that with the other sex
we should commence
immediate war. . . .[1]

BIOGRAPHY

Judith Sargent Murray's life was intertwined with the birth of the
United States. Born to wealthy shipowners Winthrop Sargent and
Judith Saunders in 1751, Judith spent most of her life on the seacoast
of Massachusetts, although she traveled as far as the Midwest with her
second husband, the founder of Universalism in the United States,
John Murray.[2] She witnessed the French-Indian War in 1782 and the
American Revolution and became friends with such important peo-
ple as Martha and George Washington.[3]

Being born into a wealthy family did not gain her access to formal
education in the early days of New England. Her brother Winthrop
Sargent, Jr., who in 1787 became Secretary of the Northwest Territory
and the first governor of the Mississippi Territory in 1798,[4] tutored
her in Greek, Latin, and math during his breaks from Harvard
College. Her earlier years were spent under the studied hand of the
Reverend John Rodgers, a minister at the Fourth Parish Church.[5]

In 1769, at eighteen, she married a trader and captain, John Stevens, who reportedly led a glamorous life and also built the finest
(most extravagant?) house in Gloucester for her.[6] During her marriage to Stevens, Judith began to write for local periodicals under the

pseudonymn of "Constantia." By 1779, she was very interested in equal education for females, having published "Desultory Thoughts upon the Utility of Encouraging a Degree of Self Complacency Especially in Female Bosoms."[7]

In 1786, her husband found himself in economic disparity and Judith had to rely upon her own family to save creditors from taking their home. Stories are told of a gallant Mr. Stevens who took a ship to the West Indies in order to avoid financial ruin. He never returned to Gloucester.[8] She eventually remarried a minister, the Reverend John Murray, whom her family supported and who had also been a house guest.

During Judith's second marriage to Murray, she discovered *The Vindication of the Rights of Woman* (1792) by Mary Wollenstonecraft. Judith had already produced her own views on equality published in 1790 in the *Massachusetts Magazine* and continued to write vociferously about everything that happened to her. While traveling with her minister-husband, she wrote vivid letters home about a Moravian Settlement and Grays' Gardens which were later printed in the *Massachusetts Magazine.*[9]

Later she authored several articles by the "Gleaner" under the title of "Repository" which became very popular. She also wrote poetry and plays, some of which were published in the *Boston Weekly Magazine,* and were performed at the Federal Street Theatre in Boston.[10] After Murray's death, she remembered him by publishing a biography of his life.

While Judith wrote constantly, most of her writings were never published. For years they lay in a stored trunk in Natchez where she had gone to live with her only daughter. Vena Field, who has written the definitive biography on Judith, mourns the loss of Judith's works:

> During all her life, Judith's most frequently expressed ambition was to be remembered by posterity. For this she labored long and earnestly, in the face of many difficulties and rebuffs. Yet she lies forgotten, far away from the scene of her literary efforts, in a lonely grave by the Mississippi. Not only is her line extinct, but the valuable manuscripts, diaries, and letters of Mrs. Murray and her husband, which had been stored in an old house on the plantation at Natchez, decayed and became illegible.[11]

PROBLEM: LACK OF EDUCATIONAL OPPORTUNITIES

Judith began her case in the historic article, "On the Equality of the Sexes" (1790),[12] by drawing attention to the present-perceived inequities between males and females. The sexes were considered to be unequal intellectually and physically. Men were believed to be superior. Yet women were born with the same faculties as men.[13] In all four areas of intellectual ability—"imagination, reason, memory, and judgment"—women could be superior if they were given the same educational advantages as men.[14]

> May we not trace its source in the difference of education, and continued advantages? Will it be said that the judgment of a male of two years old, is more sage than that of a female's of the same age? I believe the reverse is generally observed to be true. But from that period what partiality! How is the exalted and the other depressed, by the contrary modes of education which are adopted! The one is taught to aspire, and the other is early confined and limited.[15]

Speaking from an obviously privileged economic position, Judith lamented the little education given to women. It made their lives empty and full of trifles.[16] Their minds were empty and so they must fill them with "amusements" or "sexual employments."[17] Even if they found men with whom to share their lives, they soon began to detest them because they discovered that they were not their equals. They discovered that they did not have the intellectual ability to accompany their husbands in society or business.[18]

The intellectual lives of women were so pitiful that Judith wondered why males would even think them worthy of an eternal home. What would they think about for eternity?

> I would calmly ask, is it reasonable, that a candidate for immortality, for the joys of heaven, an intelligent being, who is to spend an eternity in contemplating the works of Deity, should at present be so degraded, as to be allowed no other ideas, than those which are suggested by the mechanism of a pudding, or the sewing of the seams of a garment? Pity that all such censurers of female improvement do not go one step further, and deny their future existence; to be consistent they surely ought.[19]

VIEW OF SCRIPTURE

Judith was not an ardent student of Scripture, the sacred oracles, although she knew that it had been used to argue against the equality of females.[20] Her own position was that the stories in the Bible were metaphorical: ". . . [A]nd thus regarding them, I could not persuade myself that there was any propriety in bringing them to decide in this very important debate."[21] Yet she decided to take on the biblical arguments because they were so pervasive, warning that she would be using all the "artillery" she could muster to disprove them.[22]

INTERPRETATIVE STRATEGY

Judith's line of reasoning was subtle and sometimes malicious. At the beginning of her treatise she suggested that nature is a "She" who had created all humans.[23] Murray ended her essay by claiming the superiority of women and inferring that God was indeed a female and had been in control of creation from the beginning. The best evidence of this was Eve. Most of her arguments do not quote the Bible verse by verse, but allude to passages within it. Her most obvious allusion is to the Adam and Eve story in Genesis.

ADAM AND EVE

Taking a literal point of view, she used the wording of the texts to exalt the abilities of females while damaging the ego of Adam, and thus all men. In arguing about who was most responsible for sin entering the world, Sargent Murray pointed her finger at the weaker cog, Adam. Eve was deceived by a shining angel or a seraph, not by a serpent. Judith's redefinition is supposedly based upon retranslating the Hebrew:

> Strange how blind self love renders you men; were you not wholly absorbed in a partial admiration of your own abilities, you would long

since have acknowledged the force of what I am now going to urge. It is true some ignoramuses have, absurdly enough informed us, that the beauteous fair of paradise, was seduced from her obedience, by a malignant demon, in the guise of a baleful serpent; but we, who are better informed, know the word to be rendered. Let us examine her motive—Hark! the Seraph declares that she shall attain perfection of knowledge; for is there aught which is not comprehended under one or other of the terms good and evil.[24]

Adam was the one who received the command from God not to eat of the fruit of the garden. Yes, woman made a mistake: "It doth not appear that she was governed by any one sensual appetite; but merely by a desire of adorning her mind; a laudable ambition fired her soul, and a thirst for knowledge impelled the predilection so fatal in its consequences."[25]

Adam's reason for making his fatal error rest solely on his own sensualities and sensibilities: "Blush, ye vaunters of fortitude; ye boasters of resolution; ye haughty lords of creation; blush when ye remember, that he was influenced by no other motive than a bare pusillanimous attachment to a woman!"[26]

It was a woman who had "done him in." Yes, the mother of sin made the mistake but "the father of mankind forfeited his own . . . merely in compliance with the blandishments of a female."[27]

SUMMARY: THE SOLUTION AND THE WARNING

Allowing women to study astronomy, geography, and philosophy would improve their minds and bring them closer to God.[28] They would have little time for "slander and detraction" and they might even have put their thoughts down on paper.[29] Education would not render women too knowledgeable for "domestic" duties. Once they had learned the basics they would take the information with them as they sewed or managed a household.[30]

Central to this thesis of education is the notion that females are indeed superior because they are so aligned with Nature, who controls everything. Yet Judith did not call for a revolution to subjugate or overthrow the men; she merely asked for equality in education and a respect that is well deserved. Her parting remarks about Adam's downfall at the hands of a woman may have been a subtle tongue-in-cheek warning to the men who would continue to seek to keep women in an inferior position.[31] A male was once dominated by the mental strength of a woman; it could happen again!

MATILDA JOSLYN GAGE
(1826–1898)

Let woman first prove that she has a soul,
both the Bible and the Church deny it.[1]
—An opposing speaker at Woman's Suffrage Convention of 1854

The most important struggle in the history of the church
is that of woman for liberty of thought and the right to
give that thought to the world.[2]

Woman's increasing freedom within the last hundred years
is not due to the church, but to the printing press, to
education, to free thought and other forms of advancing
civilization.[3]

BIOGRAPHY

Matilda's life pulsated with words that challenged the existence of cherished institutions and social codes. Throughout her many careers she demanded equality, fairness for all humans, and the vote for women. She used her studied and often brilliant pen to author and coauthor three volumes, including *The History of Woman Suffrage* (1889) and *Woman, Church, and State* (1900), and several pamphlets such as *Woman as Inventor* (1870) and *Who Planned the Tennessee Campaign of 1862?* (1880). She used her editorial skill in publishing and editing newspapers, such as the *National Citizen* and the *Ballot Box*, in order to raise equity issues. Early in her career she also wrote for the *Revolution*. She used her organizational skills in founding the Woman's National Liberal Union which denounced the church and clergy as tyrants.[4]

Born an only child into a wealthy and progressive physician's family in Cicero, New York, Matilda was educated in physiology, math, and Greek. Her father, Hezekiah, and mother, Helen, opened their home to reformers and advocates of equity in human rights. "She was always encouraged to think for herself."[5] By the time she was fifteen, she was enrolled at the Clinton Liberal Institute in New York. At the completion of her studies, she married Henry H. Gage, eight years her senior in 1845. They produced five children and enjoyed a thriving business in dry goods.

Throughout most of her life Matilda had physical problems that incapacitated her and therefore prohibited her from extensive travel. Yet she continually involved herself in political and social causes to advance the liberty of women. In a time when many women took on a "manly look," she chose to remain feminine in voice and dress.

Her first experience in public life found her "trembling in every limb." She addressed the National Woman's Rights Convention in 1852 on the topics of equality in law and education: "Unfortunately, she spoke so softly that few could follow her remarks; . . . she never developed an outstanding platform personality, being known rather for her writing and organizing talents."[6] By 1875, she had become the head of "both the National and the New York State suffrage associations."[7]

Matilda's closest associates included Elizabeth Cady Stanton and Susan B. Anthony, who worked with her in National Suffrage associations. Together they challenged the people of the United States and the world to recognize that women too were human beings and deserved equal treatment and rights under the law.

Later in life, Gage studied the writings of Madam Blavatsky (Theosophy), but still maintained her membership in the Fayetteville Baptist Church. She died of "an embolism in the Brain" while residing with her daughter in Chicago in 1898.[8]

THE PROBLEM

In Matilda Joslyn Gage's book, *Woman, Church, and State: A Historical Account of the Status of Woman through the Christian Ages: With Reminiscences of the Matriarchate*,[9] she produced a litany of well-researched and documented historical anecdotes and political situations where women were used and abused. She linked their oppression to religious institutions and especially to the misinterpretation of the Bible used by the clergy within Christianity. But in spite of these male-dominated cultures, there were times in history in various parts of the world when the "Matriarchate" ruled. The Mother-rule was based upon peace and justice.[10] Here is one example of the Matriarchate.

One of the most brillant modern examples of the Matriarchate was found in Malabar at the time of its discovery by the Portuguese in the XV century. The Nairs were found to possess a fine civilization, entirely under the control of women, at a period when woman's position in England and on the Continent of Europe, was that of a household and political slave. Of Malabar it has been said, that when the Portuguese became acquainted with the country and the people, they were not so much surprised by the opulence of their cities, the splendor of all their habits of living, the great perfection of their navy, the high state of the arts, as they were to find all this under the entire control and government of women. The difference in civilization between christian Europe and pagan Malabar at the time of its discovery was indeed great. While Europe with is new art of printing, was struggling against the church for permission to use type, its institutions of learning few, its opportunities for education meager; its terrible inquisition crushing free thought and sending thousands each year to a most painful death, the uncleanliness of its cities and the country such as to bring frequent visits of the plague; its armies and its navies with but one exception, imperfect; its women forbidden the right of inheritance, religious, political, or household authority—the feminine principle entriely eliminated from the divinity—a purely masculine God the universal object of worship, all was directly the opposite in Malabar.[11]

While walking through history, Gage attacked the male religious establishments, especially the clergy within Christianity (which she often spells with a lower case "c"). In the late twentieth century, "patriarchy" is a familiar word; Gage, used the term "patriarchate" to characterize the same male dominance, and for her it was corrupt. It had influenced the structures of society and the laws within governments in order to suppress women. It claimed divine right to control women using the Bible as its weapon. Over the years it had prohibited woman from taking the eucharist, entering certain buildings, studying the Bible, and speaking in a public place. Women had been pronounced to be less than human—they were told that they did not even possess a soul. Therefore, women could never be elevated to the level of the man. Women were only vessels of service. For Gage, these prohibitions and theories had become "an organized robbery of the rights of women."[12]

Throughout one lengthy chapter in her book, she quoted numerous sermons by males who were determined to keep females in their place. Here is a short example:

> Reverend Dr. Craven spoke these words to the General Presbyterian Assembly of the United States in 1876, "I believe the subject involves the honor of my God. I believe the subject involves the headship and crown of Jesus. Woman was made for man and became first in the transgression. My argument is that subordination is natural, the subordination of sex. . . . [T]here exists a created subordination; a divinely arranged and appointed subordination of woman as woman to man as man. . . . It is not allowed woman to speak in the church. Man's place is on the platform. It is positively base for a woman to speak in the pulpit; it is base in the sight of Jehovah."[13]

Here is an example of a statue passed by church members of the Hopkinson Association of Congregational Divines of New Hampshire in 1843:

> But, as to leading men, either in instruction or devotion, and as to any interruption or disorder in religious meetings, "Let your women keep silence in the churches"; not merely let them be silent, but let them keep or preserve silence. Not that they may not keep or preserve silence. Not that they may not preach, or pray, or exhort merely, but they may not open their lips to utter any sounds audibly. Let not your women in promiscuous religious meetings preach or pray audibly, or exhort audibly, or sigh, or groan, or say Amen, or utter the precious words, "Bless the Lord," or the enchanting sounds, "Glory! Glory!"[14]

VIEW OF SCRIPTURE

Gage condemned the use of the Bible by the male "Patriarchate" because they had mistranslated, interpolated, and misused it for their benefit. There were thousands of translation errors in the Bible. How could the average person trust the academics when there were so many problems with the original texts?

[W]ith no Hebrew manuscript older than the twelfth century; with no Greek one older than the fourth; with the acknowledgment by scholars of 7,000 errors in the Old Testament, and 150,000 in the New; with the assurance that these interpolations and changes have been made by men in the interest of creeds, we may well believe that the portions of the Bible quoted against woman's equality are but interpolations of an unscrupulous priesthood, for the purpose of holding her in subjection to man.[15]

Yet in spite of all of her criticisms about Christianity, she failed to abandon its Scriptures. They had meaning for her, although she did not view them as the only sacred writings or valuable information available to Christians. Science,[16] the Buddha,[17] historical evidence,[18] orphic hymns,[19] and other writings such as "The Everlasting Gospel," "The Gospel of the Holy Ghost," or Kabalistic (spelled Cabalistic by Matilda) or both could help people find the truth.[20]

While maintaining the authority of the Scriptures in her life, she accused Paul the apostle of carrying on an "enlarged Judaism." He was biased: "He brought into the new dispensation the influence of the old ceremonial law, which regarded woman as unclean."[21] "Paul, brought up in the strictest external principles of Judaism, did not lose his educational bias or primal belief when changing from Judaism to Christianity."[22] "He was the first Jesuit in the Christian church." And for her this was definitely not a compliment.[23]

INTERPRETATIVE STRATEGY

Gage viewed the Scriptures as foundational to the oppression and the subjection of women. Her hope was to create a feminist utopia where women could find all the liberties they desire. Some of her interpretations, which did not seem to follow a logical order, remythologized accepted views of ancient stories. She also attempted to explain selected vocabulary by discussing history, or the etymology from the Greek. Using prooftexts, she shored up her arguments by quoting noted authorities. Her examples always underscored equality and hinted at the superiority of the "Matriarchate."

REMYTHOLOGIZING: THE CREATION STORY

The notion of original sin is based primarily in the story of Adam and Eve. Gage accepted the teaching that the origins of sin fell upon the irresponsible pair in the garden. On the issue of whether it was Eve's fault and thus the fault of all women that sin came into the world, she quoted an outside source which was supposedly from a book printed in Amsterdam in 1700 (no specific reference is given) placing the greater responsibility upon Adam. Here are a few of the eleven reasons:

First: The serpent tempted her before she thought of the tree of knowledge of good and evil . . .

Second: That believing that God had not given such prohibition she [did] eat the fruit.

Third: Sinning through ignorance she committed a less heinous crime than Adam.

Fourth: That Eve did not necessarily mean [earn?] the penalty of eternal death, for God's decree only imported that *man* should if he sinned against his conscience.[24]

The articles contended that Adam should have been punished for his sin because the prohibition was given to him not to Eve—he was driven out of the garden; she was not. Gage also quoted Hieronymus, who suggested that Eve possessed a much finer constitution than Adam and was therefore superior to him.[25] Hieronymus contended that Eve lived ten years longer than Adam and bore him a boy and a girl every year. Gage added that Eve must have been more intelligent because she knew the three languages spoken by God, Adam, and the serpent.

DEGRADED STATE OF WOMEN IN THE BIBLE

Gage alleged that the Bible has a very low regard for women: "The sacrifice of woman to man's basic passions has ever been the distinguishing character of the Patriarchs."[26] Jephthah's daughter was killed by her father, and while Abraham did not kill Isaac he never revealed the secret plan to Sarah that he planned to sacrifice their only son.[27] Gage alleged that infanticide and prostitution were born within Patriarchate religions: "Both infanticide and prostitution with all their attendant horrors are traceable with polygamy—their origin—to the Patriarchate of Father-rule, under which Judaism and Christianity rose as forms of religious belief."[28]

THE FEMININE PRINCIPLE IS AN ESSENTIAL
PART OF THE DIVINE

To Gage, this "degraded" state of women in society and within the pages of the Bible was deplorable. Although most interpreters ignored the positive aspects of women, they were very important in the Bible. In fact, the feminine principle is an essential part of the Divine. If the origins of the names for God in the Old Testament are studied, the interpreter would find that contained within the name for the God of the Old Testament is the masculine-feminine principle; it is a "double-sexed word:"[29] "Jehovah signifies not alone the masculine and the feminine principles but also the spirit or vivifying intelligence. It is a compound word indicative of three divine principles."[30] Here is an example of her interpretative etymology: "Jehovah should be read from left to right, and pronounced *Ho-Hi;* that is to say *He-She* (*Hi* pronounce *He,*) *Ho* is Hebrew, being the pronoun and *Hi* the feminine. *Ho-Hi* therefore denotes the male and female principles, the vis genatrix."[31]

The third part of the Divine is the Holy Spirit: "Holy Ghost, although in Hebrew a noun of masculine, feminine, or neuter gender, is invariably rendered masculine by Christian translators of the Bible."[32] "In the Greek, from whence we obtain the New Testament, spirit is of the feminine gender, although invariably translated masculine."[33]

> The Holy Spirit, symbolized by a dove, is a distinctively feminine principle—the Comforter—and yet has ever been treated by the Christian Church as masculine, alike in dogmas propounded from the pulpit, and in translations of the Scriptures. A few notable exceptions however appear at an early date. Origen expressly referred to the Holy Ghost as feminine, saying, "The soul is maiden to her mistress the Holy Ghost." An article upon the "Esoteric character of the Gospels" in Madam Blavatsky's *Lucifer* (November 1887) says: Spirit or the Holy Ghost was feminine with the Jews as most ancient peoples and it was so with the early Christians; Sophia of the Gnostics and the third Sephiroth, Binah (the female Jehovah of the Cabalists,) are feminine principles "Divine Spirit" or *Ruach*, "One is She the spirit of the Elohim of Life," is said in Sepher Yetzirah.[34]

Authority for Christian living can be found in other books outside the accepted canon. Gage quoted what she termed an "early canonical book" that has been omitted from the present day Bible. In this verse, the Holy Spirit is referred to as "mother." The quote is attributed to Jesus: "My mother the Holy Ghost, took me by the hair of my head into the mountain."[35] Continuing her proof for the feminine element in the Divine, Gage analyzed other names for God found in the Old Testament: "The Hebrew word 'El Shaddai' translated, 'The Almighty' is still more distinctively feminine than Iah, as it means 'the Breasted God,' and is made use of in the Old Testament whenever the especially feminine characteristics of God are meant to be indicated."[36]

Justice for women can become a possibility when people recognize the element of the feminine within God: "It is through a recognition of the divine element of motherhood as not alone inhering in the great primal source of life but as extending throughout all creation, that it will become possible for the world, so buried in darkness, folly and superstition, to practice justice toward woman."[37]

Gage ended her book with a battle cry for women. She hoped that women would rebel against the church and all the people and institutions that had oppressed women: "During the ages, no rebellion has been of like importance with that of Woman against the tyranny of Church and State; none has had its far reaching effects. We note its beginning; its progress will overthrow every existing form of these institutions; its end will be a regenerated world."[38]

SUMMARY

Mary Daly and Rosemary Radford Ruether must be partially indebted to Matilda for many of their feminist strategies, philosophies, hopes, and dreams. While Gage's labored writing style can be placed squarely within the nineteenth century, her conclusions about the influence and history of patriarchy relative to women is foundational to much of twentieth-century feminism. She understood that religion and its influence on society was of paramount importance. Religion was not something that was on the periphery of culture; it in fact was a controlling factor in culture and especially in the lives of women. Central to that control of women was the Bible, and Gage was determined to proclaim to all the world that its pages contained the possibility of liberation, even though the clergy taught submission.

FRANCES ELIZABETH CAROLINE WILLARD
(1839–1898)

Men preach a creed; women will declare a life.
Men deal in formulas, women in facts.
Men have always tithed mint and rue and cummin
in their exegesis and their ecclesiasticism,
while the world's heart cried out for compassion,
forgiveness and sympathy.
Men's preaching has left heads committed to a catechism,
and left hearts hard as nether millstones.[1]

BIOGRAPHY

Frances Willard, a Methodist, lived the life of an emancipated woman during the nineteenth century. By the time she was fifty years old, she had become the first women president of the Ladies College in Evanston, Illinois; Dean and Professor of Aesthetics at Woman's College of Northwestern University; and president of both the Illinois Woman's Christian Temperance Union and the National Woman's Christian Temperance Union.

Her early education began at Milwaukee Female College in 1857 and later Western Female College in Evanston. From 1860 to 1868, she worked as a teacher and administrator in educational institutions. Much of her working life was spent in searching for a position that fit her capabilities. She was concerned about the lack of opportunities for woman and was pro-suffrage, although the National Woman's Christian Temperance Union never endorsed her position. She represented the conservative woman who wanted a better home life and equitable property rights and divorce laws, but not necessarily equality in public life with men: "Willard developed a broad program, advocating such diverse reforms as women police officers, kindergartens, the eight-hour day, putting a monetary value on housework, manual and physical training for girls, coeducation, raising the age of consent, and laws making men and women legal and economic equals in marriage."[2]

Her work for the NWCTU took her throughout the country. She worked with D. L. Moody in Chicago, addressed summer camps at Chautauqua meetings in New England, and traveled extensively in the southern states. "Her delicate features, close-cropped hair, and small pince-nez were familiar to millions, as was her ability to sway audiences."[3] Small in stature and always the feminine figure, Frances preferred the company of females as she lectured on the equal rights of women and the evils of strong drink. "She was loved, she was adored. Her intense, almost sexual attractiveness to members of her own sex was a major factor in her success. . . ."[4] Anna Gordon became her life companion in 1877.

The only woman to be placed in the statuary hall in Washington, D.C., Nancy Hardesty lauds her memory: "She was indeed 'Woman of the Century.' Heir to the revivalist legacy of broad-based, gospel-rooted reform, Willard sought to do everything within her power to empower and uplift women. Gathering up all the strings of women's resources and efforts, she brought together in one huge, very political organization the power to make women a force in American life."[5]

Her many books include *Woman and Temperance* (1883), *Glimpses of*

Fifty Years (1889), *Woman in the Pulpit* (1888), *A White Life for Two* (1890), and pamphlets including, "Hints and Helps in Temperance World," and "How to Win." Most of her views of woman and the Bible are found in *Woman in the Pulpit.*[6]

THE PROBLEM

According to Willard, Women were disqualified from Christian public ministry by an ecclesiastical hierarchy that in spite of its own incompetencies had survived.[7] This hierarchy (which she termed ecclesiasticism) used arguments from the Bible, an exegesis of the cloister,[8] to create church edicts[9] enforced by a white male dynasty[10] that had lost faith in itself and others:[11] "Their fear that incompetent women may become pastors and preachers should be put to flight by the survival of the church, in spite of centuries of the grossest incompetency in mind and profligacy in life, of men set apart by the laying-on of hands."[12]

The ecclesiastical authorities betrayed not only incompetencies but also prejudiced attitudes[13] and a myriad of absurd reasoning and interpretative processes. Their view of history was biased and selective.[14] "The whole subjection theory grows out of the one-sided interpretation of the Bible by men."[15] Some passages of the Bible, such as the "keep silent" injunction to women were interpreted literally with the force of law, while other passages were ignored, especially if they referred to a woman accomplishing anything.[16] In short, they not only "preach but practise the heresy that woman is in subjection to man. . . ."[17]

Other males espoused a philosophy of acculturation that accommodated the male hierarchies of foreign cultures at the expense of accurate translations of the Bible, which would have included women as equal laborers within Christianity. What does this do to the status of women in these countries?

A returned missionary from China assures me that of four separate translations of the New Testament into Chinese, all change Paul's words, Phil. iv. 3, "I intreat thee, also, true yoke-fellow, help those women which labored with me in the Gospel," into "help those true yoke-fellows," etc., leaving out the idea of woman altogether. A leading (male) missionary was asked the reason of this, and he naively replied, "Oh, it would not do, with the ideas of the Chinese, to mention women in this connection.[18]

This approach to Scripture and foreign missions was especially troubling when women were allowed to "administer the sacrament in India" but not in the United States. What made the two parts of the world so different?[19]

This "intolerant sacerdotal element has handicapped" the church from its beginnings[20] because women had been denied their equal right to serve God. One priestly writer said, "We do sometimes find a man's head on a woman's shoulders, but it is a great misfortune to her."[21] This fear of female intellectual ability may have proven to be the makings of their downfall: "The time has come when those men in high places, 'dressed in a little brief authority' within the church of Christ, who seek to shut women out of the pastorate, cannot do so with impunity."[22]

Urging women to ordain themselves in order to take their rightful place within Christianity, Willard warned the men, "Let not conservative ecclesiastical leaders try to steady the Lord's ark; let them not bind what God hath loosed; let them not retain the bondage he hath remitted, lest haply they be found to fight against God."[23]

VIEW OF SCRIPTURE

For Willard, the Bible contained the truth, was a revelation from God,[24] and was relevant for people in the nineteenth century. Voices, human voices,[25] within the Bible gave contradictory statements.[26] Jesus' words are to take precedence over Paul's: "Christ, not Paul is the source of all churchly authority and power."[27] And again, "Christ's commission only is authoritative."[28] Sayings found in Matthew came from "Christ himself," and so she also believed that the Bible records the actual words of the devil and Paul.[29]

INTERPRETATIVE STRATEGY

Willard attempted to demonstrate that traditional exegesis used by clerics is riddled with inconsistencies, prejudices, and presuppositions about woman's subjection that are self-serving.[30] She characterized their approach to Scripture as "literal,"[31] "fast and loose,"[32] "exegesis of the cloister,"[33] "one eyed,"[34] "one sided,"[35] and the so-called "scientific study of the Holy Scriptures."[36]

She began by attacking the way clergy pick and choose scriptural passages in order to fit their own points of view. She argued that if one part of the Bible is to be interpreted literally and used as an unretractable law then other passages should also be kept in a legal manner. Consider I Corinthians 7 where Paul "elevates celibacy above marriage," yet present-day ministers perform marriage ceremonies without hesitation.[37] Or the female submission requirements of I Timothy which declared that a woman learn in silence and be prohibited from teaching. Men enforced the letter of the law with regard to prohibiting women from exercising her abilities to preach, yet on the other hand, they ignored the provision of ministering without the signs of wealth. The same book says, "I desire . . . that women adorn themselves in modest apparel, with shamefastness and sobriety; not with braided hair, and gold or pearls or costly raiment."[38] Yet women came to church clothed in such a manner every week. This uneven and biased approach must be balanced: "We need women commentators to bring out the women's side of the book; we need the stereoscopic view of truth in general, which can only be had when woman's eye and man's together shall discern the perspective of the Bible's full-orbed revelation."[39]

Her own strategies included quoting noted Bible authorities from Augustine to Dean Alford,[40] redefining words,[41] recognizing that words such as "brethren" exclude the idea of female,[42] counting passages relating to woman,[43] and listing stories about women that demonstrate equality.[44]

MYTHOLOGICAL VIEW OF WOMAN

Willard created her own mythology about women and their importance in the early church.[45] For instance the traveling women of Luke
8:1–3 became fearless leaders: "What loss of caste came to those
fearless women, who, breaking away from the customs of society and
the traditions of religion, dared to follow the greatest of Iconoclasts
from city to village with a publicity and a persistence nothing less
than outrageous to the conservatives of that day."[46]

And Mary became "the first commission to declare his resurrection."[47] ". . . Christ started the church based on his resurrection, by
commissioning Mary to bear the gladdest tidings this dying world has
ever heard. . . ."[48]

Willard also attempted to draw attention to neglected passages of
Scripture that suggested the importance of woman.[49] For instance,
only God and a woman were present at the conception and birth of
Jesus.[50] Isn't that an important fact and event? Wouldn't that fact
underscore the importance of women?

WOMEN AND PUBLIC WORK

Finally, she suggested that more men would become Christians if
women were in the pulpit,[51] calling upon the clergy to recognize that
the terms "minister" and "mother" are not mutually exclusive.[52]
Ministering will not disrupt the home; it is only an extension of her
duties as a mother. "[A]nd everybody knows that, beyond almost any
other, the minister is the one who lives at home."[53]

According to Willard, there are 30 or 40 passages that support
"woman's public work" and only two against it.[54] Taking her cue
from the gospels and the Old Testament/Hebrew Bible, Willard
suggested that stories in the Gospels hold more weight than Pauline
injunctions against women. In chart form she cited Paul, and then
refuted him by quoting another verse from the Bible. Here are a few
examples:

Problem:	Refutation:	Additional Refutation:
PAUL	OTHER SCRIPTURES	PAUL
I Tim ii. 11	*Judge iv. 4, 5*	*Gal iii. 28*
"But I permit not a woman to teach, nor to have over a man, but quietness."	"Now Deborah, a prophetess, the wife of Lappidoth, she judged Isreal at that time . . ."	"There can be no male and female; for ye are dominion all one man in Christ to be in Jesus"
I Cor. xiv. 34	*Joel ii. 28, 29*	*I Cor. xi. 5*
"Let the woman keep silence for it is not permitted unto them to speak."	"And it shall come to pass afterward . . . that your . . . daughters shall prophesy . . . and upon the handmaids will I pour out my spirit."	"But every woman churches; praying or prophesying with her head unveiled to dishonoreth her head."
I Cor. xiv. 35	*Luke ii. 36–38*	*Phil. iv. 3*
"It is shameful for a woman to speak in the church."	"And there was one Anna, a prophetess . . . which departed not from the temple, worshipped with fastings and supplications night and day. And coming up at that very hour she gave thanks unto God, and spake of him to all them that were looking for the redemption of Jerusalem."[55]	"I beseech thee also help these women for they labored with me in the Gospel."

THE CREATION STORY AND THE SUPERIORITY OF WOMAN

In interpreting the Creation stories, Willard suggested that the last of Creation was the best: "If they would be consistent, all ministers who accept the evolutionary theory—and a majority of them seem to have done so—must admit that not only was woman made out of better material than man (which doubtless will cheerfully grant!), but that, coming last in the order of creation, she stands highest of all."[56]

This philosophy of the superiority of woman underpinned most of her thoughts on men. Her villification peaked in the following statement:

Men preach a creed; women will declare a life. Men deal in formulas, women in facts. Men have always tithed mint and rue and cummin in their exegesis and their ecclesiasticism, while the world's heart cried out for compassion, forgiveness, and sympathy. Men's preaching has left heads committed to a catechism, and left hearts hard as nether millstones.[57]

SUMMARY

Willard's sophisticated and biting rhetoric came at the end of a century of many battles fought for the equality of women. Having the benefits of a fine education and access to the process of powerful decision making and struggles in the academy and politics, she understood her enemy more than most other women. Her immense popularity gave her the confidence to startle the public with the view that not only are mothers better, as the cult of motherhood taught, but all women are better.

CHARLOTTE PERKINS GILMAN (1860–1935)

Birth-based religion
would steadily hold before our eyes the vision of a splendid race,
the duty of upbuilding it.
It would tell no story of old sins, of anguish and despair,
of passionate pleading for forgiveness for the mischief we have made,
but would offer always the sunrise of a fresh hope:
"Here is a new baby. Begin again!" [1]

BIOGRAPHY

Charlotte Perkins Gilman was a social theorist, critic of history and society, and an avid lecturer and writer on feminist issues. Her socialist and utopian ideals penetrated most of her rationalistic writings.

Charlotte authored several books and created her own periodical *The Forerunner* (1909), lasting seven years, the contents of which were entirely hers:

> The suffragist Carrie Chapman Catt placed Charlotte Perkins Gilman at the head of her list of America's dozen greatest women; in her time she was certainly the leading intellectual of the woman's movement in the United States. She was one of those individuals who are, in her words, "so constituted as not to fit existing conditions" and "in sharp and painful consciousness" . . . . cry out against them.[2]

Her early life was plagued by poverty, isolation, loneliness, an absent father, and a mother who avoided debts by moving away from them. Her family moved "eighteen times in fourteen years."[3] Her mother, Mary Fitch Wescott Perkins, attempted to support the family through teaching. Her father, Frederick (Beecher) Perkins worked as an editor and librarian.[4] While her brother was sent to the Massachusetts Institute of Technology, Charlotte was given a reading list by her father, and later studied commercial art at the Rhode Island School of Design. In spite of or because of her childhood, Charlotte developed into one of the greatest theoreticans of the late nineteenth century.

She was a woman whose ideas took her far into the twentieth century. She did not wear a corset, neither did she assume a traditional feminine lifestyle. She exercised rigorously and trained her body through self-denial: "At a time when fainting was considered the badge of femininity, Gilman ran a mile twice a week, learned gymnastics, and wore clothing as light and as loose as possible. The physical conditioning stayed with her. At the age of forty-two she played basketball with her daughter at Barnard, at the age of sixty-five she followed up a lecture at the University of Oklahoma by swinging two lengths of the parallel rings."[5]

She stayed in excellent physical and mental health until she married Charles Walter Stetson in 1884 and gave birth to her daughter a year later. From the onset of pregnancy until after the birth of her daughter, Charlotte became mentally ill. Relief from her nervous breakdown came only when she was on holiday away from her husband. Upon her return the mental-emotional symptoms that paralyzed her returned. She subsequently left her husband, taking her daughter to California in 1888, where they explored many writing adventures. During this time she barely supported herself, her daughter, and her mother by lecturing and writing poetry. Eventually obtaining a divorce from her, Stetson married Charlotte's best friend, Grace Ellery Channing. Throughout their lives, the three remained close friends. Charles and Grace eventually raised Charlotte's only child, Katharine. Newspapers claimed that she abandoned her child; in reality, Charlotte knew her daughter would have a better life with her husband. For years she traveled from town to town giving lectures, never having a home of her own. She wrote that she often recalled with tears the day she put her daughter on the train going east. After that painful day, she always cried whenever she saw a mother and daughter together.[6]

Eventually she married George Houghton Gilman, a cousin and attorney, who gave her a place to call home. She spent the rest of her career in New York and later Connecticut, writing and lecturing. In 1893, Charlotte published her first book of verse, *In This Our World*. Her other books include *Women and Economics* (1898), *Concerning Children* (1900), *The Home* (1903), *The Human Work* (1904), *Man-Made World* (1911), *Herland* (1915), *His Religion and Hers* (1923). She died in 1935 by committing suicide after battling painful breast cancer for three years.[7]

THE PROBLEM

Although Charlotte was very well known for her economic theories, two of her works *Herland* and *His Religion and Hers*,[8] criticized Christianity and religion in general. She believed that women's progress was retarded by males because they constructed and developed the environment, and thus Christianity, only for themselves.[9] They created a "death-based" religion or a religion built upon the concept of sacrifice that is too heavenly minded.[10]

> The death-basis for religion is so old, so deep, that we must look for its cause in our earliest beginnings, in that long, dark period of savagery which covers so extensive a proportion of human existence.[11]
> A rather conspicuous point to be noted in all these joy-promising futures is their naive masculinity. Never a feminine paradise among them. Happy Hunting-Grounds—no happy Nursing-Grounds.[12]

Not only did the males omit women from their projections of heaven, through Christianity they had taught women to feel unworthy[13] and weak[14] while dutifully serving males.[15] Men had used the Bible against women by passing on the legend of "the curse of Eve,"[16] and used the words of domination found in Genesis 3:16, "and he shall rule over you."[17] This low estimation of themselves was translated to their children.[18] "A misused, subordinate mother gives us an underrated, mistaught child."[19] Thus, the whole world was damaged.

Because of their "sex pride"[20] and love of violence,[21] men missed the point of Jesus' earthly teachings:[22] "The religion which urges most of real race-improvement is that of Jesus. He taught unmistakably of God in man, of heaven here, of worship expressed in the love and service of humanity. But our strange death-complex was too strong even for his teachings. What he taught us to pray and work for here, was ignored in our eagerness to get to heaven through his virtues."[23]

Gilman did not stop her criticism of society with the males. She chastized females who had, in their new-found freedom, sold out and taken on the values of these males. She believed in equality but not the kind that was bred and conditioned by males and which would abandon motherhood:[24]

> The kind of women bred and trained through ages of masculine selection are not such as one would trust the world to, unassisted. . . . Now that they have in large measure reached their goal of "equality with men,"—not real equality in social development but equality in immediate consitions—it is sickening to see so many of the newly freed using their freedom in a mere imitation of masculine vices.[25]

> No prisoned harem beauty, no victim of white-slavery, no dull-eyed kitchen drudge is so pitiful as these "new women," free, educated, independent, and just as much the slaves of fashion and the victims of license as they were centuries before.[26]

> These poor little slouchy creatures, painting their cheeks and powdering their noses, fluttering before our eyes as willing exponents of every passing fashion, adopting male vices, and so unutterably traitorous to the essential glory of their own sex as willingly to forego motherhood in order to share the barren pleasures of the other—are these the women from whose influences we are to expect a higher religion?

Most certainly they are not. But these are not Women. These are really more worthy of that absurd title with which men have tried to discredit the progressive women of our times—"the third sex."[27]

VIEW OF SCRIPTURE

Gilman's approach to Scripture was more philosophical than literary-critical, thus referring directly to it only a few times throughout her books. But she recognized the foundational importance of "the Book" handed down to people through the centuries, and that many hold ". . . that every word of our Scripture is true, and not contradictory of another . . ."[28] It is the Word of God.[29] Not so for Gilman—it was only a book, and it could not answer all the questions for people who lived in the twentieth century: "The remote, uncertain, contradictory views concerning a book-derived God, which have been so often shaken when the world went more wrong than usual, . . . We grovel and 'worship' and pray God to do what we ourselves ought to have done a thousand years ago . . ."[30]

While she respected the Book and found truth in it, she also recognized that males had interpreted it and used it for their own benefit. Reading the Bible is not the way to find equality or fulfillment in this life. It will take much more than a book. Her only biblical hero continued to be Jesus, clinging to Jesus' words and life as an excellent example of the proper way to live,[31] although, she deplored the idea of a male-only God.

INTERPRETATIVE STRATEGY

Gilman took a shot-gun approach to explaining passages found in the Bible, never bothering to cite her references or situate them contextually or historically. The passages she chose to quote became springboards for her own matriarchal philosophy and criticisms of patriarchy.

ADAM AND EVE: DEMYTHOLOGIZATION

She began by deconstructing the notion of the devil in favor of human error.[32] The story of Adam and Eve was only a legend, not a legal mandate for all of eternity. Gilman chose to defend Eve in this 'meaningless' story. Women had been incorrectly blamed for bringing sin into the world, which she termed a "guileless habit" of men.[33]

> The curse seems all the more unwarrantable when we read in the story itself that it was before Eve was made that Adam was commanded not to eat of the tree. She certainly was not forbidden.

> If the ancient Hebrew religion accepted the still more Assyrian legend, stating that woman was made out of Adam's rib, for his personal accomodation, and that her subsequent interest in apples was responsible for the loss of that horticultural paradise, it is not remarkable that the pious modern Hebrew still mutters his daily prayer of masculine superiority, thanking God that he was not born a woman.[34]

> One religion after another has accepted and perpetuated man's original mistake in making a private servant of the mother of the race.[35]

PAULINE MANDATE: THE SUBMISSION OF WOMEN

Women had been conditioned to live for men. They bore children for males and gave up their entire lives in order to make males happy. All religions had done the same thing to women. It is found in Paul's foundational mandate, "Wive's submit" (Ephesians 5:22): "All the laws and all the religions worked to the same end—that embodied in our Pauline instruction, "Wives submit yourselves to your husbands,"—so she submitted, to our racial degradation; or rebelled, and was destroyed."[36]

JESUS: A SINGLE VOICE.

One male stands alone against the patriarchal darkness. Jesus, himself, is a man who never condemned a woman, even if she was guilty of adultery: "Jesus was far more gentle with the Magdalene, and with the woman taken in adultery, than he was with the scribes, Pharisees, hypocrites he so condemned. But we, in spite of law, religion, and any sense of justice, continue to blame and punish the woman for acts but lightly disparaged in a man."[37]

MOTHERHOOD: A BIRTH-BASED RELIGION

Males had failed in building a peaceful and equitable world. They had used Christianity to further their own need for power over others. For Gilman, the only solution to the patriarchal and violent society was to center religion in Motherhood. It would be a life-giving, sustaining, and birth-based, instead of death-based, religion. The women should be in control, for after all else, they were superior.[38]

> It is to social relationship that life-based religion brings vital change. By the new alignment, the new attitude of humanity toward God, of men toward women, of women toward men, of both toward child, of the child toward them, and of every one of us toward society, we attain a position which allows free transmission of power.

> Seeing God as within us, to be expressed, instead of above us to be worshipped, is enough to change heaven and earth in our minds, and gradually to bring heaven on earth by our actions.[39]

Woman is the future of the world. Birthing and rearing children must be the center of her life. Through the recognition of the divine in bearing children, women will change the face of the earth. It will be a peaceful and wonderful place to live.

HERLAND

Gilman took her matriarchal theories and incorporated them into a feminist utopian serial entitled *Herland.* In this imaginary place on earth, women were in control. By accident three men crashland in Herland and begin a journey which leads them to the discovery of the true nature, strength, and abilities of women. These women also have a very different kind of religion.

> Their religion, you see, was maternal; and their ethics, based on the full perception of evolution, showed the principle of growth and the beauty of wise culture. They had no theory of the essential opposition of good and evil; life to them was growth; their pleasure was in growing, and their duty also.[40]

> Their great Mother Spirit was to them what their own motherhood was—only magnified beyond human limits. That meant that they felt beneath and behind them an upholding, unfailing, serviceable love—perhaps it was really the accumulated mother-love of the race they felt—but it was a Power.[41]

This mothering Spirit was the only hope for women to find equality within a historically dominated patriarchal world, and of course the only real hope for change.

SUMMARY

As a philosopher, Gilman recognized the importance and influence of the Bible on American culture. Its emphasis on death and war had only led to more violence and abuse. Ironically, she could not totally abandon it. Some of its high ethical and social standards could be maintained, but most of the interpretations should be abandoned. The Book did have some merit but, unfortunately, it had been used to enslave and oppress females for centuries.

The answer to the dilemma was to begin anew with a matriarchal religion that would offer an alternative and often opposite view of life and the beyond. While Gilman answers many of the criticisms of a birth-based culture, recommending communal child-care facilities and feeding stations in her other books, she could not solve the problem of birthing. In *Herland,* birthing presents no problems and men are not needed in order to conceive. Reality presents many more challenges to the problems and opportunities of child-raising.

Because of her own restricted life, Charlotte faced the darkness of a mental breakdown. Her essay entitled "The Yellow Wallpaper" is a penetrating and startling portrait of what happens to a woman who is totally dominated by a male husband and physician. This darkness of self-abandonment is faced by every woman who is governed by male interpretations of Scripture. She must not submit; she must realize her own potential, rebel, and choose life instead of the utter bleakness of service to males. Within each woman is the hope of change. Without Her there is no hope and no love.

Notes

HENRICH CORNELIUS AGRIPPA VON NETTESHEIM

1. Henrich Cornelius Agrippa von Nettesheim. *The Glory of Women: or, A Treatise Declaring the Excellency and Preheminence of Women above Men which is proved both by Scripture, Law, Reason, and Authority, Divine and Humane.* Written first in Latine by Henrich Cornelius Agrippa . . . and now translated into English for the Vertuous and Beautiful Female Sex of the Common wealth of England, by Devv. Fleetvvod (London: Robert Ibbitson, 1652), 4. See also Maurice de Gandillac, "Sur le Role du Féminin dans la Theologie D'Agrippa de Netttesheim," *Revue d'histoire et de philosophié Religionses* 55 (1, 1975): 37–47.
2. Agrippa von Nettesheim, *The Glory of Women*; see the epistle dedicatory at the front of the treatise. No page number.
3. Clyde L. Manschreck, ed., *History of Christianity: Readings in the History of the Church* (Grand Rapids: Baker Book House, 1964), 2:1–216.
4. Justo L. Gonzalez, *The Story of Christianity,* vol. 2. *The Reformation to the Present Day* (San Francisco: Harper and Row, 1984), 1–73.
5. W. N. Hargreaves-Mawdsley, ed., *Everyman's Dictionary of European Writers* (London: J.M. Dent, 1968), 5. See also Charles Nauert, *Agrippa and the Crisis of Renaissance Thought* (Urbana: University of Illinois Press, 1965) and Arlene Miller Guinsburg, "The Counterthrust to Sixteenth Century Misogyny: The Work of Agrippa and Paracelsus," *Historical Reflections* 8(1981): 3–28.
6. Anne Llewelly Barstow, *Witchcraze: A New History of the European Witch Hunts* (San Francisco: HarperCollins, 1994), 62–64.
7. Ibid., 64.
8. Ibid., 65.
9. W. N. Hargreaves-Mawdsley, ed., *Everyman's Dictionary of European Writers,* 5.
10. Ibid.

11. Agrippa von Nettesheim. *The Glory of Women*; see the epistle dedicatory at the front of the work.
12. Ibid.
13. Agrippa von Nettesheim. *The Glory of Women*, 4.
14. Ibid., 3.
15. Ibid., 5, 7, 21.
16. Ibid., 8.
17. Ibid.
18. Ibid., 22.
19. Ibid., 3.
20. Ibid., 9.
21. Ibid., 7.
22. Ibid., 20.
23. Ibid., 11, 15.
24. Ibid., 11.
25. Ibid., 12.
26. Ibid., 14.
27. Ibid., 21.
28. Ibid., 30.
29. Ibid., 18.
30. Ibid., 19.
31. Ibid., 18.
32. Ibid., 15.
33. Ibid., 18.
34. Ibid., 30.
35. Ibid., 23.
36. Ibid., 3.
37. Ibid., 31.
38. Ibid., 30.
39. Ibid., 23.
40. Ibid., see epistle dedicatory at the front of the work.
41. Ibid., 31–32.
42. Ibid., 1.
43. Ibid., 2.
44. Ibid., 3.
45. Ibid., 14.
46. Ibid., 7.
47. Ibid., 16.
48. Ibid., 20.
49. Ibid., 21.
50. Ibid., 21–22.
51. Ibid., 22.
52. Ibid.

MARY ASTELL

1. Mary Astell, *A Serious Proposal to the Ladies for the Advancement of their True and Greatest Interest* (London: R. Wilkin, 1701) and reprint (New York: Source Book Press, 1970), 18. See also Mary Astell, *Some Reflections upon Marriage* (London: John Nutt, 1700).
2. Mary Astell, *A Serious Proposal to the Ladies*, 14.
3. Florence M. Smith, *Mary Astell* (New York: AMS Press, 1966), 6.
4. Ibid.
5. Ibid., 7.
6. Ruth Perry, *The Celebrated Mary Astell. An Early English Feminist* (Chicago: University of Chicago Press, 1986), xii.
7. Florence M. Smith, *Mary Astell*, 7.
8. Ruth Perry, *The Celebrated Mary Astell*, 106.
9. Joan K. Kinnaird, "Mary Astell and the Conservative Contribution to English Feminism," *Journal of British Studies* 19(Fall, 1979):54.
10. Mary Astell. *A Serious Proposal to the Ladies*, 13.
11. Ibid., 12.
12. Ibid., 13.
13. Ibid., 135.
14. Ibid., 20.
15. Ibid.
16. Ibid., 143.
17. Ibid., 20.
18. Ibid., 159.
19. Ibid., 158.
20. Ibid., 16.
21. Ibid.
22. Ibid., 129.
23. Ibid., 14.
24. Ibid., 136.
25. Ibid., 38.
26. Ibid., 20.
27. Ibid., 38.
28. Ibid., 159.
29. Joan K. Kinnaird, "Mary Astell," *Journal of British Studies* 19(Fall, 1979): 74.
30. Ibid., 64.
31. Ibid., 73.
32. Ruth Perry, *The Celebrated Mary Astell*, 104.
33. Ibid., 103.
34. Mary Astell, *A Serious Proposal to the Ladies*, 159.
35. Ibid., 129.

JUDITH SARGENT MURRAY

1. Judith Sargent Murray, "On the Equality of the Sexes," found in Alice S. Rossi, *The Feminist Papers: From Adams to de Beauvoir* (New York: Columbia University

Press, 1973): pp. 16–24. Reprint from original articles, "On the Equality of the Sexes," *The Massachusetts Magazine*, March 1790, pp. 132–135, and April 1790, pp. 223–226.

2. Vena B. Field, *Constantia: A Study of the Life and Works of Judith Sargent Murray, 1751–1820* (Orono: University of Maine Press, 1931), 10.

3. Vena B. Field, *Constantia*, 27. See N.A. "Article IX. Mrs. Judith Murray," *The Universalist Quarterly* 19(1882): 140–151.

4. Vena B. Field, *Constantia*, 13.

5. Ibid., 15.

6. Edward T. James, ed., *Notable American Women 1607–1950: A Biographical Dictionary* (Cambridge, MA: Harvard University Press, 1971), 2:603–4.

7. Ibid.

8. Vena B. Field, *Constantia*, 22.

9. Ibid., 26.

10. Ibid., 21, 46, 33, 32.

11. Ibid., 51.

12. Judith Sargent Murray, "On the Equality of the Sexes," found in Alice S. Rossi, *The Feminist Papers: From Adams to de Beauvoir* (New York: Columbia University Press, 1973): pp. 16–24. Reprint from original articles, "On the Equality of the Sexes," *The Massachusetts Magazine*, March 1790, pp. 132–135, and April 1790, pp. 223–226.

13. Alice S. Rossi, *The Feminist Papers*, 19.

14. Ibid., 18.

15. Ibid., 19.

16. Ibid., 20.

17. Ibid.

18. Ibid.

19. Ibid., 21.

20. Ibid., 22.

21. Ibid.

22. Ibid., 22–23.

23. Ibid., 18.

24. Ibid., 23.

25. Ibid.

26. Ibid., 24.

27. Ibid.

28. Ibid., 20.

29. Ibid.

30. Ibid., 21.

31. Ibid., 18.

MATILDA JOSLYN GAGE

1. Matilda Joslyn Gage, *Woman, Church and State: A Historical Account of the Status of Woman through the Christian Ages: with Reminiscences of the Matriarchate. American Women. Images and Realities Series.* Annette K. Baxter and Leon Stein, eds. (New York: The Truth Seeker Company, 1900. Reprint New York: Arno Press, 1972), 471.

2. Matilda Joslyn Gage, *Woman, Church and State*, 525.

3. Ibid., 526.

4. "Gage, Matilda Joslyn," *American Women: Fifteen Hundred Biographies with over 1,400 Portraits.* Frances E. Willard and Mary A. Livermore, eds. (Detroit: Gale Research Company, 1973), 1:309.

5. Edward T. James, ed., *Notable American Women 1607–1950: A Biographical Dictionary* (Cambridge, MA: Harvard University Press, 1971), 2:4–7.

6. Ibid.

7. Matilda Joslyn Gage, *Woman, Church and State*, preface.

8. Edward T. James, ed., *Notable American Women 1607–1950: A Biographical Dictionary* (Cambridge, MA: Harvard University Press, 1971), 2:4–7. See also Nancy A. Hardesy, *Evangelical Feminism in the Nineteenth Century: Women Called to Witness* (Nashville: Abingdon, 1984), 66–67; 97–98.

9. Matilda Joslyn Gage, *Woman, Church and State*, preface.

10. Ibid., 20.

11. Ibid., 21.

12. Ibid., 529, 527.

13. Ibid., 479.

14. Ibid., 476.

15. Elizabeth Cady Stanton, Susan B. Anthony, Matilda Joslyn Gage, eds., *History of Woman Suffrage* (New York: Susan B. Anthony, 1889), 1:799.

16. Matilda Joslyn Gage, *Woman, Church and State*, 48.

17. Ibid., 519.

18. Ibid., 57.

19. Ibid., 46.

20. Ibid., 47.

21. Ibid., 58.

22. Ibid., 53, 58, 59.

23. Ibid., 54.

24. Ibid., 522–523.

25. Ibid., 524.

26. Ibid., 44.

27. Ibid., 43.

28. Ibid., 44.

29. Ibid., 45.

30. Ibid., 47. Gage says," *Sepher Yetzirah* here which reads, "Observe that I. H. U. is Jod, male, father; "he" is female, Binah, and U is male, Vau, Son."

31. Matilda Joslyn Gage, *Woman, Church and State*, 45.

32. Ibid., 44.

33. Ibid., 44–45.

34. Ibid., 47.

35. Ibid.

36. Ibid., 45.

37. Ibid., 48.

38. Ibid., 545.

FRANCES ELIZABETH CAROLINE WILLARD

1. Frances E. Willard, *Woman in the Pulpit* (Chicago: Woman's Temperance Publication Association, 1888), 47.
2. Karlyn Kohrs Campbell, *Man Cannot Speak for Her*, vol. 1: *A Critical Study of Early Feminist Rhetoric* (New York: Greenwood Press, 1989), 122.
3. Edward T. James, ed., *Notable American Women 1607–1950: A Biographical Dictionary* (Cambridge, MA: Harvard University Press, 1971), 3:616. See also Frances E. Willard and Mary A. Livermore, eds., *American Women* (Republished, Detroit: Gale Research Company, 1973), 2:777–780.
4. Ruth Bordin, *Frances Willard: A Biography* (Chapel Hill: University of North Carolina Press, 1986), 68–69. See also Nancy A. Hardesy, *Evangelical Feminism in the Nineteenth Century: Women Called to Witness* (Nashville: Abingdon, 1984), 21; see also 13–25; 166–167.
5. Nancy A. Hardesy, *Evangelical Feminism in the Nineteenth Century*, 25.
6. Frances E. Willard, *Woman in the Pulpit* (Chicago: Woman's Temperance Publication Association, 1888); *Woman and Temperance* (Hartford, CT: Park Publishing, 1883); *Glimpses of Fifty Years* (Chicago: Woman's Temperance Publication Association, 1889), *A White Life for Two* (1890) found in *Man Cannot Speak for Her*, vol. 2. *Key Texts of the Early Feminists.* Karlyn Kohrs Campbell, ed. (New York: Greenwood Press, 1989): 317–337.
7. Frances E. Willard, *Woman in the Pulpit*, 131, 33, 53, 47.
8. Ibid., 49.
9. Ibid., 38.
10. Ibid., 45.
11. Ibid., 47–48.
12. Ibid., 53.
13. Ibid., 13.
14. Ibid., 31.
15. Ibid., 37.
16. Ibid., 31–32.
17. Ibid., 29.
18. Ibid., 18.
19. Ibid., 55.
20. Ibid., 47.
21. Ibid., 36.
22. Ibid., 52.
23. Ibid., 45.
24. Ibid., 21.
25. Ibid., 22.
26. Ibid., 27.
27. Ibid., 40.
28. Ibid., 42.
29. Ibid., 26.
30. Ibid., 23.
31. Ibid., 17, 18.
32. Ibid., 18.

33. Ibid., 49.
34. Ibid., 34.
35. Ibid., 37.
36. Ibid., 24.
37. Ibid., 19.
38. Ibid., 20.
39. Ibid., 21.
40. Ibid., 23, 27–30.
41. Ibid., 32.
42. Ibid., 35.
43. Ibid., 34.
44. Ibid., 33, 44, 34.
45. Ibid., 37, 42.
46. Ibid., 42.
47. Ibid., 41.
48. Ibid., 59.
49. Ibid., 41.
50. Ibid.
51. Ibid., 49.
52. Ibid., 63.
53. Ibid., 55.
54. Ibid., 34.
55. Ibid., 27.
56. Ibid., 37.
57. Ibid., 47.

CHARLOTTE PERKINS GILMAN

1. Charlotte Perkins Gilman, *His Religion and Hers: A Study of the Faith of Our Fathers and the Work of Our Mothers* (New York: The Century Co., 1923), 50.
2. Charlotte Perkins Stetson, *Woman Economics: A Study of the Economic Relation Between Men and Women as a Factor in Social Evolution* (Boston, 1899), 80. See also, Edward T. James, ed., *Notable American Women 1607–1950* (Cambridge, MA: Harvard University Press, 1971), 2:39–42.
3. Judith Nies, *Seven Women: Portraits from the American Radical Tradition* (New York: Penguin, 1977), 128. See also, Karlyn Kohrs Campbell, *Man Cannot Speak for Her*, vol. 1, *A Critical Study of Early Feminist Rhetoric* (New York: Greenwood Press, 1989), 185–186; 191, 198, and Carl N. Degler, "Charlotte Perkins Gilman on the Theory and Practice of Feminism," *American Quarterly* 8(Spring, 1956): 21–39, and Gerda Lerner, "Women's Rights and American Feminism," *American Scholar* 40(1971): 235–48.
4. Judith Nies, *Seven Women: Portraits from the American Radical Tradition* (New York: Penguin, 1977), 128.
5. Ibid., 131.
6. Ibid., 127–143.

7. Riegel, Robert E., *American Feminists* (Lawrence: University of Kansas Press, 1963), 163–173.
8. Charlotte Perkins Gilman, *His Religion and Hers: A Study of the Faith of Our Fathers and the Work of Our Mothers* (New York: The Century Co., 1923); *Herland* (New York: Pantheon Books, 1979) Introduction by Ann J. Lane.
9. Ibid., 7.
10. Ibid., 223, 21, 36.
11. Ibid., 37.
12. Ibid., 20.
13. Ibid., 114.
14. Ibid., 115.
15. Ibid., 9, 245.
16. Ibid., 44.
17. Ibid., 164.
18. Ibid., 295.
19. Ibid.
20. Ibid., 57.
21. Ibid., 36.
22. Charlotte Perkins Gilman. *His Religion and Hers*, 35. See also a wonderful essay by Gilman, "Are Women Human Beings?," in Ronald W. Hogeland, ed., *Women and Womanhood in America* (Lexington: D.C. Heath and Co., 1973), 133–135.
23. Ibid., 36.
24. Ibid., 239.
25. Ibid., 54.
26. Ibid., 95.
27. Ibid., 236.
28. Ibid., 21.
29. Charlotte Perkins Gilman. *Herland*, 114.
30. Charlotte Perkins Gilman. *His Religion and Hers*, 12.
31. Ibid., 159.
32. Ibid., 12.
33. Ibid., 43.
34. Ibid., 44.
35. Ibid., 217.
36. Ibid., 246.
37. Ibid., 130.
38. Ibid., 160.
39. Ibid., 292.
40. Charlotte Perkins Gilman. *Herland*, 102. See Alice S. Rossi, *The Feminist Papers: From Adams to Beauvoir* (New York: Columbia University Press, 1973) 566–571 for a discussion of the "Militant Madonna."
41. Charlotte Perkins Gilman, *Herland*, 111–112. See Frances Barkowski, *Feminist Utopias* (Lincoln: University of Nebraska Press, 1989), 23–48, for a comparison of Gilman's work with Monique Wittig's *Les Guérillères*.

Chapter 5

THE FEMALE
AS DIVINE

INTRODUCTION

Modern western culture boasts no real goddesses. Mary, the mother of Jesus, is venerated but as many claim not in the same way as her son. Both of the women in this chapter present feminine views of the Divine. Both Joanna Southcott and Anna Bonus Kingsford, natives of England, claimed to receive messages telepathically which offered solutions for the troubles of humankind. Joanna, a domestic worker, believed that God was speaking through her to the world. She would be the New Eve who would restore peace and prosperity to all. She interpreted all of the Bible through the lens of gender. Her following numbered as many as 100,000 and are known as the Southcottians today.

Kingsford was a medical doctor and a physician whose messages from the other realm revealed that the Divine was a duality, both male and female. She recognized that males had violated the rights women and animals. Their hostility developed because of their denial of the feminine side of God within themselves. She and Edward Maitland, her secretary and companion, created the Christian Theosophical Movement.

Central to the messages of both Southcott and Kingsford-Maitland was the Bible. Anna interpreted the Bible against the background of the history of religions using a mystical approach. Joanna allowed the Scriptures to flow only through her and created a symbolic or metaphorical interpretation that almost always centered on women.

JOANNA SOUTHCOTT (1750–1814)

Now, Joanna, look and see. . . .[1]
Many abroad have judged me an imposter. . . .

. . . [T]hey judged me a good woman, and that too much
learning had made me mad,
or deranged my senses, and I may add, made me a fool;
for I cannot be a good
woman, nor a sensible woman, if I can mock God,
and deceive men,
and trifle with eternity."[2]

Our eyes were so dazzled with the glorious prospect set
before us . . . we became like
the man taken out of the dark room . . . the light so
overpowering him that he could
not see . . . the idea of having one of the GODHEAD to
reign over us was
overwhelming, after so long tyrannized over by man,
under evil influence. . . .[3]

THE TIMES: A PROPHETESS AMONG MANY

J. F. C. Harrison and Brian Manning have skillfully created fascinating books which discuss the emergence of religious women in seventeenth-, eighteenth-, and nineteenth-century England.[4] Joanna Southcott was not alone. For many and diverse socio-political reasons, women began to emerge as leaders within such groups as the Quakers, Dissenters, Levellers, Methodists, Shakers, Swedenborgians, and others. They exercised their freedoms through boycotts, riots, marches, and by petitioning the government and criticizing the religious authorities. Some called them "fishwives," "scum," "oyster women," "Billingsgate wenches," "lusty lasses,"[5] and the "London Mob:"[6] "The unusual part played by women in petition and in politics, Leveller and non-Leveller, challenged generally accepted ideas about the place of women in seventeeth-century

English society. Women asserted that they had some political rights, not excluding the right to express their views and influence important decisions by means of petitions to parliament."[7]

Women began to fearlessly teach and preach in spite of being labeled witches and beaten within inches of their lives. Some of the women that crisscrossed the lands fulfilling the will of God in their lives were Mary Bateman, Mary Evans, Sarah Flaxmer, Ann Lee, and Widow Hughes. Other women who followed similar footsteps throughout Europe were Catherine Theot, Anna Maria van Schurman, and Elspeth Simpson (or Luckie Buchan) whose life overlapped Joanna Southcott's.[8]

ELSPETH SIMPSON (LUCKIE BUCHAN), 1738–1791

Elspeth Simpson was one of those women who had visions and challenged the religious establishment with her personal interpretations of female images in the Bible.[9] Unfortunately, she left no personal legacy of sermons or other materials which can be analyzed. Yet she is an important person to consider because she was one of many women who began to claim her right to interpretation of the Bible and her own revelations that she was indeed the long-awaited woman in the book of Revelation. Here is her story.

Elspeth was a Scottish woman born in "the parish of Fordyce, in Banffshire,"[10] who was orphaned at the age of three. Raised by strangers who belonged to the Scotch Episcopal Church, Elspeth could claim very little formal education.[11] After an adventurous youth, Elspeth chose a Mr. Buchan of Ayr to be her mate and father of her children. After moving to Banff, Mr. Buchan returned to Glasgow because of the failure of his pottery business. Elspeth remained and opened a school for small children. It was about this time in 1774 that she began to experience visions from God.[12] The visions absorbed her so much that she abandoned her responsibilities for her school and her children. In 1781 she returned to live with Mr. Buchan in Glasgow.

The Reverend Hugh White and many other interested people in Irvine began to form a group of followers who began to call Elspeth, "Friend Mother in the Lord," while to the profane she was only Luckie Buchan, the witch-wife who had cast her glamour over the weak-headed minister and other dupes."[13] Elspeth declared that she was the woman clothed with the sun in Revelation 12, and the Reverend Hugh White was her child. Later, she claimed that she was the Spirit of God.[14] Apparently she taught other doctrines which included the abrogation of all marriage vows and the raising of one's own child. For her creative interpretations of Scripture, her neighbors responded by rock throwing, beating, and running her out of town.[15] Naked, beaten, and bleeding she crept back to the Reverend White's, and he took her back to Mr. Buchan in Glasgow.

After regaining her strength in 1783, on advice of a follower, Elspeth went to Muthill, a superstitious town with a miraculous well, to begin her preaching and interpreting once again: "They might believe in holy wells and other forms of mild superstition, but there was something too uncanny about his strange prophetess from the South. They were especially doubtful about a woman teaching religion at all, and expressed a desire to hear rather what the college-bred Rev. High White might have to say on these things."[16]

In Muthill she attracted a sizable following but was soon compelled to leave the town, with her followers in tow.[17] Finally welcomed at New Cample Farm, the group of about sixty people settled into the barn and waited for their translation to heaven. When the translation did not take place, the Buchanites (as they were now called) were tormented by the nearby churches and constables.[18] After a failed attempt at prolonged fasting and incidents of economic insecurity, Friend Mother died in 1791 leaving her followers to carry on her beliefs.

BIOGRAPHY OF JOANNA SOUTHCOTT

Joanna was born into this legacy of women rebels adopting their methodologies and strategies later in life. She lived in England during a time of war, national unrest, state repression, and depression at the end of the eighteenth and beginning of the nineteenth century. Many prophets emerged from the working classes claiming to have been sent by God to heal political problems and social wounds. Some declared that it was the end of time. Not many were as successful or as accurate as Joanna: "Joanna's record of prognostication was impressive. She foretold the war with France, the poor harvests of 1794, 1795 and 1797, and the effects of the rain in 1799 and the sun in 1800 on the crops. She foretold the naval mutiny of 1797, and confounded Pomeroy by accurately predicting the death of the Bishop of Exeter."[19]

Joanna's life as a domestic servant and upholsterer in Devonshire lasted until she began to hear voices at the age of forty-two. She received prophesies first through her dead mother in 1792 and then through the Spirit of God. She wrote as a preface to her book on full assurance of the end of the times, "In this book I shall insert the manner of my mother's coming to me. . . ." and "the fulfillment of my Mother's words took place in . . ."[20] Her father claimed, "as the spirit of Elijah fell on Elisha, so hath the Spirit of thy mother fallen on thee."[21]

Investing her own money, she published a pamphlet in 1801 entitled *The Strange Effects of Faith* and continued with scores of other booklets, eventually totalling over 4,500 pages of published material.[22] Many of her interpretations were written in verse and dictated to secretaries. It is reported that Joanna's handwriting was almost impossible to read and her spelling so poor that it needed to be translated before it could be understood.

Her prophecies had a profound effect upon several Anglican clergy and working-class laity who began to support her writings. Soon she moved to Exeter and lived with loyal friends. Later her flock drew her to London to live with Jane Townley who with her maid, Ann Underwood, became her benefactress and secretary.[23]

Joanna was a prophetess who interpreted the Bible in such a way that it offered a future of hope and comfort to struggling men and women. George Turner, a follower, wrote these words many years after the death of Joanna: "Our eyes were so dazzled with the glorious prospect set before us . . . we became like the man taken out of the dark room . . . the light so overpowering him that he could not see . . . the idea of having one of the GODHEAD to reign over us was overwhelming, after so long tyrannized over by man, under evil influence. . . ."[24]

Joanna claimed to be the New Savior, the Woman clothed with the Sun, the New Eve found in the book of Revelation. She offered hope to thousands that personally felt the oppression from male aristocracy and tyranny.[25]

Joanna had no formal education in interpreting the Bible. Her musings were spirit-led and dictated: "[B]ut now, with the simple, the

Lord will deal simply, and I am but a simple woman, and was never brought up to high learning. . . ."[26] "But I never read any books, at all; but write by the Spirit as I am directed. I should not like to read any books to mix my senses with any works but those of the Spirit by whom I write."[27]

Organized religion seemed to play an important part in her life as a child but lost its appeal in her later years. Having only a brief experience with the Methodists, she rejected their tenets for a journey that soon created her own following: "My religion is that of the established church of England; but being of St. Paul's mind, to try all, prove all things, and to hold fast that which is good . . . I attended constantly my church, forenoons and afternoons, and received the sacrament; at the same time I also attended Mr. Wesley's preachers. . . ."[28] ". . . [B]ecause they made so great a profession of faith, their unbelief was a stumbling block to me."[29]

Her flock may have numbered as many as 100,000, while the Southcottians today boast only a few members.[30]

COMPETITION WITH RICHARD BROTHERS

In the midst of her meteoric rise, hints of a controversy with another millennial prophet, Richard Brothers, were intermingled within the poetic lines of her mystical prophecies. Apparently he challenged her call from God and claimed that she was taking money from her converts when she delivered her sealed prophecies.

In 1802, he published an attack on Southcott entitled *Dissertation on the Fall of Eve*.[31] Mr. Brothers preached doom and gloom and directed his hostile prophecies at monarchs such as George III of England.[32] Consequently he was imprisoned for several years and kept forcibly silent in an insane asylum.[33] During his imprisonment he used precise mathematical dimensions to predict and describe and draw the New Jerusalem. Joanna did not pay any attention to his accusations, drawings, or prophecies until he was about to gain his freedom.

From 1802 to 1809, Joanna's prophecies were written on paper and then enclosed by a seal with Joanna's signature or "seal," then given to followers that had made a profession of faith in her and her prophecies. The seal read: "The sealed of the Lord, the Elect and

Precious, Man's Redemption to Inherit the Tree of Life, to be made
Heirs of God and Joint Heirs with Jesus Christ."[34]

Seals were a way of marking the people similarly to those who were
sealed in the Book of Revelation. Some counted as many as 14,000
people who had received personal revelations from Joanna. Thousands of seals were stored in a trunk which would be opened at a
specified day at the end of time.

In about 1814, Joanna announced that she was to bear Shiloh (a
name associated with Mr. Brothers), who would be the new Messiah.
According to historians, she had a hysterical pregnancy, although
reportedly thirty medical physicians verified her condition.[35] Her
death came shortly after she was to give birth at the age of sixty-
four.[36]

VIEW OF THE BIBLE

Generally, Joanna's prophecies about future events were based upon
interpretations of biblical stories or phrases. To her, the Bible was a
book of mysteries that needed to be solved. It held the key to understanding all the solutions to problems and future events. For hundreds of years men had been trying to understand the Bible but they
had failed. Recognizing that theology represented a selectivity in
texts, Joanna accused males of ignoring important biblical texts.[37]
They were blind to the real meaning of passages, predictions, and
role models in the Bible. They needed to listen to a woman: "I believe
the Bible as it is revealed to me by the Spirit; but I cannot rely on the
judgment of any man; as the best of men differ so much in opinions
and judgment. On whom then shall I rely? The judgment of men
contradicts one the other. Therefore, I rely on the revelation given
unto me from the Spirit of the Lord."[38]

For her the Bible was inspired by God[39] and contained the actual
words of Jesus[40] that needed to be explained to people correctly.
Truths found in the Bible will ultimately be proved to be accurate at
the end of time when the earth passes away.

For earth, I say, must pass away,
To make my Bible true.[41]

The end will prove my Bible true.
I made the woman, at the first
To be your helpmate at the last.[42]

Then, as perfect God I must fulfill my word in the woman,
and complete the bliss in man; and she must be his helpmate
for good; as perfect man, I must bring the shadow to
the substance, to resemble man in every perfection I ordained
for him and designed for him.[43]

INTERPRETATIVE STRATEGY: GENDER BASED

A hundred years after the death of Joanna, a faithful follower by the name of Alice Seymour attempted to collect Southcott's writings and explain them. The following quote is attributed to Joanna: "Fear not ye women; fear not . . . My Mother; fear not, My Sister—I will be your Savior—I will be your Conqueror—I will tread the liar between My Feet; he shall feel the weight of my fury; he shall tremble and fall before ME."[44]

Joanna interpreted almost everything in the Bible through the lens of gender. Rejecting male opinion and interpretation, she launched prophesies that predicted that only through a woman would the earth be restored. Only through a woman would Adam's sin at the beginning of time be neutralized. Woman would be the perfect helpmate who would rescue all of humankind by vanquishing Satan. She would be the New Eve or the Bride. Men must seek out a woman and they must understand and mimic the strategies whereby women find answers to their questions and longings: "Men of wisdom must act like the Queen of Sheba to find out the wisdom of Solomon."[45]

In attempting to explain Joanna's prophecies and person, William Sharp in 1806 penned these words: "The reader must keep his attention fixed to the Fall which came through the Woman—the promise was made to the Woman—Christ was born of the Woman—and the Redemption from the Fall must come through the Woman at last, as the Fall came through her at the first. I am convinced that Joanna has for about twenty years, in various ways, been in preparation. . . ."[46]

William Roundell Wetherell quoted Joanna in 1803. He confirmed that Joanna taught that it was through a woman that all the problems of misunderstanding and hatred in the world would be solved: "The fullness of the Gentiles is come; and the Almighty has sent his Son in Spirit to a Woman, as predicted in Scripture, to perform the grand Work of reconciling all differences in Religion, and bringing the whole World under one Faith; to clear up every Mystery, and make the nations unite in Brotherly Love."[47]

He recognized the present prejudices exhibited by learned men: "Some worthy and pious Men of dignified Character have called it Blasphemy for any earthly Woman to assume the Name of the Bride, or Wife of the Lamb, though our Saviour himself, when upon Earth, said, whosoever did the will of his heavenly Father was his Mother, Sister and Etc. . . . and shall Man presume to dictate to his Maker what Instrument he shall chose?"[48]

TYPES AND SHADOWS OF THE FUTURE

For Joanna, biblical stories about women were only types, shadows, correspondences, allegories, or models of events in the future. Esther as well as other strong female characters in the Bible foreshadowed the coming of the New Eve. Someday a woman would cure the world and reign as the New Eve.[49]

Sometimes Joanna quoted the Bible as if to suggest that the literal meaning was the obvious one, but then at other times she interpreted the story in the Bible as it related to present-day events. Here is her own explanation of the methodology she used in interpreting the Bible: "Watch the Scriptures, weigh the whole together, draw the link; lengthen the chain, see, if one link will join with another—compare the whole together—see, if it adds link to link, chain to chain, like the dawning morning, higher and higher, brighter and brighter, to the perfect day: or like a flower in the bud, opening more and more until the full blown flower appears."[50]

According to Alice Seymour, "Joanna was sometimes commanded to pen her own thoughts, and then the Lord explained them by His Spirit. She was ordered to read the Bible through, and draw her own observations. She wrote Seven Books of the True Explanations of the Bible, as given to her by the Spirit. . . ."[51]

Alice warns the reader that "all the meaning of a text does not appear at the first perusal."[52] J. F. C. Harrison says, "Her writings are full of the imagery (mostly biblical) of brides, bridesmaids, bride-grooms, marriages, wedding feasts, wedding guests, as well as adul-tery, fornication, and sodomy."[53]

Barbara Taylor, a modern scholar, gives this assessment of her strat-egy: "[H]er language abounded in images of male villany and female defiance which aroused women to an anticipation of greater glory."[54]

JOEL'S PROPHECY

Here is an example of Southcott's reinterpretation of Joel 2:28 which prophesied that young women would prophesy and old men would dream dreams: "Many good men and women have had their eyes so fixed on the gathering at the day of Pentecost, that they have not seen that the prophecy was at that time only partially fulfilled, and that it was only a shadow of a yet greater fulfilment. The Spirit was not poured out upon all flesh, neither did the handmaids prophesy, and the young men see visions."[55]

THE FALL

The story of the Fall is central to Joanna's prophecy that she would be the New Eve who would vindicate all women and crush the powers of Satan. Here is a sample of her argumentation:

> To this I answer from the Fall. I took thy writings from thee to clear up every mystery; for know, I said the same hand that brought the knowl-edge of evil, should bring the knowledge of the good. Now if you take the same hand, without calling the woman the same hand, you must say it must be brought by Eve, to lay the foundation for another to claim and build thereon. So, I tell thee, the hand is alike; it cannot be changed to man; and perfectly so, I tell thee, as they hand began the writing, from My Spirit, so the hand of woman shall end. Then now discern what is meant by the same hand, it is not meant the hand of Eve, that plucked the evil, and brought the knowledge of the evil, shall bring the knowledge of the good; and yet, I tell thee, the foundation was as much laid by her, in speaking the truth, and casting her claim on the serpent, as the foundation of thy writings was first laid by thy

hand. And as men blame the foundation that was laid by thee, and thousands judge it foolishness what thou has penned, perfectly so, I tell thee, is the mystery of the Fall: they do not discern the promise; her first reasoning; and her second truth; neither do they discern the fault in Man; neither do they discern how soon the curse came on again from Noah, after the world was drowned, that he pronounced upon his son. These things were not discerned by men; therefore, the blame lied upon the woman, without discerning that Adam was as easy to fall, by the weakness of the woman, as she was by the subtilty of the serpent. But, see how the blame was cast. These things men do not discern, therefore they go on, as Adam began to cast the blame upon the woman; and My honour can never be cleared, for giving the woman for his helpmate, if I do not clear My honour, to fulfil My promise and make her for his good. . . .

Therefore I tell thee, all I mean by another hand of woman is, to finish what thou has begun; and to pen the words, that I shall deliver to thee and thou to them. . . .[56]

Or again, this poem which is found in *The Express*:

> Then see ye plain, ye sons of men,
> The way I've led all on.
> It was to Woman, not to Man,
> I in this power did come.[57]

> So Woman here in Love Appear
> You'll find my Love is strong
> To see you all from Adam's Fall.
> If Eve brought in the first,
> Of sorrow here that did appear
> Then I'll bring in the Last;
> For Joy shall come the same to Man;
> So now the WOMAN see!
> MY CHURCH upon HER it must stand,
> AS WOMAN joined with ME.[58]

REVELATION AND THE CREATION STORY

Here is a sampling of her rhythmic prophecies based upon interpretations of the Book of Revelation and the Creation story in Genesis:

The Woman and the Serpent's seed—
  I'll bring all to your view:
So let the Serpent's seed appear
  The Woman's seed shall come. . . .[59]

And Satan's kingdom fall.
The Woman, see, shall now be free—
  Then now behold the BONE
That lives so strong by faith in ME,
  With courage stands alone.
Can it be done by her weak hand?
  Then heavens must silent be,
To let a Woman so explain,
  And say she writes by ME . . .
  When I the BONE return,
You all will see the mystery,
  And tears of joy will come.[60]

CONCLUSION

According to J. F. C. Harrison, Joanna's doctrine of woman "was a form of feminism: for she sought to redress the balance of guilt brought by the original fall and make woman the 'perfect helpmate' of man."[61] But Joanna's contributions did more than restore the image of Eve; her unique feminist-matriarchal interpretation (or the doctrine of woman) lay in her unswerving belief in the goodness and strength of females. Similar to her male ("patriarchal") colleagues, she decided that she could interpret the Bible solely through the knowledge and experiences of a female. Why not—males had been doing it for hundreds of years and had they solved the problems of her country? Neither had they ushered in an age of peace and prosperity.

According to Joanna, whether or not the males in government or the religious hierarchies recognized it, it would be a female that would bring peace and solve the problems of the earth. The Spirit of God was present on earth in the form of a female. She was a mouthpiece for the Divine. Hope for the future was not found in armies, monarchs, or even in any other sect; it was found in the plain speech of a maidservant. According to Joanna, this truth confounded and would eventually save the world.

POSTSCRIPT

Ann Lee, a factory worker in England, believed it, but she also believed that *she* would be the One to usher in a new era of peace, prosperity, and equality. In 1774, she led a group of followers, who were eventually named The United Society of Believers in Christ's Second Appearing, the Shakers, to America to await the new age of peace, equality, and prosperity.

ANNA BONUS KINGSFORD (1846–1888)
AND
EDWARD MAITLAND (1824–1897)

---

*She is the Beginning of Wisdom
wherein God makes the heavens and the earth;
the substantial waters upon whose
face He, the Energising Will, moves at every fresh act
of creation, and the ark or
womb from which all creatures proceed. . . .
"For She is the spiritual substance which,
polarising interiorly, is—God; and coagulating exteriorly,
becomes—in the outermost—Matter.* [1]

*She is to him very "mother of the living," and without
her is no life. . . .
Thus is she mediator between man and God, to draw
them together to herself.* [2]

A COLLABORATION OF MYSTICAL LOVE

After traveling around the world for most of his life, Edward Maitland found a "twin-soul" in Anna Bonus Kingsford in his own country, England. In 1874, when he finally spoke with Anna, he was fifty and she was twenty-eight years old. Instantly they knew that their views of life and religion were similar. Edward had a history within Anglicanism but Anna, believing it to be the only true church, became a Roman Catholic in 1870. In 1874 she left her husband in order to study medicine in Paris, France, because women were not admitted to the universities in England. In France she continued her advocacy of woman's rights "with a special emphasis on womanly attributes."[3] After receiving her degree she practiced medicine in London.[4]

Together Kingsford and Maitland began a life-long association that would carry them to Switzerland, France, Italy, and back to London again.[5] Among the many publications which they created together, they produced *The Perfect Way*,[6] a very popular, esoteric or mystical interpretation of Christianity. In 1882 the authors attempted to explain their book in these terms:

"The Perfect Way" seeks to consolidate truth in one complete whole, and by systematising religion to demonstrate its Catholicity. It seeks to make peace between Science and Faith; to marry the Intellect with the Intuition; to bring together East and West, and to unite Buddhist philosophy with Christian love, by demonstrating that the basis of religion is not historical, but spiritual—not physical, but psychic—not local and temporal, but universal and eternal.[7]

Although Kingsford and Maitland lectured, researched, composed, traveled, and lived together, they claimed that their relationship was purely spiritual. He would edit and rearrange material that she would receive mystically. In spite of many debilitating illnesses, including asthma, tuberculosis, and possibly psychological disorders, Maitland attended to Kingsford until the day she died. This relationship caused some to gossip because Anna was legally married to an Anglican clergyman, the Reverend Algernon G. Kingsford, to whom she had bore one child. Sources suggest that the marriage was in name only and both parties enjoyed their freedoms apart from one another.

Kingsford and Maitland began lectures in what might be termed "Theosophy" in London in 1881 in a rented room, at No. 11 Chapel Street in Park Lane.[8] After meeting the members of the British Theosophical Society or the London Lodge of the Theosophical Society in 1883, Anna was offered the presidency and Maitland, the vice presidency of that organization. Their affiliation did not last long because both Anna and Edward disagreed with the Lodge's interpretation and application of Buddhism. Anna and Edward taught "Christian" theosophy which was too narrow for the British group.[9] Soon they formed the Hermetic Society and in 1884 Maitland became president of the Esoteric Christian Union.

Anna collaborated on other projects with Maitland including *Keys of the Creeds* (1875). In addition, she wrote a book of verse, a book on health and beauty, and several works of fiction before her death in 1888 at forty-two. After her death, Maitland spent most of his energy writing his remembrances of his "twin soul" in a biography entitled *Anna Kingsford; her life, letters, diary* (1896). He also published two of her books; *Dreams and Dream Stories* (1888) and *Clothed with the Sun* (1889). Maitland died, alone, in 1897 at the age of seventy-three.

THE PROBLEM

Kingsford and Maitland thought that organized Christian religion had become too materialistic and power hungry. Its leaders were perverted. They had suppressed the feminine side of God and even worse, they voiced their bitterness against women. "For, in her intuition of Spirit, they recognise their chief enemy."[10] Therefore, "orthodox Christianity" was defective.[11] The real reason that the entire world had not been regenerated was that the church only appealed to the mind.[12] "Christianity has failed, that is, not because it was false, but because it has been falsified." Here are a few of their views of the problem.

Biblical exegesis was bankrupt:

> Critical analysis—that function of the mind which, in its nature destructive, is, . . . has laid an unsparing axe to the forest of ancient tradition. The science of Biblical exegesis had made it obvious to every percipient mind that sacred books, so far from being infallible records of actual events, abound with inaccuracies, contradictions, and interpolations; that sacred persons, if they existed all, had histories differing widely from those narrated of them. . . .[13]

The feminine side of God had been ignored and had bankrupted everyone:

To this divorce between the elements of masculine and feminine of man's intellectual system, is due the prevailing unbelief. For, converted thereby into superstition, religion has been rendered ridculous; and instead of being exhibited as the Supreme Reason, God has been depicted as the Supreme Unreason. Against religion, as thus presented, mankind has done well to revolt. To have remained subject, had been intellectual suicide. Wherefore the last person entitled to reproach the word for its want of faith, is the Priest; since it is his degradation of the character of God that has ministered to unbelief. Suppressing the "woman," who is the intuition, by putting themselves in her place, the priests have suppressed also the man, who is the intellect.[14]

Males made hasty decisions and shed and ate the blood of animals: "They are the authors, too, of those hasty impulses by yielding to which people do in a moment mischief which a life-time cannot efface or repair."[15]

VIEW OF SCRIPTURE

For Anna and Edward in *The Perfect Way*, the Christian Bible contained the primary Scriptures, the Word of God.[16] Yet, they admitted, that God had many avenues whereby mystical disclosures were made to humans.[17] The knowledge that is gained from the Bible mirrors the soul. In *The Credo of Christendom*, Anna revealed an illumination she received concerning the Scriptures: "I am shewn that there is but little of real value in the Scriptures. They are a mass of clay, comparatively modern, with here and there a bit of gold."[18] And while some might criticize their view for being outside the mainstream of Christian interpretation, the authors actually believed that they had discovered the true interpretation and purpose of the Bible. Their unique view of the Bible was foundational to all of their beliefs:

Now, all Scripture given by inspiration of God is mystical; and, in its esoteric sense, deals not with material things, but with spiritual realities, the mystic intention of the things named being alone implied, and by no means the things themselves. And this rule holds good alike of those two divisions of Scripture which are called respectively the Old and New Testament."[19]

> For that object is—as was the object of all sacred mysteries, whether of
> our Bible or other—to enable man anew so to develop the Soul, or
> Essential Woman, within him, as to become, through Her, a perfect
> reflection of the universal Soul, and made, therefore, in what, mysti-
> cally, is called the image of God.[20]

Kingsford and Maitland argued that only the mystical interpretation is real and meaningful. The accepted historical-critical approach
to the Bible yielded empty words with empty traditions. The priests
who interpreted the Bible had corrupted its meaning. Yet at times
when Anna and Edward were attempting to disprove an accepted view
of Scripture, they actually employed historical-critical reasoning and
scholarship themselves. For example, they disputed the Mosaic authorship of the Pentateuch and claimed that these books were written
by greedy priests who trampled their better half, woman.[21] They
claimed that many if not all of the stories in the Old Testament
originated in Egypt and were finally written down by Ezra or Esdras.[22]
Even today, the very Bible that is read by most people was corrupted by
the Pharisees by their use of alteration and interpolation.[23]

The Gospels of the New Testament are parables[24] and must be
understood as "spiritual significations."[25] Matthew represented the
lower and physical plane while Mark appealed to the rational. Luke
began the ascent of the soul and intuition, and the crowning Gospel
is John, "being in the highest degree interior, mystic, and spiritual."[26]

INTERPRETATIVE STRATEGY

As stated earlier, Kingsford and Maitland used what they term to be a
"mystical" interpretation of the Bible.[27] But their conclusions were
informed by extensive research in the history of religions. They often
referred to Greek and Egyptian mythology, Plato, Aristotle, Philo,
readings from the early church writers, the Koran,[28] Christian and
Jewish Apocryphal writings, Hermetic texts, the "Kabbala," as well as
traditions about the Buddha.[29]

Throughout their work, they used inclusive language and established an interpretation of the Divine which was androgynous. They
knew that the story of Eve had been used to demean women into a

second-class existence. They sought to redeem the Adam and Eve myth by pointing to a woman who would restore life to its highest order.

Their research and interpretations of the Bible were used to create a feminist critique of Christianity, both Protestant and Catholic. In a brief litany against the major founders and movers of Christianity, Maitland and Kingsford declared that all of them had denegrated woman: Luther did not better the condition of woman; Calvin always favored the male over the female. Even general Protestantism "finds in its definition of the Substance of Existence, place only for the masculine element."[30]

EVE AND ADAM

The Perfect Way concerns itself mainly with interpreting the stories of the Creation and the Fall in Genesis 1–2. The interpersonal relationship of Adam and Eve was the allegory through which Kingsford and Maitland developed their views about humans who are in search of God. Eve and her power over Adam was always central to the discussion. This parable or allegory was interpreted in four distinct ways or "significations:" Physical and Social; Rational and Philosophical; Psychic and Personal (Ethical); Spiritual and Creative (Cosmic).[31]

At times their interpretation changed little from the accepted tradition but on other occasions the stories became vehicles to vent their hostility toward organized Christianity and at the same time grounded their belief in vegetarianism. Here is an example of hyperbole: "If it were possible for this ruined and disobedient Adam to 'eat and live for ever,' that eternal life would necessarily be the eternal hell of the Calvinists. . . ."[32]

In the physical and social interpretation, the symbol of Eve represented the fall of the church.[33] And this Eve, a She, disobeyed the Divine Will and betrayed the world. Evidence of this "fallen state" is the shedding of blood and eating the flesh of animals.[34]

In the rational and philosophical reading, the story became a symbol for the decline of (real) religion. Adam and Eve became idolaters, i.e., they chose "the tendency toward matter and sense."[35] This may mean that they chose the material world and its stimuli over the mystical one in which they were living.

The psychic and personal interpretation view asserted that Eve represents superstition and a loss of real faith by people who belonged to the church of this world:[36] "Hence the fact that she is naked and empty must be studiously concealed, and all approach forbidden, that no one not concerned to keep the secret may spy upon her darkened shrine."[37]

Finally in the Edenic allegory, the spiritual and cosmic interpretation drew upon allusions to Greek and Egyptian myths that place woman in the center of sacred space. Eve, although she failed, in the end she will bruise the head of the serpent and become the "Woman-Messias:" "She it is who, by Her Intuition of God, bruises the head of the Serpent of Matter, and Her sons they are who get the victory over him."[38] "And the curse will be removed, Paradise regained, and the second Sabbath of the Golden Age achieved, only when this "woman" is again invested with her rightful supremacy."[39]

While Eve is charged with the cause of the fall, she was never viewed negatively. The very fact that Adam followed her dictates so quickly demonstrated her own inherent decision-making powers over those of males.

Maitland concluded by suggesting that the best way to interpret Genesis 1–2 is by correlating it with the book of Revelation. Revelation reveals the doctrine of the Woman, suppressed by the priesthoods of the world and revealed as the "crowning recognition as the foundation of that true Christianity."[40]

The Fall is essentially a story about sin. Woman instigated Adam and "together they become sensual and debased."[41] Yet there is hope: "So, She who has been the cause of the Fall, shall be the means also of redemption."[42] The story of the woman clothed with the sun and the bride become metaphors for the surviving soul and redeemers of the world.[43] The future hope for all the world is in the hands of a woman.

> Put away Blood from Among you!
> Destroy your Idols!
> Restore your Queen![44]

> That the time of the rising of this Celestial Virgin and
> the rehabilitation of truth by the Woman-Messias of the
> Interpretation is near at hand. . . .[45]

PAULINE PERVERSION

Maitland and Kingsford did not worship the great Christian missionary, Paul. Quoting Pauline biblical texts referring to women, the authors suggested that he "aggravated and reinforced—to Christianity, the traditional contempt of his race for woman:"[46] "Thus enforced, the doctrine of the subjection of the woman became accepted as an integral part of the Christian system, constituting in it an element of inevitable self-destruction."[47]

They blame Paul's conclusions about woman on a perverted interpretation of the Fall of Adam and Eve which he obtained from the Talmud. This misconception about woman was also taught by the fathers or rather "step-fathers" of the church.[48]

[F]or the most part [they] vied with each other in their depreciation of woman; and denouncing her with every vile epithet, held it a degradation for a saint to touch even his own aged mother with the hand in order to sustain her feeble days. And the Church, falling under a domination exclusively sacerdotal, while doctrinally it exalted womanhood to a level beside, though not to its place in, the Godhead, practically substituted priestly exclusiveness for Christian comprehension. For it declared woman unworthy, through inherent impurity, even to set foot within the sactuaries of its temples. . . .[49]

DUALITY, ANDROGYNY, AND THE PERSON OF GOD

In the process of discussing their interpretations the authors used nonsexist and inclusive language. They asserted that there was a duality within every human being. Part of that duality involved the soul or "She."[50] Males may have intellect but it is the Mother who has wisdom. Here is a proposed prayer to be used at the Eucharist:

May this holy Body and Blood, Substance and Spirit, Divine Mother and Father, inseparable Duality in Unity, given for all creatures, broken and shed, and making oblation for the world, be everywhere known, adored, and venerated! May we, by means of that Blood, which is the Love of God and Spirit of Life, be redeemed, indrawn, and transmuted into the Body which is Pure Substance, immaculate and every virgin, express Image of the Person of God![51]

Not only did they suggest that woman or the feminine is part and parcel of the Godhead, they hinted that God or the essential foundation of God within the Scriptures is female: "She is the Beginning or Wisdom wherein God makes the heavens and the earth; the substantial waters upon whose face He, the Energising Will, moves at every fresh act of creation, and the ark or womb from which all creatures proceed. . . . For She is the spiritual substance which, polarising interiorly, is—God; and coagulating exteriorly, becomes—in the outermost—Matter."[52]

Males are so blind that they cannot recognize that it is woman who supports and makes them into the person that they have become: "Doing this with all his heart, he finds that She makes him, in the highest sense, Man."[53]

Maitland and Kingsford, as their arguments progress, suggested that a "She" may be the link between humanity and divinity.

> . . . [T]hat whereby the man attains to manhood is woman. It is his power to recognise, appreciate, and appropriate her, that stamps him physically, man. [She] . . . who, gathering him round herself as center, redeems him and makes him into a system of capable self-perpetuation, supplementing and complementing meanwhile his masculine qualities, as will, force, and intellect, with her feminine qualities, as endurance, love, and intuition.[54]

> She is to him very "mother of the living," and without her is no life. . . . Thus is she mediator between man and God, to draw them together to herself.[55]

Even Jesus is a duality containing both the male and the female within him: "And the vision of Deity under a definite form, dual and human—or androgynous, though not as ordinarily apprehended—has been univeral and persistent from the beginning; . . ."[56]

In the end it is God the Mother and the Father who rules and generates the universe: "For, whenever and whenever creation—or manifestation by generation—occurs, God the Father co-operates with God the Mother—as Force, moving in Substance—and produces the Utterance, Word, Logos, or Adonai—at once God and the Expression of God."[57]

Humans have the ability to be made in the image of God. But first they must embrace their own male-female duality: "And hence it is also, that, in order to be made in the image of God, the individual must comprise within himself the qualities masculine and feminine of existence, and be, spiritually, both man and woman."[58]

CONCLUSIONS AND OBSERVATIONS

While Kingsford and Maitland's mystical interpretations of the Bible often seem contrived, they reveal an understanding and concern for the problems within traditional Christianity. They recognized the alienated state of many. This alienation was evidenced in the hostile relationship between males and females as well as how humans viewed animals and other humans as prey. The authors longed for life on a higher plane that was not governed by animal appetites, that is, human emotions. (Perhaps they had achieved this in their own lives?) This life can only be achieved by recognizing the woman in every person. Discovery of the essential mother or female, or Eve, or the bride, within one's self could be the spark that could change life forever.

Kingsford and Maitland are included in this study because they were quoted so often by nineteenth-century women such as Elizabeth Cady Stanton and Matilda Joslyn Gage. No one could possibly estimate the influence they had on the women's rights movements in England and the United States.[59] No one knows how many other people knew their work and quoted them in the cause for equality.

Notes

JOANNA SOUTHCOTT

1. Joanna Southcott, *The Full Assurance that the Kingdom of Christ is at Hand from the Signs of the Times* ([London]: S. Rouseau, [1806]), 49.
2. Joanna Southcott, *Letters &c.* (London: E. Spragg, [1801]), 4.
3. Joanna Southcott, *Letters &c.* (London: E. Spragg, [1801]), 3. J.F.C. Harrison, *The Second Coming, Popular Millenarianism 1780–1850* (New Jersey: Rutgers University Press, 1979), 121.
4. J.F.C. Harrison, *The Second Coming, Popular Millenarianism 1780–1850* (New Jersey: Rutgers University Press, 1979), 24–134; Brian Manning, *Politics, Religion and the English Civil War* (New York: St. Martin's Press, 1973), 179–224; 255–259. See

also James K. Hopkins, *A Woman to Deliver Her People: Joanna Southcott and English Millenarianism in an Era of Revolution* (Austin: University of Texas Press, 1982) and Clarke Garrett, *Respectable Folly: Millenarianism and the French Revolution in France and England* (Baltimore: John Hopkins University Press, 1975), 210–229.

5. Brian Manning, *Politics, Religion and the English Civil War*, 180, 181, 200.
6. Barbara Taylor, "The Woman-Power: Religious Heresy and Feminism in Early English socialism," Susan Lipshitz, ed., *Tearing the Veil: Essays on Feminism* (London: Routledge and Kegan Paul, 1978), 119–144.
7. Brian Manning, *Politics, Religion and the English Civil War*, 209.
8. J.F.C. Harrison, *The Second Coming*, 8.
9. John Cameron, *History of the Buchanite Delusion: 1783–1846*, (Kilmarnock: R. G. Mann, 1904).
10. Ibid., 2.
11. Ibid., 3.
12. Ibid., 5.
13. Ibid., 16.
14. Ibid., 67.
15. Ibid., 18–19.
16. Ibid., 26.
17. Ibid., 31.
18. Ibid., 59.
19. J.F.C. Harrison, *The Second Coming*, 104.
20. Joanna Southcott, *The Full Assurance*, 1.
21. Joanna Southcott, *Letters &c.*, 14.
22. Joanna Southcott, *The Strange Effects of Faith* (London: 1802).
23. J.F.C. Harrison, *The Second Coming*, 89, 92.
24. J.F.C. Harrison, *The Second Coming*, 121. Found also in Samuel Jowett, *To the Believers of Joanna Southcott's Visitation* (Leeds: 1844), 7.
25. Barbara Taylor, "The Woman-Power. Religious heresy and Feminism in Early English socialism," Susan Lipshitz, Editor. *Tearing the Veil: Essays on Feminism* (London: Routledge and Kegan Paul, 1978), 120.
26. Joanna Southcott, *Letters &c.*, 9.
27. Joanna Southcott, *Letters &c.*, 11.
28. J.F.C. Harrison, *The Second Coming*, 87 and Joanna Southcott, *The Strange Effects of Faith* (London: 1802), 84.
29. Joanna Southcott, *The Full Assurance*, 11–12.
30. Jennifer S. Uglow, ed., *The International Dictionary of Women's Biography* (New York: Continuum, 1982), 438.
31. Richard Brothers, *A letter to His Majesty, and One to her Majesty. Also a Poem, with a Dissertation on the Fall of Eve and an Address to Five Eminent Councillors* (London, 1802).
32. G. R. Balleine, *Past Finding Out: The Tragic Story of Joanna Southcott and Her Successors* (New York: The Macmillan Company, 1956), 32.
33. Ibid., 35.
34. Ibid., 41.
35. Ibid., 61.

36. Anne Crawford, ed., *The Europa Biographical Dictionary of British Women* (Detroit: Gale Research Company, 1983), 374.

37. Alice Seymour, *The Express containing The Life and Divine Writings of Joanna Southcott* (London: SPCK, 1956), 1:37.

38. Joanna Southcott, *The Second Book of Visions* (London: E. Spragg, 1803), 65.

39. Ibid., 65.

40. Joanna Southcott, *The Full Assurance*, 33.

41. Ibid., 36.

42. [Joanna Southcott], *The Second Book of Visions*, 50.

43. Joanna Southcott, *The Full Assurance*, 42.

44. Alice Seymour, *The Express*, 1:52.

45. Joanna Southcott, *Letters &c.*, 6.

46. William Sharp, *An Answer to the World* (London: Rousseau, 1806), 8.

47. William Roundell Wetherell, *A Testimony of Joanna Southcott, The Prophetess: Sent by the Lord, To Warn the People of His Coming* (London: S. Rousseau, 1803), 10.

48. Ibid., 11.

49. Joanna Southcott, *The Full Assurance*, 60, 31,

50. Joanna Southcott, *The Second Book of Visions*, 55–56.

51. Alice Seymour, *The Express*, 1:18.

52. Ibid., 1:32.

53. J.F.C. Harrison, *The Second Coming*, 107.

54. Barbara Taylor, "The Woman-Power: Religious Heresy and Feminism in Early English Socialism," Susan Lipshitz, ed., *Tearing the Veil: Essays on Feminism* (London: Routledge and Kegan Paul, 1978), 120.

55. Alice Seymour, *The Express*, 1:32.

56. Ibid., 1:30–31.

57. Alice Seymour, *The Express*, 65 and Barbara Taylor, "The Woman-Power: Religious Heresy and Feminism in Early English Socialism," Susan Lipshitz, ed., *Tearing the Veil: Essays on Feminism* (London: Routledge and Kegan Paul, 1978), 121.

58. Ibid., 1:67.

59. Joanna Southcott, *The Full Assurance*, 55.

60. Joanna Southcott, *The Full Assurance* Ibid., 55–56.

61. J.F.C. Harrison, *The Second Coming*, 109.

KINGSFORD AND MAITLAND

1. Anna Bonus Kingsford and Edward Maitland, *The Perfect Way or, the Finding of Christ* (London: John M. Watkins, 1923), 57.

2. Ibid., 183.

3. Leslie A. Shepard, ed., *Encyclopedia of Occultism and Parapsychology*. 3 vols. (Detroit: Gale Research Company, 1984), 2:724–725.

4. Anne Crawford, ed., *The Europa Biographical Dictionary of British Women* (Detroit: Gale Research Company, 1983), 242.

5. Edward Maitland, *Anna Kingsford: Her Life Letters Diary and Work*. 2 vols. (London: George Redway, 1896), 2:73–116.

6. Anna Bonus Kingsford and Edward Maitland, *The Perfect Way.*
7. Edward Maitland, *Anna Kingsford,* 2:77.
8. Ibid., xxxix.
9. Ibid., xxv.
10. Ibid., 78.
11. Ibid., ix.
12. Ibid., xi.
13. Ibid., 26.
14. Ibid., 11.
15. Ibid., 79.
16. Ibid., 177.
17. Ibid., v, 62, 63.
18. Ibid., 88.
19. Ibid., 179.
20. Ibid., 61.
21. Ibid., 97.
22. Ibid., 152.
23. Ibid.
24. Ibid., 230.
25. Ibid., 225.
26. Ibid., 230–231.
27. Ibid., 285.
28. Ibid., 279, 281,
29. Ibid., 251, 165.
30. Ibid., 280.
31. Ibid., 153–170.
32. Ibid., 159.
33. Ibid., 156.
34. Ibid., 161.
35. Ibid., 162.
36. Ibid., 163.
37. Ibid., 165.
38. Ibid., 60.
39. Ibid., 156.
40. Ibid., 187.
41. Ibid., 188.
42. Ibid., 189.
43. Ibid., 192–194.
44. Ibid., 175.
45. Ibid., 170.
46. Ibid., 273.
47. Ibid., 275.
48. Ibid., 279.
49. Ibid., 280.
50. Ibid., 15.
51. Ibid., 117.
52. Ibid., 57.

53. Ibid.
54. Ibid., 182.
55. Ibid., 183.
56. Ibid., 261.
57. Ibid., 293.
58. Ibid., 262.
59. See C. Despard, *Theosophy and the Woman's Movement* (London: Theosophical Publishing House, 1913) and Bill Quinn, "The Feminine Principal," *American Theosophist* 64(1976): 102.

Chapter 6

AFRICAN AMERICAN
READING

How long shall the fair daughters of Africa
be compelled to bury their
minds and talents beneath a load of iron pots and kettles?[1]

Princes shall come out of Egypt;
Ethiopia shall soon stretch her hands unto God . . .
Oh God, thou art terrible out of thy holy places,
the God of Israel is he that giveth strength and power unto his people.

PSALM 68: 31, 35 *KJV*

O woman, woman! Upon you I call; for upon your exertions
almost entirely depends whether the rising generation
shall be any thing more than we have been or not.[2]

INTRODUCTION: THE HISTORICAL SITUATION OF
RELIGIOUS BLACK WOMEN

Book after book about African American women from the seventeenth century onward details the injustices that black women encountered from the white socio-political structures and from the black males within their own churches.[3] As early as 1641, black women were baptized as Christians but, "Black conversion to Christianity in North American Colonies was token and generally without positive impact upon white attitudes toward Africans."[4] Even in the twentieth century the ordination of black females to the ministry is a controversial subject. Jacquelyn Grant suggests that black males "monopolized the ministry as a profession. . . . The black church fathers were unable

200

to see the injustices of their own practices, even when they paralleled the injustices of the white church against which they rebelled."[5]

Searching for and discovering African American or black women writers who employed the Bible as the primary evidence for arguing for the equality of women has not been an easy task. The pressures of society on black women are and were enormous. If she was a slave then her future lay in the hands of her master. If she was a free woman, she was expected to be the primary person attending to household duties. Yet economics prohibited her from becoming the ideal domestic "woman." Her husband often was paid low wages and in order to supplement his pay, she would work in some domestic capacity outside her own home. There was very little time for education, reading, or writing. Free black women often lived on the edge of economic disaster and thoughts of the ministry were out of the question.

Many black women were deeply religious, having heard Bible stories throughout their lives, and committed to achieving equality for themselves and their peers. Their ideals of equality were rooted in their own personal experience and religious convictions. Their writings rarely offer sections which deal with the equality of women from a biblical perspective. Perhaps their assumptions about the nature of equality needed no written proofs.

Some of these African American women were preachers. In 1836, Jarena Lee published an account of her life, ministry, and search for ordination which she never obtained: "I now told him that the Lord had revealed it to me, that I must preach the gospel. . . . He then replied, . . . But as to women preaching, he said that our Discipline knew nothing at all about it—that it did not call for women preachers."[6]

And while she claimed equality for herself and others because Christ's death on the cross was for both men and women, and the call of God upon her life, she did not leave an extensive legacy of treatises aimed at proving the equality of women. This is also true of Mary Church Terrell[7] and Amanda Berry Smith. Amanda's autobiography details an amazing life of service but does not make extensive use of the Bible on the issues of equality.[8]

Sojourner Truth's wonderfully witty comments proving that women were indeed physically stronger and perhaps superior to men were rooted in a relationship with Jesus, her God. Sojourner, a slave who had won freedom, an itinerate preacher and teacher, did not need the Bible to prove equality; she had lived it.[9]

Anna Julia Hayword Cooper wrote about the need for education for black women in the South in 1892. While criticizing the church for its corruptions and oppression of the poor and women, she tenaciously held on to the view that the basis of true liberation is found in the Gospels. This is her brief statement of the importance of Scripture and the role of women in society:

> The idea of the radical amelioration of womankind, reverence for woman as woman regardless of rank, wealth, or culture, was to come from that rich and bounteous fountain from which flow all our liberal and universal ideas—the Gospel of Jesus Christ.[10]

> [T]hroughout his life and in his death he has given to man a rule and a guide for the estimation of woman as an equal, as a helper, and a friend, . . .[11]

MARIA W. MILLER STEWART (1803–1879)

BIOGRAPHY

> I expect to be hated of all men,
> and persecuted even unto death,
> for righteousness and truth's sake.[12]

A free black living in Boston in the early part of the nineteenth century, Stewart, in spite of all of the cultural pressures against women addressing the public, spoke out against the injustices of slavery and the abuse of women. Her sometimes militant voice challenged listeners to change their ethics and lifestyles in order to usher in an age of equality for all people. She believed that it would be the people of Ethiopia who would someday rule the world.

Independent biographical information on Stewart is sketchy. Published with her *Meditations* and in a collection of her works entitled *Productions,* are short, personal biographies of about three pages.[13] Born a free black in Hartford, and orphaned when she was five years old, she became the bond servant of a minister for whom she worked until she was fifteen. During that time she studied the Bible but was prevented from pursuing any type of public education. There is some evidence to suggest that in her youth, she was almost illiterate.

In 1826 she married James W. Stewart, a prosperous ship's outfitter, who died mysteriously within three years. Much of his estate was stolen, according to Louise Hatton, by unscrupulous businessmen. Stewart was left without her inheritance and penniless.[14] She was befriended by David Walker, a independent-thinking free black who in 1829, "denounced American slavery as the most vicious form of bondage known to history."[15] His book *Walker's Appeal*, resulted in a bounty being placed on his head by southern slaveholders. Within the year he was dead from the same disease as her husband (possibly poison).[16]

Stewart experienced firsthand what the violent white political system could do to those it controlled. During the 1830s, she experienced some type of conversion and began to write and publish her thoughts. She was determined to speak out against the injustices of her time, no matter what the cost to her personally: "The spirit of God came before me and I spake before many . . . reflecting on what I had said, I felt ashamed . . . And something said within my breast, 'press forward, I will be with thee.' And my heart made this reply, 'Lord, if thou wilt be with me, then I will speak for thee as long as I live."[17]

Stewart was invited to speak at several civic organizations after publishing three of her speeches in the *Liberator*, a chronicle of the antislavery movement. They included the Afric-American Female Intelligence Society and African Masonic Hall in Boston. Subsequently, she was harassed for her views, even by her friends, and left the city of Boston to lead a life of obscurity for almost fifty years.

During this time of obscurity she became a teacher in New York and joined a literary society. Moving to Baltimore, where she again taught, she ended up working as a matron in the Freedman's Hospital in Washington. Having learned that she was entitled to a navy pension from her late husband, she reunited with Lloyd Garrison who had been one of the publishers of the *Liberator*. In 1879, she reissued her speeches and meditations. No one has discovered a journal or other works written during the fifty year period of obscurity. That she republished her earlier thoughts suggests that Stewart maintained her radical views for her entire life.

VIEW OF SCRIPTURE

Stewart embraced the Bible as the word of God. Its words and stories filled her life and her speeches: "During the years of childhood and youth, it was the book I most studied. . . ."[18] She felt as if her words came directly from God. "Again; why the Almighty hath imparted unto me the power of speaking thus, I cannot tell."[19] In many of her writings, she quotes or summarizes the Bible as if its words were her own.

> . . . I believe, that for wise and holy purposes, best known to himself, he hath unloosed my tongue and put his word into my mouth, in order to confound and put all those to shame that have rose up against me. For he hath clothed my face with steel, and lined my forehead with brass. He hath put his testimony within me, and engraven his seal on my forehead. And with these weapons I have indeed set the fiends of earth and hell at defiance.[20]

She casts herself in the image of a redeemer or a prophet remembering that God had raised up prophets in times past and promised that he could do it again.[21]

THE PROBLEM: WHITE TYRANNY OVER BLACKS

Stewart's assessment of the problems in society targeted both the white establishment and the black culture itself. The basis of the problem was sin. Slavery was wrong.[22] Americans had abused blacks and had treated them like animals and considered them to be an inferior race.[23] The hard labor required of them deadened the mind. People were prejudiced and based their opinions about others on the color of their skin rather than on their intellect.[24] White women took advantage of black women in order to make their lives easier.[25]

> We have been imposed upon, insulted and derided on every side; and now, if we complain, it is considered as the height of impertinence. We have suffered ourselves to be considered as dastards, cowards, mean, fainthearted wretches; and on this account, . . . many despise us, and would gladly spurn us from their presence.[26]

Most of our color have dragged out a miserable existence of servitude from the cradle to the grave. And what literary acquirements can be made, or useful knowledge derived, from either maps, books, charts, by those who continually drudge from Monday morning until Sunday noon? O, ye fairer sisters, whose hands are never soiled, whose nerves and muscles are never strained, go learn by experience![27]

BLACK APATHY

Yet the problems confronting African Americans may have been, in part, caused by their own lack of discipline, pride in themselves, and rampant immorality (sin).[28] They did not seek to obtain an education which would help them to change their lives, and perhaps create a few heroes among them.

> I would ask, is it blindness of mind, or stupidity of soul, or the want of education, that has caused our men who are 60 or 70 years of age, never to let their voices be heard, nor their hands be raised in behalf of their color? . . . Have the sons of Africa no souls? feel they no ambitious desires? shall the chains of ignorance forever confine them? . . . But where is the man that has distinguished himself in these modern days by acting wholly in the defence of African rights and liberty? There was one, although he sleeps, his memory lives.[29]

Even those African Americans who had become educated, who had become ministers of the Gospel, were "blind leaders of the blind."[30] Blacks could be their own worst enemy, said Stewart. They often failed to respect and help each other. They had no vision of the future.

> It appears to me that there are no people under the heavens so unkind and so unfeeling towards their own, as are the descendants of fallen Africa. I have been something of a traveller in my day, and the general cry among the people is, 'Our own color are our greatest opposers;' and even the whites say that we are greater enemies toward each other, than they are toward us.[31]

> And why is it, my friends, that we are despised above all the nations upon the earth? Is it merely because our skins are tinged with a sable hue? No, nor will I ever believe that it is. What then is it? Oh, it is

because that we and our fathers have dealt treacherously with one another, and because many of us now possess that envious and malicious disposition, that we had rather die than see each other rise an inch above a beggar. No gentle methods are used to promote love among us, but much is done to destroy it.[32]

Blacks failed to see that they could take their meager earnings and build a business or an independent life for themselves. They wasted away their wages, again, never thinking of the future: "We have spent more than enough for nonsense, to do what building we should want."[33]

Yet at a speech given at Franklin Hall, she took issue with the perceptions of laziness among African-Americans promulgated by the white establishment.

I observed a piece in the *Liberator* a few months since, stating that the colonizationists had published a work respecting us, asserting that we were lazy and idle. I confute them on that point. Take us generally as a people, we are neither lazy nor idle; and considering how little we have to excite or stimulate us, I am almost astonished that there are so many industrious and ambitious ones to be found; although I acknowledge, with extreme sorrow, that there are some who never were and never will be serviceable to society. And have you not a similar class among yourselves?[34]

Stewart offered solutions to these problems by first pointing to the great power and influence of women in their culture and then to the necessity of self-sacrifice which may result in the loss of lives.

INTERPRETATIVE STRATEGY

Steeped in the verses and traditions of the Bible, Stewart quoted the Bible as if the words came from her own lips. She viewed herself in the line of the ancient prophets. She interpolated, restated, and summarized passages so that it was often difficult to trace their origins. Richardson suggests that her favorite books were Jeremiah and Lamentations.[35] In Jeremiah-like fashion, in Stewart's *Meditations,* a cloud of doom seems to hover over her prayers and hopes for the black community.

Stewart addressed her hopes for the future to black women, perhaps alluding to the parable of the wise and foolish maidens in Matthew 25. They have an awesome responsibility because they will raise the children of tomorrow:

> O, ye daughters of Africa, awake! awake! arise! no longer sleep nor slumber, but distinguish yourselves. Show forth to the world that you are endowed with noble and exalted faculties."[36]

> O, ye mothers, what a responsibility rests on you! You have souls committed to your charge, and God will require a strict account of you. It is you that must create in the minds of your little girls and boys a thirst for knowledge, the love of virtue thus early formed in the soul will protect their inexperienced feet from many dangers.[37]

WOMEN IN THE BIBLE AS ROLE MODELS

While Stewart addressed the women in her audience frequently, her strongest statement of equality and perhaps superiority was found in her "Farewell Address to her friends in Boston" in 1833. Attempting to defend her call to preach, she cited a litany of strong female models in the Bible: "What if I am a woman; is not the God of ancient times the God of these modern days? Did he not raise up Deborah, to be a mother, and a judge of Israel? Did not Queen Esther save the lives of Jews? And Mary Magdalene first declare the resurrection of Christ from the dead?"[38]

Opting for Jesus' example and relationship toward women, she concluded that Paul, if he had known of the present circumstances of women, would not object to women "pleading in public for our rights." In fact, women thoughout the ages have had a "voice in moral, religious, and political subjects."[39]

Not only have women been involved in important issues throughout history, it appears that God "more readily communicates himself to women." Stewart's proofs for this assertion came from the ancient religions of Greece, Rome, Egypt, and even that of the Jews. And later she listed women in philosophy and languages, as well as those who were poetesses, Divines, and scholars:[40] "And in the most barbarous nations, all things that have the appearance of being supernatural, the mysteries of religion, the secrets of physic, and the rites of magic, were in the possession of women."[41]

She warned her listeners that God could choose to raise up similar women in order to change the present. Those who ridiculed them would be termed sinful: "For God makes use of feeble means sometimes, to bring about his most exalted purposes."[42]

FEMININE SYMBOLIC IMAGERY

Perhaps the most stunning use of the Bible is her intepretation of the Whore of Babylon in the Book of Revelation. The Whore is America!

> It appears to me that America has become like a great city of Babylon, for she has boasted in her heart . . . She is indeed the seller of slaves and the souls of men; and she has made the Africans drunk with the wine of her fornication. . . .[43]

> Oh, America, America, foul and indelible is they stain. Dark and dismal is the cloud that hangs over thee, for the cruel wrongs and injuries to the fallen sons of Africa. The blood of her murdered ones cries to heaven for vengeance against thee. Thou art almost become drunken with the blood of her slain; thou has enriched thyself through her toils and labors . . . And thou has caused the daughters of Africa to commit whordoms and fornications; but upon thee be their curse.[44]

In apocalyptic fervor, she predicted that this nation would fall. It is only a matter of time. No matter what the nation does to them, God is greater and in a veiled threat of annhiliation, she warned that the ten plagues of Egypt could be at their doorstep at any moment.[45] In a tract entitled "Religion and the Pure Principles of Morality," Stewart hinted at the possibility of violence: "All the nations of the earth are crying out for liberty and equality. Away, away with tyranny and oppression! And shall Afric's sons be silent any longer? Far be it from me to recommend to you either to kill, burn, or destroy. But I would strongly recommend to you to improve your talents; let not one lie buried in the earth."[46]

In a speech delivered to the African Masonic Hall, she asserted that if the "free people of color" united their efforts together nothing could stop them.[47] She warned her audience to make themselves ready for she believed that out of Ethopia (Psalm 68) would come princes and princesses who would rule the world:

> It is useless for us any longer to sit with our hands folded, reproaching the whites: for that will never elevate us.[48]

> And were it not that the King eternal has declared that Ethiopia shall stretch forth her hands unto God, I should indeed despair.[49]

> . . . in God's own time, and his time is certainly best, he will surely deliver you with a mighty hand and with an outstretched arm.[50]

Cheryl Townsend Gilkes suggests that an Afrocentric reading of Psalm 68 united the historic black community by giving them hopes of liberation. Afrocentric interpretations of the Bible concentrated on neglected texts and interpreted them to fit into the present political situation. "The reference to 'Ethiopia' became a promise that affirmed their humanity, ethnic identity and community."[51]

THE ULTIMATE PRICE

Finally, Stewart made the theoretical jump from possible violence to a willingness on her part to die for her faith and her cause. She left these parting words with the people at the African Masonic Hall.

> The unfriendly whites first drove the native American from his much loved home. Then they stole our fathers from their peaceful and quiet dwellings, and brought them hither, and made bond-men and bond-women of them and their little ones; they have obliged our brethren to labor, kept them in utter ignorance, nourished them in vice, and raised them in degradation; and now . . . They would drive us to a strange land. But before I go, the bayonet will pierce me through.[52]

SUMMARY

Stewart's brave and yet rash statements did not come true in her life. She did not literally walk in the footsteps of Jesus. She was not a martyr. She was not killed for her cause, she merely left town to avoid harassment. Her radical words were the cry of a zealot who wanted "change" more than anything else in life. In fact, life would not be worth living if the changes did not occur.

She saw herself as a prophetess called of God to change the world. She recognized the importance of mothers within the African American community and encouraged them to change the future by educating their children in virtue. She argued for the equality of women in order to prove to the people that God could send a woman to bring the good news of change, of impending revolution. She argued, that, indeed, it was women who were more likely to have a relationship with the Divine. She argued for the equality of all people based upon Genesis 1:26. God had formed them and "he hath made all men free and equal."[53]

Her hope for the future of African Americans lay in her belief in their essential goodness and talents. If they had the educational or cultural opportunities they could again be a mighty people. The reign of terror exercised by the whites of America had to end. It could not go on forever. The next generation of rulers would come from their courageous and historic country of Ethiopia. The rulers would be Africans. God was on the side of the oppressed, the hopeless. A woman brought this message to them.

Notes

1. Maria W. Stewart, *Productions of Mrs. Maria W. Stewart presented to the First African Baptist Church and Society of the City of Boston* (Boston: Friends of Freedom and Virtue, 1835), 16.
2. Marilyn Richardson, ed., *Maria W. Stewart, America's First Black Woman Political Writer: Essays and Speeches* (Bloomington: Indiana University Press, 1987), 55. This quote was taken from an address delivered before the African-American Female Intelligence Society of America in 1832.
3. Katie G. Cannon, *Black Womanist Ethics* (Atlanta: Scholars Press, 1988), 78–83. See Ida Delores Young, *Between the Voices of our Ancestors: Afrocentric Strategies*, "Symbols, Forms of Revolution, and the Philosophical Implications of the Rhetorical Discourse of Abolitionist Maria W. Stewart (1803–1879)," Ph.D. dissertation, Temple University, 1992, who interprets Stewart using an modern Afrocentric model.
4. Lillian Ashcraft Webb, "Black Women and Religion in the Colonial Period," *Women and Religion in America*, vol. 2., *The Colonial and Revolutionary Periods*, Rosemary Radford Ruether and Rosemary Skinner Keller, eds. (New York: Harper and Row, 1983), 236.

5. Jacquelyn Grant, "Black Women and the Church," in *All the Women are White, All the Blacks are Men, But Some of Us are Brave*, Gloria T. Hull, Paricia Bell Scott, and Barbara Smith, eds. (New York: The Feminist Press, 1982), 142.

6. Jarena Lee, *The Life and Religious Experience of Jarena Lee, a Coloured Lady. Giving an Account of the Call to Preach the Gospel* (Philadelphia: N.P, 1836), 13. See also Dennis Dickerson, ed., *Religious Experiences and Journal of Mrs. Jarena Lee* (Nashville: Legacy Publishing, 1991).

7. Bell Hooks, *Ain't I a Woman: Black Women and Feminism* (Boston: South End Press, 1981), 162.

8. Jacquelyn Grant, "Black Women and the Church," 143–144; Amanda Berry Smith, *An Autobiography: The Story of the Lord's Dealings with Mrs. Amanda Berry Smith, the Colored Evangelist* (Chicago, N.P., 1893).

9. Bell Hooks, *Ain't I a Woman*, 159–160. Also see, Olive Gilbert, ed., *Sojourner Truth: Narrative and Book of Life* (1850–1875) (Chicago: Johnson Publishing, 1970) and Margaret Washington, ed., *Narrative of Sojourner Truth* (New York: Random House, 1993). See also Karen Baker-Fletcher, "Anna Julia Cooper and Sojourner Truth: Two Nineteenth-Century Black Feminist Interpreters of Scripture," in *Searching the Scriptures: A Feminist Introduction*, Elisabeth Schüssler Fiorenza, ed. (New York: Crossroad, 1993), 41–51, who suggests that Sojourner had much more to say on the subject, although her narrative was written by Olive Gilbert.

10. Anna Julia Haywood Cooper, *A Voice from the South* (Ohio: Aldine Printing House, 1892), 14–17.

11. Anna Julia Haywood Cooper, *A Voice from the South*, 18. See Karen Baker-Fletcher, "Anna Julia Cooper and Sojourner Truth: Two Nineteenth-Century Black Feminist Interpreters of Scripture," in *Searching the Scriptures: A Feminist Introduction*, Elisabeth Schüssler Fiorenza, ed. (New York: Crossroad, 1993), 41–51, who suggests that Cooper had much more to say on the subject.

12. Marilyn Richardson, *Maria W. Stewart*, 52.

13. Maria W. Stewart, *Meditations* (Washington: N.P., 1879), 7–9; Maria W. Stewart, *Productions*, 3–5.

14. Maria W. Stewart, *Meditations*, 7–9.

15. Marilyn Richardson, *Maria W. Stewart*, 6.

16. David Walker, *Walker's Appeal in Four Articles Together With a Preamble . . .* (Boston: David Walker, 1830).

17. Marilyn Richardson, *Maria W. Stewart*, 19.

18. Marilyn Richardson, *Maria W. Stewart*, 15; Maria W. Stewart, *Meditations*, 24.

19. Bert James Loewenberg and Ruth Bogin, eds., *Black Women in Nineteenth-Century American Life: Their Words, Their Thoughts, Their Feelings* (University Park: Pennsylvania State University Press, 1976), 198.

20. Ibid.

21. Ibid., 195, 199.

22. Ibid., 186, 189–190.

23. Marilyn Richardson, *Maria W. Stewart*, 29.

24. Bert James Loewenberg and Ruth Bogin, eds., *Black Women in Nineteenth-Century American Life*, 193.

25. Ibid., 194.

26. Ibid., 195.

27. Ibid., 194.
28. Maria W. Stewart, *Productions*, 32.
29. Bert James Loewenberg and Ruth Bogin, eds., *Black Women in Nineteenth-Century American Life*, 196.
30. Marilyn Richardson, *Maria W. Stewart*, 52.
31. Ibid., 53.
32. Ibid., 54.
33. Maria W. Stewart, *Productions*, 17.
34. Maria W. Stewart, *Productions*, 53.
35. Bert James Loewenberg and Ruth Bogin, eds., *Black Women in Nineteenth-Century American Life*, 195; and Marilyn Richardson, *Maria W. Stewart*, 15.
36. Maria W. Stewart, *Productions*, 6.
37. Ibid., 13.
38. Bert James Loewenberg and Ruth Bogin, eds., *Black Women in Nineteenth-Century American Life*, 198.
39. Ibid.
40. Ibid., 199.
41. Ibid.
42. Ibid.
43. Maria W. Stewart, *Productions*, 71.
44. Ibid., 18.
45. Bert James Loewenberg and Ruth Bogin, eds., *Black Women in Nineteenth-Century American Life*, 190.
46. Marilyn Richardson, *Maria W. Stewart*, 29.
47. Bert James Loewenberg and Ruth Bogin, eds., *Black Women in Nineteenth-Century American Life*, 197.
48. Maria W. Stewart, *Productions*, 60.
49. Ibid., 54.
50. Ibid., 21.
51. Cheryl Townsend Gilkes, "Mother to the Motherless, Father to the Fatherless: Power, Gender, and Community in an Afrocentric Biblical Tradition," *Semeia* 47(1986): 63, 68, 69.
52. Maria W. Stewart, *Productions*, 72.
53. Marilyn Richardson, *Maria W. Stewart*, 29.

Chapter 7

TRANSLATION AS INTERPRETATION

INTRODUCTION

Every translator is biased. Every lexicon and linguistic tool employed to determine the meaning of a word or phrase is biased and limited in their experiences of the languages and usages of those languages 2,000 or 4,000 years ago. People who compile grammars and lexicons have a philosophical predisposition concerning how meaning should be derived and which ancient resources should be used and included as relevant examples to define words and the relationships of those words.

Each translator must determine which manuscripts are more "accurate" or "plausible" based on certain principles before the process of translation can begin. Recently a scholar accused another colleague of mine of choosing readings from manuscripts in the Bible which "fit" into a certain feminist ideology. He accused her of failing to search for "truth." According to this scholar, she was not following the time-honored guidelines of textual critics.

The scholars discussed the historic process of the collection of manuscripts which occurred primarily under the reigns of Roman emperors. The feminist scholar suggested that the very compilation and editing of many of these manuscripts was in itself biased, and transcribers could have purposely omitted phrases about the strength, authority, and relationship of women during the founding years of Christianity. The other scholar had never questioned the

213

process or the history. He may never have questioned the guidelines that textual critics follow in determining the best reading available for a passage of Scripture.

Most of us are not aware of our biases, and so it is with well-meaning scholars who devote their lives to the translation of the Bible. Their own ideologies or belief systems propel them into the time-consuming and tedious work of translation, but those very ideologies prevent them from viewing the Bible from multiple points of view. Even when translation committees are assembled, the publishers choose certain individuals who represent certain traditions and will produce a translation which will "fit" within their ideological mindset.

Julia Smith experienced dissonance when she attended a local Congregational church in Connecticut over a hundred years ago. There was something wrong with the preaching and the way the Bible was translated. She was determined to discover the exact words of the Bible for herself, and so she translated the Old Testament (Hebrew Bible or First Testament), Apocrypha, and the New Testament from the Hebrew, the Latin, and the Greek several times.

JULIA EVELINA SMITH (1792–1886)

So that by this means the gospel is made vulgar,
and more open to the laity,
and even to women who can read . . .[1]

HISTORICAL SITUATION: NINETEENTH CENTURY

Julia's long life spanned a century of growth and conflict that would shape issues and problems of the twentieth century. She was born during the presidency of George Washington and watched a nation develop from its infancy into a major world power that had a habit of neglecting the rights of others as it conquered new lands. Railroads, electricity, the phonograph, the Indian Wars, slavery, and the Civil War buttressed corsetted women with Victorian values, bloomers, and children working in factories during the Industrial Revolution. Julia experienced these social upheavals while living in rural Connecticut on a farm in Glastonbury.[2]

BIOGRAPHY

Independence of thought, habit, and mind characterized the life of Julia Smith. From the time she was very young she knew that she wanted more out of life than learning how to dress, dance, or please the boys. Studying was more important to her than socializing. Her desire for knowledge outweighed almost everything. She wanted to learn and nothing was going to get in her way, not even her father. A story is told about Julia expecting her father to return from Hartford, Connecticut, with a new Latin grammar with English explanations for her. When he arrived home without it, she was so distressed that she saddled up the horse and road all the way by herself from Glastonbury to Hartford to buy the book.[3]

Born into a Congregational family whose father, Zephaniah, left the ministry for law and later explored the teachings of William Miller, Julia learned to appreciate diverse thinking. Julia's mother, Hannah, helped lay the foundation for the extraordinary journey Julia would take later in life, by teaching her and her four sisters French, Latin, and Greek.[4] In 1810, Julia continued her studies by attending a boarding school in New Haven where she studied French with the Value family.[5] By 1823, at the age of thirty-one she was offered a position at the Troy Female Seminary in New York[6] which lasted about a year. For whatever reasons, her health or homesickness, she returned to Glastonbury and lived on the family farm with her sisters for most of the rest of her life. Her greatest achievement was in translating the Bible five times. She translated the Greek New Testament, the Greek Septuagint, and the Latin of the Vulgate.[7] Before she could translate the Hebrew Old Testament or Hebrew Bible, she had to master Hebrew.

Susan Shaw assumes that Julia attended The First Congregational Church of Glastonbury on a semiregular basis,[8] although other sources suggest that the family was too independent to have membership in any church.[9] Julia's alliance with the Congregational church was challenged by the preaching of William Miller, who predicted that the world was coming to an end in 1842,[10] and by the defection from the congregation by her good friend, Emily Moseley.[11] Miller spent many years of his own life translating and comparing Scriptures in order to prove a single author. His vigorousness spawned Julia's own work of retranslating the Bible.[12] Julia and her four sisters including Emily had a habit of meeting regularly every Sunday to study the Bible. "[S]ometime in 1847, Julia, the Smith sisters, and Emily Moseley, agreed to meet every Sunday to 'read over what [Julia] had translated'."[13]

Julia's purpose for translating the Bible into English may be found in a news article in the *New York Sun* in 1875: "My purpose in this was to see whether no new and clearer light might not thus be thrown upon passages whose meaning is ambiguous and whose construction is disputed. . . . It struck me that if we could consult the original text whenever any passage in the Bible was referred to, it would be a good thing, and we determined to make a literal translation for that sole reason. . . ."[14]

Julia never intended for the translation to be published. It was, for her, a way of worshipping, a way of understanding the ways and mysteries of God. Yet, after her property was sold to her neighbor for lack of payment for taxes, Julia felt as if she needed to prove to the world that women were as good as men, perhaps even better.

In 1873, Julia and her sole surviving sister, Abby, received a bill for property tax on their farm. They were outraged. Taxes were levied against them even though they could not vote. They began a campaign to challenge the government's right to levy taxes to disenfranchised people. This was not the first time that the Smith family had fought for the rights of others. Early in her life Julia, watched her mother write antislavery petitions which were presented to Congress with a host of signatures. "Julia was the local distributor for the *Charter Oak*, an anti-slavery newspaper."[15]

By 1874, the government had taken seven of their cows for payment in back taxes and their neighbor had bought fifteen acres of their farm for a mere $78.35 at an illegally run auction held by the tax collectors. The land was reportedly worth $2,000. It took years of writing letters, protesting, and searching for legal counsel before the Smith's regained their property.

In the process of their campaign, the Smith sisters received national attention and invitations from prestigious organizations. They were invited to speak at the National Woman's Suffrage Association, The Senate Committee on Privileges and Elections in Washington, and before a committee of the legislature in Hartford. Eventually Julia collected their correspondence, articles, and speeches into a book that detailed their fight for equal treatment before the law in Connecticut entitled, "*Abby Smith and Her Cows, with a Report of the Law Case Decided Contrary to Law* (1877).[16]

Julia's decision in 1876 to publish her translations of the Bible was in response to the treatment she had received by the males in government. For her it was a way of proving that women were not second-rate citizens. They could do more than any man: "We wanted them to understand that the woman who knew not enough to manage what she rightfully and lawfully owned had actually done what no man had ever done. . . . Never have I considered myself above others for having translated the Bible. Still I think we ought to be respected enough for men not to break their own laws to get possession of our property."[17]

Julia's work has been virtually ignored by historians. The committee set up to create *The Woman's Bible* by Elizabeth Cady Stanton[18] used selections of Julia's translation for their work, but in general, most researchers do not refer to her efforts.[19] Writing a tribute to Julia Smith in an appendix to *The Woman's Bible*, Francis Ellen Burr quotes Henry de Knyghton's praise for the first translation of the Bible into English by John Wyclif,

> This Master John Wyclif hath translated the gospel out of Latin into English, which Christ had intrusted with the clergy and doctors of the church that they might minister it to the laity and weaker sort, according to the state of the times and the wants of men. So that by this means the gospel is made vulgar, and more open to the laity, and even to women who can read, that it used to be to the most learned of the clergy and those of the best understanding! . . . I'm afraid Julia Smith would have set his old head buzzing. . . .[20]

The all-male translating committee of *The Revised Standard Version of the Bible* (*RSV*), published in 1888, totally disregarded Julia's work.

Julia died at the age of ninety-three, in 1886, eight years after the death of her sister Abby, and six years after her marriage to her first and last husband, Andrew Parker.

TRANSLATING THE BIBLE

Why did Julia spend most of her spare time translating the Bible? Obviously she was enamoured with the languages and any hobby can become a fascinating, compelling experience. Perhaps Julia thought that the Bible contained answers to her own personal questions. Susan Shaw who has written the only modern account of Julia's life concludes, "Her motives for translation came from adventist theology which claimed Scripture as the prophetic voice calling out to the believer, and her interest had been to see the thematic connections from Alpha to Omega, and not to create a vehicle by which to challenge the patriarchal status-quo."[21]

Yet, it would appear that Julia's very life choices challenged the patriarchal status quo. She chose to be a very distinctive type of person who cared little for social customs or requirements. She must have had suspicions that English versions of the Bible were biased or inadequate in some way. She may not have used the word "patriarchal," but she surely recognized the absence of women among the hierarchy within Christianity. Choosing to worship together on Sunday in their own home with a friend is an obvious criticism of the church which apparently did not meet the intellectual, emotional, or social needs of the sisters and Emily.

JULIA SMITH'S VERSION (*JSV*)[22]

Julia's work should be studied against the background of Hebrew, Greek, and Aramaic by biblical scholars. In a brief comparison of Julia's translation (*JSV*), with the *Authorized King James Version* (*KJV*), and the *Revised Standard Version* (*RSV*), it appears that at least fourteen verses were translated by Julia with the intention of changing the traditional interpretation about women. Below is a list of some of the differences in her translation compared with the *RSV* and the *KJV* with an analysis of her work.

GENESIS 2:18

> KJV: "I will make him an help meet for him."
> RSV: "I will make him a helper fit for him."
> JSV: "I will make for him a help as before him."

Both the *RSV* and *KJV* seem to suggest that the helper will adjust or mold itself to the man. It will become whatever the man needs. Julia obscures this possible interpretation by emphasizing that the helper will be available but she does not use the words "fit" or "for" which suggest possession. The helper is "before" which could refer to time past or to a spacial proximity.

GENESIS 2:25

> KJV: "the man and his wife"
> RSV: "the man and his wife"
> JSV: "the man and his woman"

Using "woman" instead of "wife" may be a small change but Julia translated it literally. There was no contract and thus no "wife."

GENESIS 3:20

> KJV: "And Adam called his wife's name Eve . . ."
> RSV: "The man called his wife's name Eve . . ."
> JSV: "And Adam will call his wife's name Life . . ."[23]

The name "Life" is much more symbolic than "Eve," since Eve was the mother of all humans. What a different perception readers would have about woman if other translators had used the term "Life." Lillie Devereux Blake, a member of the committee charged with writing *The Woman's Bible* said this about Julia's translation, "It is a pity that all versions of the Bible do not give this word instead of the Hebrew Eve. She was Life, the eternal mother, the first representative of the more valuable and important half of the human race."[24]

GENESIS 7:2

> KJV: "Thou shalt take to thee by sevens, the male and his female."
> RSV: "Thou shalt take to thee seven and seven, the male and his female."
> JSV: "Thou shalt take to thee seven; seven male and female."

These verses are taken from the story of Noah and the ark. Notice that Julia does not assume that the female is a mate of any other male. There is no matching or subordination; she does not use the possessive "his female."

GENESIS 16:2

> KJV: "And Abram hearkened to the voice of Sarai."
> RSV: "And Abram hearkened to the voice of Sarai."
> JSV: "And Abram will listen to the voice of Sarai."

These verses are taken from the story of Sarah requesting Abraham to sleep with a concubine in order to gain an heir. Julia used the future tense "will listen" instead of the past tense "listened." She makes it seem as if Sarah will be in control permanently.

JUDGES 4:4

> KJV: "Now Deborah, a prophetess, the wife of Lapidoth, she judged Israel at that time."
> RSV: "Now Deborah, a prophetess, the wife of Lappidoth, she judged Israel at that time."
> JSV: "And Deborah, a woman, a prophetess, wife to Lapidoth, she judged Israel in that time."

Notice that Julia adds the term "woman" which clarifies her sex and she is not "wife of" but "wife to." Here Julia omits the perception of possession of woman by the man again.

JUDGES 4:5

KJV: ". . . and the children of Israel came up to her for judgment."
RSV: ". . . and the children of Israel came up to her for judgment."
JSV: ". . . and the sons of Israel will go up to her for judgment."

At first glance one would conclude that the *KJV* and the *RSV* were using nonsexist, inclusive language by employing the term "children." Julia translates the verse literally. Clearly, if anyone is going to Deborah for advice and council, it is the men. Julia suggests that she indeed did rule over the "sons of Israel."

LUKE 8:3

KJV: ". . . which ministered unto him out of their substance."
RSV: ". . . which ministered unto them of their own substance." (Footnote in margin: Many ancient authorites read him.)
JSV: ". . . who served him from possessions to them."

This verse is found in a passage that describes and lists women who follow Jesus. Julia chooses to use the term "serve" instead of "minister." The term "minister," employed by the *RSV*, leaves the impression that the women are serving tables. The women are one step removed from Jesus. Julia's translation links the woman directly to Jesus. Obviously she had access to different manuscripts of the Greek Bible because she chose a reading which suggests that the women took care of Jesus' own personal financial needs. They served "him" by donating their own things. (I prefer to translate it, "They served with him.") Julia is sensitive to the capabilities of ancient women and managing their own money in order to finance and build the career of Jesus.

ACTS 2:17

KJV: ". . . and your old men shall dream dreams."
RSV: ". . . and your old men shall dream dreams."
JSV: ". . . and your elder dream dreams."

This phrase is from the famous passage predicting that daughters shall prophesy. It is not only the men who will dream dreams. By choosing to use "elder" instead of "old men," she includes herself, a woman, in the prophecy. And it is no longer in the future tense, it is a present activity.

I CORINTHIANS 11:3

KJV: ". . . the head of woman is man."
RSV: ". . . the head of the woman is the man."
JSV: ". . . the head of the woman the man."

This passage in I Corinthians deals with head covering and women who prophesy. The *RSV* translation is clear, the man is the authority. The *KJV* suggests that all men are in authority over all women. Julia obscures those conclusions by not including a verb. The readers can draw their own conclusions.

I CORINTHIANS 14:28

KJV: "Let him keep silence in the church."
RSV: "Let each of them keep silence in the church."
JSV: "Let him be silent in the church."

This passage is found in the context of a later passage in I Corinthians that instructs women to keep silent in the churches and has been used to exclude women from worship and leadership positions within Christianity. The *RSV* suggests that all people are to keep silent. Julia agrees with the *KJV*; only the males are to keep silent. This translation would match the later translation about the females. So both sexes were told to remain quiet in the church depending upon the situation.

EPHESIANS 5:22

KJV: "Wives, submit yourselves unto your own husbands, as unto the Lord."

RSV: "Wives, be in subjection unto your own husbands, as unto the Lord."

JSV: "Women yield ye obedience to your own husbands, as in the Lord."

This is one of the most famous submission passages used to keep women in a subordinate position. Julia agrees with the *KJV* and the *RSV*, women are to "yield" to their "own" husbands. She does not use the word "submit" which suggests slavery. She also translates the phrase "as in the Lord" in place of the very strong "as unto the Lord." The yielding is not absolute and it is only within Christian circles.

COLOSSIANS 3:18

KJV: "Wives, submit yourselves unto your husbands, as is fitting in the Lord."

RSV: "Wives be in subjection to your husbands, as is fitting in the Lord."

JSV: "Women, place yourselves under your own husbands, as was permitted in the Lord."

Julia uses neither of the inflammatory words of "submit" or "subject" in this famous subordinate passage. She uses "women" instead of "wives" again. This generalizes the verse in the same way that "own husband" particularizes it. The last phrase "as was permitted" softens the type of subordination required of women. While both the *RSV* and the *KJV* used commands at the beginning of the sentence, Julia gently says "place yourselves," (reflexive) suggesting that the women are again in control of the situation.

I TIMOTHY 2:11–12

KJV: "Let the woman learn in silence with all subjection. But I suffer not a woman to teach, nor to usurp authority over the man, but to be in silence."

RSV: "Let a woman learn in quietness with all subjection. But I permit not a woman to teach, nor to have dominion over a man; but to be in quietness."

JSV: "Let the woman, in freedom from care, learn in all subjection. And I trust not the woman to teach, neither to exercise authority over the man, but to be in freedom from care."

This passage has been used for centuries to prohibit women from preaching and leadership positions within the church. The most obvious difference in Julia's translation is that she omits the word "silence." In both instances, she translates it "in freedom from care." Instead of using "permit" or "suffer not," she softens the word into "trust not" which almost makes it an individual preference and not a command etched in concrete for eternity, as it has been traditionally interpreted. Woman does not "usurp" authority. There is no hint of a mutiny or rebellion. A woman may have authority over the man but this verse suggests that the writer prefers that women do not exercise that option if they are in a state of "freedom from care."

CONCLUSION

No one really knows what was in the mind of Julia when she translated the Bible. Some of the differences in the translations could be typographical or publishing errors. Yet, after a brief survey of a few passages contained in Julia's monumental translation, it can be concluded that she did intentionally translate the Bible in order to change the traditionally accepted subordinate views about women. In Julia's translation, women are stronger, more independent, and have a measure of control over their lives.

Notes

1. Susan J. Shaw, *A Religious History of Julia Evelina Smith's 1876 Translation of the Holy Bible: Doing More Than Any Man Has Ever Done* (San Francisco: Mellen Research University Press, 1993), 261.

2. John A. Garraty, *The American Nation: A History of the United States* (New York: Harper and Row, 1975) and C. Willett Cunnington, *Feminine Attitudes in the Nineteenth Century* (New York: Macmillan Company, 1936).

3. Susan J. Shaw, *A Religious History of Julia Evelina Smith's 1876 Translation of the Holy Bible*, 99.

4. Susan J. Shaw, Ibid., 98.

5. Susan J. Shaw, Ibid., 100.

6. Ibid., 102.

7. Ibid., 151.

8. Ibid., 114.

9. Edward T. James, ed., *Notable American Women 1607–1950: A Biographical Dictionary* (Cambridge, MA: Harvard University Press, 1971), 3:303.

10. Susan J. Shaw, *A Religious History of Julia Evelina Smith's 1876 Translation of the Holy Bible*, 117.

11. Susan J. Shaw, Ibid., 144–145.

12. Ibid., 147.

13. Ibid., 146.

14. Ibid., 147.

15. Edward T. James, ed., *Notable American Women 1607–1950: A Biographical Dictionary* (Cambridge, MA: Harvard University Press, 1971), 3:303.

16. Julia Smith, *Abby Smith and Her Cows, with a Report of the Law Case Decided Contrary to Law* (1877).

17. Susan J. Shaw, *A Religious History of Julia Evelina Smith's 1876 Translation of the Holy Bible*, 172.

18. Elizabeth Cady Stanton, ed., *The Woman's Bible* (New York: European Publishing Company, 1898; Reprint: Seattle: Coalition Task Force on Women and Religion, 1974).

19. Susan J. Shaw, *A Religious History of Julia Evelina Smith's 1876 Translation of the Holy Bible*, 243–246.

20. Ibid., 248.

21. Ibid., 261.

22. Julia E. Smith, *The Holy Bible Containing the Old and New Testaments. Translated Literally from the Original Tongues* (Hartford, CT: American Publishing Company, 1876). I attempted to find a *Revised Standard Version* at about the same time her version was published; I used, *The Holy Bible Containing the Old And New Testaments. Translated out of the Original Tonues. Being the Version set forth A.D. 1611 compared with the most Ancient Authorities and Revised* (Oxford: The University Press, 1885).

23. We do not know how Julia Smith learned Hebrew—whether she had a tutor or was self-taught, or what grammars she may have used—but it is clear from her translation of Gen. 3:20 as well as of Gen. 16:2 and Judges 4:5 that she was either unaware of or deliberately chose to ignore the Hebrew usage

known as the waw consecutive. According to one classic text, *Gesenius' Hebrew Grammar* by E. Kautsch (2d English edition, 1910, prepared from the 26th German edition; 1st German edition, Halle, 1813): "One of the most striking peculiarities in the Hebrew *consecution* of tenses is the phenomenon that, in representing a series of past events, only the first verb stands in the perfect, and the narration is continued in the imperfect. Conversely, the representation of a series of future events begins with the imperfect, and is continued in the perfect. . . . This progress in the sequence of time is regularly indicated by a pregnant *and* (called *wāw consecutive*), which in itself is really only a variety of the ordinary *wāw copulative,* but which sometimes (in the imperf.) appears with a different vocalization" (¶49, a, 1).

24. Susan J. Shaw, *A Religious History of Julia Evelina Smith's 1876 Translation of the Holy Bible,* 245.

CONCLUDING OBSERVATIONS

The search for documents arguing for the equality of women using the Scriptures as a primary text began over six years ago in the Yale Divinity Library. At least one hundred names and literatures were identified. Numerous other names were added later. Very few of the original names are included in this volume because documents were unavailable or lost.

The search led me down many empty pathways. It is much easier to describe the historical importance of a person than to discover his or her written materials and then analyze them for their literary strategy and content. Historians often describe interpretations of the Bible by important historic persons. After studying the original documents about those people, I often determined that they had only one or two sentences to say on the subject and that the historian had elaborated substantially on the historic person's view of the Bible.

This collection of analyses is only the beginning of an area of research that must be pursued. There are thousands of men and women who wrote on the subject of equality and the Bible. There are hundreds of people who could not be included in this volume. And while an attempt has been made to analyze and classify the kind of strategies employed through the centuries, none of the complicated writings in this volume fit neatly into any typical literary critical, or historical critical categories. Hopefully, new categories and methodologies will be identified, named, and developed in the future.

The textual history of the Bible must also be investigated through feminist critical eyes. The process of identifying androcentric choices of readings has already begun. The presuppositions about the importance of determining the "original" or most ancient text must be examined. Textual strategies and "laws" should be evaluated in light of the historical circumstances which necessitated their creation. Greek and Hebrew lexicons and grammars should be studied to determine if there is an inherent patriarchal bias in how languages are taught and learned.

And finally, on a personal note, the discovery of these people, their relationships, and their writings has enriched me immensely. It may seem trivial, but it was heartening to view so many people during the past 500 years who have struggled so valiantly with similar circumstances and prejudices prevalent in my own "world" and culture today. I will never forget those voices. Their voices have been silent for too long. They are no longer lost.

SELECTED
BIBLIOGRAPHY

AGRIPPA VON NETTESHEIM, HENRICUS CORNELIUS. *The Glory of Women: or, A Treatise Declaring the Excellency and Preheminence of Women above Men which is proved both by Scripture, Law, Reason, and Authority, Divine and Humane.* Written first in Latine by Henricus Cornelius Agrippa . . . and now translated into English for the Vertuous and Beautiful Female Sex of the Common wealth of England, by Devv. Fleetvvod (London: Robert Ibbitson, 1652).

ALVES, RUBEM. *What Is Religion?* (New York: Maryknoll, 1984).

ANDERSON, BONNIE S. and JUDITH P. ZINSSER, *A History of Their Own, from Prehistory to the Present,* vol. 1 (New York: Harper and Row, 1988).

ANDOLSEN, BARBARA HILERT. *Daughters of Jefferson, Daughters of Bootblacks* (Georgia: Mercer University Press, 1986).

ANDREWS, WILLIAM, ed. *Sisters of the Spirit* (Bloomington: Indiana University Press, 1986).

ASTELL, MARY. *A Serious Proposal to the Ladies for the Advancement of their True and Greatest Interest* (London: R. Wilkin, 1701) and reprint (New York: Source Book Press, 1970), 18.

————. *Some Reflections upon Marriage* (London: John Nutt, 1700).

BACON, MARGARET H. *Liberating Women: The Life of Lucretia Coffin Mott* (New York: Walker & Co, NY, 1980).

BAINTON, ROLAND H. *Women of the Reformation in Germany and Italy* (Minnesota: Augsburg, 1971).

BALLEINE, G. R. *Past Finding Out: The Tragic Story of Joanna Southcott and Her Successors* (New York: The Macmillan Company, 1956).

————. *Women of the Reformation in France and England* (Boston: Beacon Press, 1973).

BARTKOWSKI, FRANCES. *Feminist Utopias* (Lincoln: University of Nebraska Press, 1989).

BASS, DOROTHY C. AND SANORA HUGHES BOYD. *Women in American Religious History. An Annotated Bibliography and Guide to Sources* (Boston: G. K. Hall, 1986).

BEAVER, R. PIERCE. *American Protestant Women in World Mission: A History of the First Feminist Movement in North America* (Grand Rapids: Eerdmans, 1968).

BENSTOCK, SHARI. *Feminist Issues in Literary Scholarship* (Bloomington: Indiana University Press, 1987).

BORDIN, RUTH. *Frances Willard: A Biography* (Chapel Hill: University of North Carolina Press, 1986).

BOYD, NANCY. *Three Victorian Women Who Changed Their World: Josephine Butler, Octavia Hill, Florence Nightingale* (New York: Oxford University Press, 1982).

BOYLAN, ANN M. "Evangelical Womanhood in the Nineteenth Century: The Role of Women in Sunday Schools," *Feminist Studies* 4 (1978): 62–80.

BRAITHWAITE, WILLIAM C. *The Beginnings of Quakerism.* Second Edition. Henry J. Cadbury, ed. (Cambridge: The University press, 1912).

BRINK, J. R., ed. *Female Scholars: A Tradition of Learned Women before 1800* (Montreal: Eden Press Women's Studies, 1980).

BROWN, ANTIONETTE LOUISA. "Exegesis of I Corinthian XIV., 34, 35 and I Timothy II. 11, 12," *Oberlin Quarterly* 4 (1849): 358–373.

BROWN, JOANNE C. AND BOHN, CAROLE R., eds. *Christianity, Patriarchy, and Abuse: A Feminist Critique* (Nashville: The United Church Press, Pilgrim Press, 1989).

CAINE, BARBARA. *Victorian Feminists.* (New York: Oxford University Press, 1992).

CAMERON, JOHN. *History of the Buchanite Delusion: 1783–1846,* (Kilmarnock: R. G. Mann, 1904).

CARMODY, DENISE. *Feminism and Christianity: A Two-Way Reflection* (New York: University Press of America, 1990 a reprint of 1982).

CAMPBELL, KARLYN KOHRS. *Man Cannot Speak for Her.* 2 vols. (New York: Greenwood, 1989).

CANNON, KATIE G. *Black Womanist Ethics* (Atlanta: Scholars Press, 1988).

CASTRO, GINETTE. *American Feminism: A Contemporary History* (New York: University Press, 1990).

CAZDEN, ELIZABETH. *Antionette Brown Blackwell: A Biography* (New York: The Feminist Press, 1983).

CHRIST, CAROL P., ed. *Womanspirit Rising: A Feminist Reader in Religion* (New York: Harper and Row, 1992).

CLARK, ELIZABETH and HERBERT RICHARDSON, eds. *Women and Religion: A Feminist Sourcebook of Christian Thought* (New York: Harper and Row, 1977).

COOPER, ANNA JULIA HAYWOOD. *A Voice from the South* (Ohio: Aldine Printing House, 1892).

COTT, NANCY F. *The Bonds of Womanhood: Woman's Sphere in New England, 1780–1835* (New Haven: Yale University Press, 1977).

CROSS, BARBARA M. *The Educated Woman in America: Selected Writings of Catharine Beecher, Margaret Fuller, and Carey Thomas* (New York: Columbia University, 1965).

DALY, MARY. *Beyond God the Father: The Church and the Second Sex* (Boston: Beacon Press, 1985).

DAVIS, CHARLES T. and HENRY LOUIS GATES, JR. *The Slave's Narrative* (New York: Oxford, 1985).

DEMERS, PATRICIA. *Women as Interpreters of the Bible* (New York: Paulist, 1992).

DONOVAN, JOSEPHINE. *Feminist Literary Criticism: Explorations in Theory* (Lexington: University of Kentucky Press, 1975).

———, ed. *Feminist Theory: The Intellectual Traditions of American Feminism* (New York: Ungar, 1985).

FERGUSON, MOIRA. *First Feminists: British Women Writers 1578–1799* (Bloomington: Indiana University Press, 1985).

FIELD, VENA B. *Constantia: A Study of the Life and Works of Judith Sargent Murray, 1751–1820* (Orono: University of Maine Press, 1931).

FOX, GEORGE. *A Collection of Many Select and Christian Epistles and Testimonies. Written on Sundry Occasions, by that Ancient, Eminent, and Faithful Friend and Minister of Christ Jesus.* Second Edition. (London: T. Soble, 1698).

———. *Gospel Truth Demonstrated in a Collection of Doctrinal Books, Given forth by that Faithful Minister of Jesus Christ, George Fox: Containing Principles Essential to Christianity and Salvation, held Among the People called Quakers.* 3 vols. A reprint of the 1706 edition. (New York: Isaac T. Hopper, 1831).

———. *The Woman learning in Silence, or the misterie of the Woman's subjection to her husband: as also the daughter prophesy* (London, 1656). Also found in *Gospel Truth Demonstrated of The Words of George Fox* (1831) (Reprint: New York: AMS Press, 1975).

FOX, MARGARET FELL. *A Brief Collection of Remarkable Passages . . . . Relating to the birth, Education, Life, of Margaret Fell Fox* (London: Printed and sold by J. Sowle, 1710).

———. *Womens Speaking Justified, Proved and Allowed by the Scriptures* (1688). First printed in 1666. (Reprinted by William Andrews Clark Memorial Library, 1979).

GAGE, MATILDA JOSLYN. *Woman, Church and State: A Historical Account of the Status of Woman through the Christian Ages: with Reminiscences of the Matriarchate. American Women. Images and Realities Series.* Annette K. Baxter and Leon Stein, eds. (New York: The Truth Seeker Company, 1900. Reprint New York: Arno Press, 1972).

GARRETT, CLARKE, *Respectable Folly: Millenarians and the French Revolution in France and England* (Baltimore and London: John Hopkins University Press, 1975).

GIFFORD, CAROLYN DE SWARTE. *The Ideal of the New Woman according to the Woman's Christian Temperance Union* (New York: Garland, 1987).

GILKES, CHERYL TOWNSEND. "Mother to the Motherless, Father to the Fatherless: Power, Gender, and Community in an Afrocentric Biblical Traditon," *Semeia* 47(1986): 57–85.

GILMAN, CHARLOTTE PERKINS (STETSON). *Herland.* Reprint of 1915 edition. New York: Pantheon Books, 1979).

———. *His Religion and Hers: A Study of the Faith of Our Fathers and the Work of Our Mothers* (New York: The Century Co., 1923).

———. *Woman Economics: A Study of the Economic Relation Between Men and Women as a Factor in Social Evolution* (Boston, 1899).

GRANT, JACQUELYN. *White Women's Christ and Black Women's Jesus: Feminist Christology and Womanist Response* (Missoula: Scholars Press, 1989).

GREAVES, RICHARD L. *Triumph over Silence: Women in Protestant History* (Connecticut: Greenwood Press, 1985).

GREEN, ANN. *Women in American Religious History* (Boston: G.K. Hall, 1986).

GREENE, DANA, ed. *Lucretia Mott: Her Complete Speeches and Sermons* (Lewiston, NY: The Edwin Mellen Press, 1980): 215.

GRIMKÉ, SARAH M. *Letters on the Equality of the Sexes and the Condition of Woman. Addressed to Mary S. Parker, President of the Boston Female Anti-Slavery Society* (New York: Burt Franklin, 1838).

HALLADAY, CARL. R. *Biblical Exegesis: A Beginner's Handbook* (Atlanta: John Knox Press, 1973).

HARDESTY, NANCY A. *Women called to Witness: Evangelical Feminism in the Nineteenth Century* (Nashville: Abingdon, 1984)

HARRISON, J.F.C. *The Second Coming: Popular Millenarianism, 1780–1850* (London: Routledge and Kegan Paul, 1979).

HAYS, MARY. *Appeal to the Men of Great Britain on Behalf of Women.* With an Introduction by Gina Luria (London: J. Johnson, 1798. Reprint, New York: Garland Publishing Company, 1974).

HILAH, THOMAS F. *Women in New Worlds: Historical Perspectives on the Wesleyan Tradition* (Nashville: Abingdon, 1981).

HOGELAND, RONALD W. *Women and Womanhood in America* (Lexington: D. C. Heath, 1973).

HOOKS, BELL. *Ain't I a Woman? Black Women and Feminism* (Boston: South End Press, 1981).

HYMOWITZ, CAROL and MICHAELE WEISSMAN, *A History of Women in America* (New York: Bantam, 1978).

IRWIN, JOYCE L. *Womanhood in Radical Protestantism 1525–1675* (Lewiston, NY: The Edwin Mellen Press, 1979).

JOHNSON, DALE A. *Women in English Religion 1700–1925* (Lewiston, NY: The Edwin Mellen Press, 1983).

KELLISON, BARBARA. *The Rights of Women in the Church* (Dayton: Herald and Hanner Office, 1862, 1867).

KINGSFORD, ANNA BONUS and EDWARD MAITLAND, *The Perfect Way or, the Finding of Christ* (London: John M. Watkins, 1923).

KITCH, SALLY L. *Chaste Liberation* (Chicago: University of Illinois Press, 1989).

KLEIN, RALPH W. *Textual Criticism of the Old Testament. From the Septuagint to Qumran* (Philadelphia: Fortress Press, 1974).

KNOX, R. A. *Enthusiasm: A Chapter in the History of Religion* (London: Oxford, 1950).

KOONTZ, GAYLE GERBER and WILLARD SWARTLEY, eds. *Perspectives on Feminist Hermeneutics.* Occasional Papers No. 10 (Indiana: Institute of Mennonite Studies, 1987).

LEE, JARENA. The Life and Religious Experience of Jarena Lee, a Coloured Lady. Giving an Account of the Call to Preach the Gospel (Philadelphia: N.P, 1836), 13. See also Dennis Dickerson, ed. *Religious Experiences and Journal of Mrs. Jarena Lee* (Nashville: Legacy Publishing, 1991).

LENZ, ELINOR and BARBARA MYERHOFF. *The Feminization of America: How Women's Values are Changing our Public and Private Lives* (New York: St Martin's Press, 1977).

LOADES, ANN, ed. *Feminist Theology: A Reader* (Louisville: John Knox, 1990).

LOEWENBERG, BERT JAMES and RUTH BOGIN, eds. *Black Women in Nineteenth Century American Life. Their Words, Their Thoughts, Their Feelings* (University Park: Pennsylvania State University, 1976).

LERNER, GERDER. *The Grimké Sisters from South Carolina, Pioneers for Women's Rights and Abolition* (New York: Schocken Books, 1971).

———. *The Grimké Sisters from South Carolina: Rebels against Slavery* (Boston: Houghton Mifflin Company, 1967).

MACHAFFIE, BARBARA J. *Her Story: Women in Christian Tradition* (Philadelphia: Fortress Press, 1986).

————. *Readings in Herstory: Women in Christian Tradition* (Minneapolis: Fortress Press, 1992)

MAITLAND, EDWARD. *Anna Kingsford: Her Life Letters Diary and Work.* 2 vols. (London: George Redway, 1896).

MANNING, BRIAN, ed., *Politics, Religion, and the English Civil War* (London: Edward Arnold, 1973).

MARSHALL, SHERRIN, ed. *Women in Reformation and Counter-Reformation Europe. Private and Public Works* (Bloomington: Indiana University Press, 1989).

MAYESKI, MARIE ANN. *Women: Models of Liberation* (Kansas City: Sheed and Ward, 1988).

MOTT, LUCRETIA COFFIN. "The Laws in Relation to Woman. Remarks, Delivered at the National Women's Rights Convention, Cleveland, Ohio, 1853," *National Women's Rights Convention. Proceedings* (Cleveland: Gray Beardsley, Spear and Co., 1854).

————. "The Argument that Women do not Want to Vote. Address, Delivered to the American Equal Rights Association, New York, May 9–10, 1867," in *Proceedings of the First Anniversary of the American Equal Rights Association* (New York: Robert J. Johnston, 1867).

MURRAY, JUDITH SARGENT. "On the Equality of the Sexes," found in Alice S. Rossi, *The Feminist Papers: From Adams to de Beauvoir* (New York: Columbia University Press, 1973): 16–24. Reprint from original articles, "On the Equality of the Sexes," *The Massachusetts Magazine*, March 1790, pp. 132–135, and April 1790, pp. 223–226.

NIES, JUDITH. *Seven Women: Portraits from the American Radical Tradition* (New York: Penguin Books, 1977).

NYE, A. *Feminist Theory and the Philosophies of Man* (New York: Croom Helm, 1988).

O'NEILL, WILLIAM L. *Feminism in America: A History* (New Brunswick, NJ: Transaction Publishers, 1989).

PALMER, PHOEBE. *The Promise of the Father* (Boston: H. Degen, 1859; Reprint: New York: Garland Publishing, 1985).

PERRY, RUTH. *The Celebrated Mary Astell: An Early English Feminist* (Chicago: University of Chicago Press, 1986).

PRIMAVESI, ANNE. *From Apocalypse to Genesis: Ecolotry, Feminism and Christianity* (Minneapolis: Augsburg, 1991).

PROCHASKA, F. K. *Women and Philanthropy in Nineteenth Century England* (New York: Oxford University Press, 1980).

RENDAL, *The Origins of Modern Feminism: Women in Britain, France and the United States, 1780–1860* (New York: Schocken Books, 1984).

REUTHER, ROSEMARY RADFORD. *Religion and Sexism: Images of Woman in the Jewish and Christian Traditions* (New York: Simon and Schuster, 1974).

REYNOLDS, D. S. "The Feminization Controversy: Sexual Stereotypes and the Paradoxes of Piety in the Nineteenth Century America," *New England Quarterly* 53(1980): 96–106.

RICHARDSON, MARILYN, ed. *Maria W. Stewart, America's First Black Woman Political writer: Essays and Speeches* (Bloomington: Indiana University Press, 1987).

ROSSI, ALICE S. *The Feminist Papers: From Adams to de Beauvoir* (Boston: Northeast University Press, 1988).

RUSSEL, LETTY M., ed. *Feminist Interpretation of the Bible* (Philadelphia: Westminster, 1985).

RYAN, MARY P. *Womanhood in America* (New York: New Viewpoints, 1975).

FIORENZA, ELISABETH SCHÜSSLER, ed. *Searching the Scripture: A Feminist Introduction* (New York: Crossroad, 1993).

SERNETT, MILTON C. *Black Religion and American Evangelicalism, White Protestants, Plantation Missions, and the Flowering of Negro Christianity, 1787–1865* (Metuchen, NJ: Scarecrow Press, 1975).

SEYMOUR, ALICE. *The Express Containing The Life and Divine Writings of Joanna Southcott* (London: SPCK, 1956).

SHAW, SUSAN J. *A Religious History of Julia Evelina Smith's 1876 Translation of the Holy Bible. Doing More Than Any Man Has Ever Done* (San Francisco: Mellen Research University Press, 1993).

SIMON, RICHARD. *A Critical History of the Text of the New Testament* (R. Taylor, 1689).

SMITH, BARBARA. *Toward a Black Feminist Criticism* (New York: Out and Out Books, 1977).

SMITH, FLORENCE M. *Mary Astell* (New York: Columbia University Press, 1912).

SMITH, HILDA L. *Reasons' Disciples: Seventeenth Century English Feminists* (Chicago: University of Illinois Press, 1982).

SMITH, JULIA E. *Abby Smith and Her Cows, with a Report of the Law Case Decided Contrary to Law* (1877).

———. *The Holy Bible containing the Old and New Testaments. Translated Literally from the Original Tongues* (Hartford, CT: American Publishing Company, 1876).

SMITH, PAGE. *Daughters of the Promised Land: Women in American History* (Boston, Little, Brown, and Co., 1970).

SOUTHCOTT, JOANNA. *The Full Assurance that the Kingdom of Christ is at Hand from the Signs of the Times* (London: S. Rouseau, 1806).

———. *Letters &c.* (London: E. Spragg, 1801)

———. *The Strange Effects of Faith* (1802)

SPRUNGER, KEITH L. "God's Powerful Army of the Weak: Anabaptist Women of the Radical Reformation," in Richard L. Greaves, ed. *Triumph over Science* (Westport, CT: Greenwood, 1985).

STANTON, ELIZABETH CADY. *The Woman's Bible* (New York: European Publishing Company, 1898. Reprint: Seattle: Coalition Task Force on Women and Religion, 1974).

STEWART, MARIA W. *Productions of Mrs. Maria W. Stewart presented to the First African Baptist Church and Society of the City of Boston* (Boston: Friends of Freedom and Virtue, 1835).

STONEBURNER, CAROL and JOHN, eds. *The Influence of Quaker Women on American History. Biographical Studies* (Lewiston, NY: The Edwin Mellen Press, 1986).

STUARD, SUSAN MOSHER. "Women's Witnessing: A New Departure," in *Witnesses for Change: Quaker Women over Three Centuries.* Elisabeth Potts Brown and Susan Mosher Stuart, eds. (London: Rutgers University Press, 1989).

THISTLETHWAITE, SUSAN B. *Sex, Race, and God: Christian Feminism in Black and White* (New York: Crossroad, 1989)

THOMAS, KEITH, "Women and the Civil War Sects," *Past Present* 13(1958): 42–62.

TOLBERT, MARY ANN, ed. *The Bible and Feminist Hermeneutics. Semeia 28* (Minneapolis: Scholars Press, 1985), 119.

WELTER, BARBARA. *"The Cult of True Womanhood 1820–1860," American Quarterly* 18(Summer, 1966): 162.

WILLARD, FRANCES E. *Woman in the Pulpit* (Chicago: Woman's Temperance Publication Association, 1888).

WOLLSTONECRAFT, MARY. *A Vindication of the Rights of Woman* (New York: Norton, 1967).

INDEX

Aaron, 59
Abby Smith and her cows, 217
Abigail, 31, 67, 129
Abishag, 129
Adam, 122
Adultery, 94
African American, 7, 210
African-American Female Intelligence
    Society, 203
African American Reading, 200
African Masonic Hall, 203, 208, 209
Afrocentric Interpretations, 209
Agrippa von Nettesheim, 7, 121, 123–
    130
Allegory, 41, 48, 99
American Woman Suffrage Association,
    107
Analogous Interpretation, 93
Androcentric, 3, 5, 121, 226
Androgynous, 31, 190, 193–194
Anna, 23, 43, 59, 67, 73, 130
Anti-feminist, 3
Anti-woman, 3
Anthony, Susan B., 55, 97, 144
Antoinette Brown Blackwell, 86, 111, 114
Association for the Advancement of
    Woman, 107
Astell, Mary, 95, 122, 131–137

Barstaw, Anne Lleywellyn, 124
Bateman, Mary, 176
Biblical Exegesis, 188
Birth-based Religion, 164
Birth Control, 96
Blackwell, Antoinette Louisa Brown, 7,
    87, 105–114
Blasphemy Act, 28
Blavatsky, Madam, 100, 144, 150
Book of Revelations, 180, 184
Brachen, Rachel, 53
Bride, 181, 195
Buch, Florence, 107
Buchanites, 177
Buddhism, 188
Burr, Francis Ellen, 217

Canonical Criticism, 48, 66
Celibate, 137, 155
Children of Light, 27
Christian Theosophical Movement, 174
Christian Theosophy, 188
Church Ferrell, 201
Clinton Liberal Institute, 144
Collier, Rebecca, 53
Complementary Relationship, 35
Constantia, 139
Cooper, Anna Julia Hayword, 202
Cosmic Interpretation 191
Creation, 34, 41, 102, 129, 157, 184
Critical Analysis, 188
Cromwell, Oliver, 26
Cult of Motherhood, 158

Daughter, 31, 41–42, 53, 59, 67, 73–75,
    101, 130, 149, 207
Daughters: of Africa, 208; of
    Zelophehad, 103
Death-based Religion, 160
Deborah, 31–32, 52, 59, 67, 72–73,
    103–104, 207, 220–221
Demythologization, 103
Dispensation, 29
Divine Light, 58
Divorce, 94
Doll, 47, 56
Dorcas, 31, 99
Double-sexed Word, 149
Douglas, Frederick, 96
Duality, 193–194

Ecclesiasticism, 153
Edenic Allegory, 192
Egalitarian, 3, 6, 23, 30
Elder Woman, 32
Elect Lady, 74
Elizabeth, 105
Emancipation, 8
Equality, 6, 31, 36–37, 41, 49–53, 68, 75,
    93–95, 102, 113, 122, 128–129, 133,
    140, 142, 154–155, 165, 195, 201,
    210, 226

Equality in Human Rights, 144
Esoteric Christian Union, 188
Esther, 103, 130, 182
Ethical-Theological Interpretation, 19
Ethiopia, 209–210;
    people of, 202
Etymology, 128, 147, 149
Evans, Mary, 176
Eve, 34–35, 41, 49–50, 52, 58, 72, 85–
    86, 93, 122–123, 128–129, 134, 148,
    161, 163, 183, 185, 190–193, 195, 219
Exegesis, 2, 11, 153, 155

Fall, The, 192
Father Rule, 149
Fellow Laborers, 31
Female Anti-Slavery Society, 45
Female Messiah, 6
Female Ministers, 53
Feminine Imagery, 31, 42
Feminine Principle, 149
Feminine Side of God, 36, 188
Feminist, 2, 5, 8, 54
Feminist Biblical Interpretation, 4–5
Feminist Hermeneutics, 5
Feminist Literary Criticism, 5
Feminist-Matriarchal, 185
Feminism, 4, 5, 6
Feminist Studies, 3
Feminist Utopia, 147, 165
Field, Vena, 139
Figurative, 93
First Women's Rights Convention, 97
Flaxmer, Sarah, 176
Foreshadowing, 182
Fox, George, 23, 26–36
Fox, Margaret Fell, 23, 26, 28–29, 37–43
Friend Mother, 177;
    See also Elspeth Simpson.
Fuller, Margaret, 5

Gage, Jacquelyn, 200
Gage, Matilda Joslyn, 7, 97, 122, 143–
    150, 195,
Giles, Cheryl Townsend, 209
Gilman, Charlotte Perkins, 123, 158–
    165

Girls, 207
God in the Image of a Female, 36
Gordon, Anna, 152
Grimké, Angelina, 44, 45
Grimké, Sarah Moore, 24, 37, 44–53,
    96
Gynocentric, 7

Hagar, 99
Handmaids, 62, 183
Hannah, 32
Hays, Mary 7, 86, 88–94
Hayes, John H., 16
Helpers, 31
Helpmate, 185
    Helpmeet, 34, 51, 73;
    Meet Helps, 30, 31
Herland, 160, 165. See Gilman.
Hermeneutics, 2, 11, 121
Hermetic Society, 188
His Religion and Hers, 160. See Gilman.
Historical-Critical Interpretation, 40,
    48, 190
Hughes, Widow, 176
Herodias, 103
History of Interpretation, 20
Holiness, 63
Hardesty, Nancy, 152
Huldah, 32, 52, 59, 67, 73, 103

Illinois Woman's Christian Temperance
    Union, 152
Inclusive Language, 48, 190, 221
Inner Light, 30
Inquisitions, 124
Interpolation, 146
Interpretative Strategy, 206;
    Interpretation, 11, 12, 153

Jael, 59
Joanna, 34
Judith, 125, 130, 140
Junia, 74, 250
Kellison, Barbara, 23, 24, 70–75
Kingsford, Anna Bonus and Edward
    Maitland, 7, 174, 186–194; The
    Perfect Way, 189, 191

Ladies College, 152
Leah, 32
Lee, Ann, 176
Lee, Jarena, 201
Liberation, 5
Liberator, 203, 206
Literary Critical Interpretation, 48
Literal Interpretation, 19, 23, 74, 93, 128
London Lodge of the Theosophical Society, 187

Martha, 23, 43, 130
Matriarchal, 3
Maidservant, 185
Maitland, Edward, 7, 186, 174, 186–194
Male-Female duality, 195
Male-dominated, 4, 145
Mary, 23, 31, 34
    Magdalene, 31, 207, 40, 43, 67, 129, 164, 174, 196, 201
Matriarchal, 121, 123, 165
    Mother Rule, 145; Matriarchal Philosophy, 162; Matriarchate, 122, 145, 148
Masculine-Feminine Principle, 149
Masculine Women, 91
Massachusetts Magazine, 139
Metaphorical, 174
Methodist, 63
Milwaukee Female College, 152
Miriam, 32, 52, 59, 67, 73, 103,
Mistranslation, 146
Moseley, Emily, 216
Mother, 32, 101, 129, 134, 135, 142, 150, 156, 158, 181, 193, 195, 207, 210, 215, 219,
Motherhood, 164
Mothering Women, 37
Mother Spirit, 165
Mott, Lucretia Coffin, 24, 37, 46, 54–61, 96
Murdock, Marian, 107
Murray, Judith Sargent, 7, 122, 138–142
Mystical Interpretation, 174, 189, 190, 195

Naomi, 32
National Woman's Christian Temperance Union, 152
National Woman's Suffrage Association, 217
New Eve, 174, 178, 181, 182, 183
New Savior, 178
New York State Suffrage Association, 144
Nodiah, 73
Nonsexist, 221

Oberlin Collegiate Institute, 106
Occult, 124

Palmer, Phoebe, 23, 24, 59, 62–70, 74, 99
Parker, Mary S., 44
Partners, 30
Patriarchy, 151, 162, (Patriarchate), 146 149; Patriarchal, 1, 5, 126, 165, 218, 227
Paul and Pseudo Pauline Texts, 12, 34, 36, 39, 40, 41, 51, 59, 68, 71, 75, 99, 102, 110, 133, 147, 154, 155, 156, 163, 193
Phoebe, 53
Physical and Social Interpretation, 191
Priestcraft, 56
Priscilla, 43, 53, 59, 67, 74, 99, 130, 133, 135,
Prooftext, 50, 147
Prophesying, 26
Prophetess, 24, 32, 41, 59, 73, 109, 130, 175, 177, 210;
    Prophet, 178
Proto-Feminist Interpretation, 8, 131
Psychic, Personal, and Ethical Interpretation, 191–192

Quaker, 23, 24, 25, 27, 29, 37, 39, 45, 54, 55; Friends, 27, 30, 38
Queen of Sheba, 181

Rachel, 32, 104, 130
Racism, 7

Rahab, 101, 130
Rational and Philosophical
    Interpretation, 191
Rebekah, 31, 100, 130
Redefinition of Words, 48
Remythologizing, 93, 147, 148
Retranslation, 48, 50
Revisionist, 7
Ruth, 31, 32, 46, 49, 51, 73, 99, 100, 129,
    130, 149, 220,

Schüssler Fiorenza, Elizabeth, 5, 17
Serpent, 41, 42, 44, 72, 148; Satan,
    28
Sexism, 7
Sewall, Mary, 53
Shaw, Susan
Shiloh, 180; Richard Simon, 16, 17, 20
Significations, 191
Silence of Women, 112, 153, 155, 224
Simpson, Elspeth, 176; Buchan, Luckie,
    7, 176
Sister, 101, 181
Slavery, 45, 54, 208,
Smith, Amanda Berry, 7, 201
Smith, Julia Evelina, 7, 100, 214–224
Sophia, 150
Southcott, Joanna, 7, 174, 175–185; The
    Strange Effects of Faith, 178
Stanton, Elizabeth Cady, 7, 46, 55, 86,
    95–104, 130, 144, 195, 217; The
    Woman's Bible, 86, 87, 97, 98, 105,
    217, 219,
Stewart, Maria W. Miller, 7, 202–209
Stone, Lucy
Stuart, Susan Mosher, 29
Subjection of Women, 51, 56, 61, 112,
    113, 127, 135, 153, 224
Submission of Women, 122, 151, 163,
    223
Symbolic Interpretation, 19, 41, 48, 128,
    174

Tabitha, 74
Textual Criticism, 18, 48
Theot, Catherine, 176
Theosophy, 187
The Third Sex, 162
Tolbert, Mary Ann, 5
Transcendentalism, 55
Translation as Interpretation, 146, 213
Troy Female Seminary, 86, 215
Truth, Sojourner, 7, 201
Tryphosa, 59, 74,
Tryphena, 59, 74
Typological Interpretation, 40, 42

Unitarians, 55
Utopia, 158

Van Schurman, Anna Maria, 176
Vashti, 103, 129
Veil, 102
Virgin, 32, 36, 41, 194

Walker, David 203; Walker's Appeal, 203
Ward, Julia Howard
Wollenstonecraft, Mary, 88, 139
Weaker Vessel, 24, 51
Weston Female College, 152
Widow, 31, 32, 36, 41
Willard, Frances Elizabeth Caroline, 7,
    63, 122, 151–157
Wisdom, 194
Witchcraft, 124
Witch Hunts, 124
Woman, Mythological View, 156
Woman's College of Northwestern
    Temperance, 152
Woman-Messias, 192
Woman Movement, 4
Women's Meetings, 192
Women's National Liberal Union,
    143
Women's State Temperance Society,
    97
Women at the Tomb, 43

INDEX OF SCRIPTURE REFERENCES

Example: Genesis 1:26. The number 1 refers to the chapter and after a colon: the number 26 refers to the verse in Genesis. Page numbers where the verse can be located will follow a comma. Books are in the acceptable order of the Christian Canon.

Old Testament/Hebrew Bible/First Testament

Genesis, 113, 128, 129

    Chapters 1–2, 191, 192
    Chapter 1, 210
    1:26, 101, 210
    2, 102
    2:15, 42
    2:18, 219
    2:25
    3:16, 161
    3:20, 219
    7:2, 220
    16:2, 220
    46, 104

Exodus

    Chapter 32, 104
    38:29

Leviticus

    24:10, 101

Numbers, 103

    Chapter 30, 74

Deuteronomy, 101

Judges

    4:4, 220
    4:5, 157, 221

Psalm

    Chapter 68, 209
    68:11, 68

Proverbs, 129

    9:1–3, 36

Isaiah

    Chapter 54, 42

Jeremiah

    31:22, 42

Ezekiel

    13:17–18, 59

Joel

    2:28, 60, 67, 157, 183

New Testament

Matthew, 154

    19:3, 94
    Chapter 25, 207

Mark 16:11, 51

    Luke 2:36–38, 157
    8:1–3, 34, 74, 156
    8:3, 221

John 1:12, 31

Acts

   2:17, 75, 221
   2:18, 67
   12:2, 112

Romans 5:12, 50

I Corinthians, 68, 106, 108, 110, 113

   Chapter 7, 155
   Chapter 11, 24, 36, 40, 99, 53
   11:3, 222
   11:5, 35, 157
   11:12, 35
   11:14, 142
   14, 24, 53, 111
   14:27, 35
   14:28, 74, 222
   14:34, 35, 36, 40, 60, 102, 109, 110, 157

II Corinthians 11:3, 50

Galatians

   3:28, 38, 68, 157

Ephesians, 133

   Chapter 5, 68
   5:22, 24, 35, 51, 163, 223
   6:21, 60

Philippians

   4:3, 153, 157

Colossians, 133

   3:18, 51, 223
   4:7, 60

II Thessalonians 3:11–12, 112

I Timothy, 65, 106, 108, 110, 113, 133, 155,
Chapter 2, 24, 40, 68

   2:4, 50
   2:8–9, 53
   2:8–10, 41
   2:9, 102
   2:10, 60
   2:11–12, 35, 109, 112, 157, 224
   2:13, 41

I Peter, 67

   3:7, 51
   3:22, 51
   3:31, 74

Revelation

   Chapter 12, 177